SHAKESPEARE WITHOUT TEARS

SHAKESPEARE WITHOUT TEARS

BY MARGARET WEBSTER

WITH AN INTRODUCTION BY
JOHN MASON BROWN

New York WHITTLESEY HOUSE London
McGRAW-HILL BOOK COMPANY, INC.

SHAKESPEARE WITHOUT TEARS

Copyright, 1942, by the McGraw-Hill Book Company, Inc.

THIRD PRINTING

PUBLISHED BY WHITTLESEY HOUSE
A division of the McGraw-Hill Book Company, Inc.

Printed in the United States of America by The Maple Press Co., York, Pa.

Introduction

BEAUMONT and Fletcher, and Massinger and Ford, are names that march into the classrooms as if they were boarding the Ark. In the American theatre Shakespeare and Webster (Margaret, not John) are just now becoming almost as inseparably linked. Any play-goer who has sat before the productions Miss Webster has made with Maurice Evans of RICHARD II, the uncut HAMLET, HENRY IV, PART I, MACBETH, and—to a lesser extent—TWELFTH NIGHT, can advance at least four and a half excellent reasons why this should be so. To these, this book, known so appropriately as *Shakespeare without Tears*, adds a fifth, which is one of the most cogent of the lot.

"When I began to write," boasted Mr. George Bernard Shaw in his famous valedictory to dramatic criticism, "William was a divinity and a bore. Now he is a fellow-creature; and his plays have reached an unprecedented pitch of popularity." Miss Webster is a director who must be thanked for having performed much the same services for Shakespeare on the contemporary American

v

stage that Mr. Shaw rendered him as a critic in the London theatre of the nineties.

She, too, has approached Shakespeare knowing that he is neither a divinity nor a bore. But, instead of exposing his weaknesses as Mr. Shaw rejoiced in doing with all his critical brilliance in order to have Shakespeare's virtues properly appreciated, Miss Webster has applied herself as a director to protecting his scripts from these weaknesses in order to project their virtues.

The critic and the director have at least this much in common. The good critic may not be able to direct but the good director must be an able critic. For the good director is a critic in action; a critic turned creator; a reviewer whose responses and perceptions are stated before, not after, a production is made; in short, a midwife with opinions. It is not surprising, therefore, to find that the same Miss Webster, who as a director has again and again delivered Shakespearean scripts into the land of the living, has written in the following pages some of the most acute and quickening Shakespearean criticism to have been produced in our time.

She knows Shakespeare as few scholars do, and writes of him in a way to make professional critics at once humble and envious. The source of her strength in directing or discussing his plays is that, much as she admires him and sensitive as she is to his wonders, she sees Shakespeare as a "fellow-creature" whose first interest was the profession they both happen to have followed.

Miss Webster is not frightened by Shakespeare. She reads his texts sympathetically, permitting his imagination to set her own imagination free. Although she responds to the magic of his verse, she never forgets (as so many have been tempted to do) that by his own choice Shakespeare was primarily a playwright; a man of the theatre who wrote for actors, not for pedants; for groundlings, not for students; and who had a professional's pride in his medium.

When Arthur Hopkins and Robert Edmond Jones failed bravely many years back with an experimental production of MACBETH, they announced their aim as having been "to release the radium of Shakespeare from the vessel of tradition." Miss Webster is not interested in breaking away from the vessel of tradition. The radium of Shakespeare is her sole concern. It is this radium which she, more than any other director of our day, has been able to reveal again and again in the theatre, and which she now shares and discloses in the pages that follow.

Miss Webster approaches Shakespeare without artyness, without stunts, and with a palpable love for, and understanding of, both his poetry and his plays. Moreover, she approaches him with her eyes open and her mind quickened, rather than deadened, by exceptional knowledge. She knows there is no such thing as a final interpretation of any of his plays. But her eyes and ears are vigilantly alert for all those characterizing and dramatic values which lurk in, and between, his lines, and which lesser directors have permitted to slip by unnoticed. If she has a genius for redeeming his plays from the College Board Examiners and making audiences forget that his works were ever compulsory reading in the classrooms, it is because she can hear the heart beat in these dramas which the bedside manner of countless teachers has persuaded many to accept as dead.

Although Miss Webster is a scholar and a critic, what keeps her knowledge alive and her perceptions creative is that she is a theatre person. She has learned her Shakespeare on a stage rather than near a blackboard. She comes from a long line of distinguished English actors. Her great-grandfather was Benjamin N. Webster, a leading actor-manager in his day. Her mother is Dame May Whitty and her father, Ben Webster, whose activities occupy more than two and a half pages in *Who's Who in the Theatre*. Her professional debut in London was made as Gentlewoman in John Barrymore's HAMLET. And she is herself an accomplished actress, as all American playgoers can testify who saw her Mary of Magdala in FAMILY PORTRAIT, her Andromache in THE TROJAN WOMEN, and, most memorably, her Masha in the Lunt-Fontanne production of THE SEA GULL.

Miss Webster was born in New York in 1905 when her father and mother were acting in this country. As a matter of cold fact, she was born in what is now a parking lot on 58th Street but what was then an apartment house owned by Finley Peter Dunne, better known as Mr. Dooley. As a girl Miss Webster twice appeared in England with Ellen Terry; studied in Paris; and was still under twenty when at a dramatic school in London she first met Maurice Evans.

Thereafter came fruitful years of apprenticeship, touring the provinces with Sir Philip Ben Greet's company, and several seasons at that best of Shakespearean universities, London's Old Vic. Meanwhile she had appeared in and directed several West End productions. It was not until 1937–1938 that, with Mr. Evans, she rediscovered RICHARD II for theatregoers in this country. Thereafter followed the uncut HAMLET, HENRY IV, TWELFTH NIGHT, and 1941's exciting MACBETH, productions which have deserved the widespread praise and popularity they have won.

It is reported that the occasion of one of Miss Webster's girlhood appearances with Ellen Terry was a Nativity play. According to the story, Miss Webster had to walk down a long aisle and then climb up on to a stage and up some steps before speaking the prologue. All this she is rumored to have done with so much success that when her piece was delivered and she was preparing to make her exit, Miss Terry's golden voice was heard to ring out from the wings, "Very good, Peggy, very good."

The chroniclers insist this unexpected praise, from so high a source, so unnerved Miss Webster that she thereupon proceeded to trip on her robes and tumble headlong into the audience. What is more important from the point of view of both Shakespeare and his admirers is that she has not tripped often since. Considering what she has done for Shakespeare in the theatre, and is now doing for him in this volume, only a person possessed of an Englishman's gift for understatement would think of thanking her in such restrained terms as "Very good, Peggy, very good."

JOHN MASON BROWN

NEW YORK CITY.

Contents

CONCLUSION

Part One

CHAPTER ONE

First Person Singular

IN the Forty-second Street library of New York City
there is a room whose walls are lined solid with trays
of filed index cards. The labels on these trays progress
lightly but inexorably from "Guinea to Guitry" and
from "Providence to Prune." But among them are nine
devoted exclusively to "Shakespeare." It would seem
that the addition of even one small card to this massive
array of scholarship would require an explanation and
an apology.

Let us assume, to begin with, that Shakespeare was
Shakespeare. This new card will have no place under
"Bacon, Sir Francis," nor under "Oxford, 17th Earl of."
Fashions in Shakespearean pretenders change, and, at
the time when all playwrights and historical novelists
favored Lord Leicester as the hero of Queen Elizabeth's
secret love life, Shakespearean mystics pinned their
faith to the dry and mighty Lord Bacon. Nowadays the
Earl of Essex has won the allegiance of the historical

3

romanticists, and the Earl of Oxford has secured a large following of literary devotees. In the meanwhile, however, painstaking scholarship has unearthed and codified a numberless array of tiny records which, taken together, form an impressive, one would almost say an impregnable, case for the despised player from Stratford-on-Avon. But there is no arguing with a Baconian or an Oxford addict. You cannot dispute logically with an act of faith nor tear down a religion with puny extracts from the tangled records of minor litigation around the year 1600. Players and playwrights and theatre people as a whole will naturally prefer to believe that the writer of the thirty-seven plays was a member of their own craft. Let us assume that Shakespeare was Shakespeare.

My second assumption, one upon which alone this book may be justified, is that the plays can be kept alive, in the fullest and most vivid sense, only through the medium of the living theatre, of whose inheritance they constitute so rich a part. They were written to be acted, to be seen and heard. "The onely grace and setting of a tragedy," wrote one of Shakespeare's contemporary playwrights, "is a full and understanding Auditory." The living theatre, too, has an obligation to keep before its public the work of the greatest dramatist who ever wrote in English, not as an academic chore, but as vital entertainment which will enrich the theatre-going lives of many thousands of people. Any theatre with blood in its veins will produce its own playwrights, deal with the problems of its day, provide a commentary and weave a pattern around the events of its own time. But as long as the English language is loved and freely spoken, as long as the imaginations of men can be caught up and glorified by great dramatic power, Shakespeare will remain a living playwright.

I can make no pretension to deep Shakespearean scholarship. I first made his acquaintance many years ago, just about the time when I first learned to master in print such a sentence as "The cat sat on the mat." My mother was then moved to observe that "To be or not to be" should lie equally within my power and indignantly repudiated on my behalf any such intermediaries as Lamb's *Tales*. Nevertheless, I did acquire a volume of stories from the plays, illustrated in color with pictures of vaguely medieval beings, all highly affable and apparently boneless. I remember particularly Rosalind, with a Robin Hood cap and a boar spear that would certainly have snapped if it had encountered any objective stronger than a chicken; Beatrice, emerging from behind the hedge like a large pink pincushion, and Lear, with a slightly depressed expression and the longest, whitest beard blown in every direction at once. The fascination these stories held for me has since caused me to wonder whether Shapespeare's plots are really quite as silly as critical sophistication suggests.

At school I fell in love with RICHARD II and MACBETH. I do not remember that this was due to particularly imaginative teaching. Perhaps the soil of my mind had been thoroughly prepared by four generations of theatrical ancestors, most of whom had had a bout with Shakespeare at one time or another. But it is a matter of the gravest regret that most children learn to regard Shakespeare as an undesired task to be mastered as superficially as is consistent with the necessity of pleasing a given body of examiners. Few of them are led to know and understand the people in the Shakespeare plays or to appreciate the music of his spoken verse. Little is done to feed the eagerness of their imaginative curiosity or to quicken their sense of the power and beauty of their own language; and their minds are crammed with a mass of basically irrelevant detail, which they thankfully reject as soon as possible. If, in later years, they are lured into a theatre where Shakespeare is being played, they are astonished to find that there is really nothing difficult about him and that he can even supply very reasonable entertainment.

My own Shakespearean education, after the inevitable collegiate appearances as Portia and Puck, was greatly advanced by Sir Philip Ben Greet, in whose company I played many plays in many places, usually in the open air and under the oddest conditions, apt to be productive of more hilarity than art. The Ben Greet productions were not of the highest standard, but his companies were filled with eager young people, none of them awed by the works of the master and all of them ready to tackle anything. You had to learn to make a running exit of anything from twenty to a hundred yards, tossing blank verse blithely but audibly over your left shoulder as you went; to play Lady Macbeth up and down a fire escape and convince an audience of irreverent school children that you really were sleepwalking at the same time; to climb stone walls in an Elizabethan farthingale, crawl behind a hedge or two, and emerge in view of the audience unruffled in dress or speech; and to be heard in great open spaces above the sound of the wind and the tossing branches of the trees above your head. You had to sink or swim. There wasn't much finesse about it, but it gave you a sense of freedom and of power. You had the feeling that Shakespeare himself would have felt at home there and enjoyed the sensation of driving the play clear through against the odds, as you hold a boat against a high wind.

After various interludes, I had the good fortune to play a season at the Old Vic in London and to meet there a tradition of Shakespearean production which in its essentials is probably as sound as any now practiced in the English-speaking theatre. Playing parts which ranged from Audrey in AS YOU LIKE IT to Lady Macbeth, watching the work of distinguished actors and directors through many seasons, and feeling the collaboration between actors and audiences continuously but quite unself-consciously devoted to the Shakespeare plays, I learned many things. Here Shakespeare was both exciting and familiar; the atmosphere was full of challenge, not of awe. I realized the enormous value of this sense of comradeship among actors, audience, and author. Here, too, Shakespeare was played almost uncut. The Old Vic public would have resented blue-pencil evasions of difficult passages, on the part of the director or the actors. This led, necessarily, to a much closer study of Shakespeare's dramatic intention in its less facile aspects. It resulted in a greater appreciation of his theatre reasoning and also in a healthier respect for the full texts which recent scholarship has unearthed from beneath a mass of wanton "editing." Nevertheless, the audiences expected entertainment, "theatre," in its best sense. Entertainment, it appeared, was not incompatible with scholarship.

My first directorial task was a curious one. Eight hundred women of the county of Kent in England combined together, through their village institutes, to give an outdoor performance of HENRY VIII. Each village contributed to the "crowd" for one of the big scenes, and only a dozen principal characters remained constant throughout the play. The experience I gained in handling this massive problem taught me, principally, two things: firstly, that anybody, man or woman, young or old, fat or thin, tall or short, can, with the aid of the famous Holbein stance and make-up, look the living image of Henry VIII; secondly, that every member of any Shakespearean crowd is as important as the principal speakers in the scene. These village women, some of them unable to read the text itself, were lost at first, listening sheepishly and uncomprehendingly to the flood of speeches. But when I gave to each of them an identity, a character, an individuality of her own, they played with an impassioned conviction that made the crowd scenes genuinely thrilling.

I realized, too, that the problems of Shakespearean production are not basically different in the amateur and professional theatre. In these days, when so many of his plays are left to the devoted labors of student societies, collegiate bodies, and amateur groups, it is valuable to remind oneself that the problems, and the rewards, of producing Shakespeare are not, by any means, confined to the professional stage.

With the direction of RICHARD II for Maurice Evans in New York in February, 1937, my first professional Shakespearean production, I began to. glimpse the enormous opportunities which lie before the producer of Shakespeare in the United States. This play was virtually unknown to American audiences; the most that was hoped of it was an "artistic" success; yet it enjoyed a record-breaking run in New York, as well as two extensive road tours. The uncut HAMLET, which followed, was also produced for the first time in the American commercial theatre, and HENRY IV, PART I, though it had been done by the Players' Club in 1926, had never been considered as having potential value for the theatrical manager with a living to earn. Yet both of them, as well as the better known TWELFTH NIGHT, which was produced by the Theatre Guild with Mr. Evans and Miss Helen Hayes, found eager audiences all over the country. The reputation and personal quality of the stars were undoubtedly a great factor in this result; but it seemed that Mr. Shakespeare was still one of America's most popular dramatists.

The aim of Mr. Evans's productions has been a collaboration with both author and audience. We have tried honestly to interpret the author's intention, as nearly as we could divine it, to the audiences for whom the productions were intended. We have never supposed that we were providing any definitive answer to the problems of the plays, especially those of the inexhaustible HAMLET.

We have had to face a number of difficulties of which we only gradually became aware. There was, for instance, the minor one of accent. Several actors went so far as to refuse parts in the productions on the grounds that they either could not "speak English" or were afraid that by so doing they would endanger their chances of future employment as gangsters. We tried to obtain some homogeneity of speech that was neither dude English nor localized American, pertaining neither to Oxford University nor Akron, Ohio. We found that actors were plainly frightened of Shakespeare, particularly of the verse, and were initially disinclined to regard his characters as real people. Audiences were frightened, too; but they also proved, I found, eager and swift, very ready to respond, the kind of audience that Shakespeare himself might have wished for.

From both actors and audience we were confronted with the inhibitions which result from regarding Shakespeare as high-brow stuff. At a performance of HAMLET in a Middle Western city, the balconies were crowded with school children, noisy, skeptical, restless. Owing to a shortage of ushers, a couple of cops were called in to keep a watchful eye on them; the cops were very conscious of their responsibilities, and, when the children, as quick as they were critical, began to laugh at Polonius, they were cowed by a fiercely respectful "shush" from the police force; poor Polonius played frantically to solemn faces throughout the afternoon.

One of the most vital tasks which confront the Shakespearean producer in America is the breaking down of this unwholesome reverence for the Bard. There is at present no tradition as to the production or playing of Shakespeare, and this freedom is, in itself, an opportunity. The repertory companies which used to tour the country have been forced out of business by economic conditions and the competition of new forms of entertainment. There have been individual, and blazing, performances by stars who have had the vision and the ability to avail themselves of Shakespeare—John Barrymore, Jane Cowl, Katharine Cornell, and others. But there has been no standard against which succeeding actors and directors could measure the truth of interpretation newly divined, little informed knowledge of the plays and of their author. Tradition is sometimes a useful yardstick. It need not be merely a collection of fusty and outworn shreds from the theatrical wardrobe of an earlier time. The modern theatre, confused and uncertain upon this as upon almost every other topic, vacillates between excessive respectfulness and a determination to be novel at any cost. Considering its more recent ancestry, this is not altogether surprising.

In America and England the nineteenth century wore itself out in a blaze of star actors, playing Shakespeare very much as he had been played for the preceding hundred and fifty years, using the plays as vehicles for the principal players, blissfully unaware of the power of their craftsmanship as the uncut texts have since revealed it. Edwin Booth in America was the last of the giants, the latest glory of a long period which had been distinguished by superlative actors and ridiculous plays. In England the succession devolved upon Sir Henry Irving, whose particular twist of genius was complemented and graced by the radiant humanity of his leading lady, Ellen Terry. Like Booth, he was a single-minded man of the theatre. His productions at the Lyceum Theatre, which he also played extensively in America, followed the long-established precedent. They interpreted Irving rather than Shakespeare.

But even in the 1890's the voice of rebellion was beginning to be heard, and it was no uncertain one. "In a true republic of art," wrote the critic of the *Saturday Review*, "Sir Henry Irving would ere this have expiated his acting versions of Shakespeare on the scaffold. He does not merely cut the plays, he disembowels them." The prophet of the new scholarship and the new criticism was Mr. George Bernard Shaw.

Mr. Shaw was no Bardolater. "Oh, what a *damned* fool Shakespeare was!" he wrote, in a moment of exasperation. And repeatedly he inveighs against Shakespeare's "monstrous rhetorical fustian, his unbearable platitudes, his sententious combination of ready reflections with complete intellectual sterility." But he never ceased trying to goad producers, Irving, Tree, Augustin Daly, and the rest, into doing the plays as "the wily William planned them." The interchange of letters between Shaw and Ellen Terry prior to her first appearance as Imogen with Irving in 1896 provides an invaluable object lesson in lucid critical thinking, supplemented and humanized by the truth and simplicity of an actress's feeling.

The apostle of the new Shakespeare did not have long to wait for the results of his campaign. In October, 1897, Forbes-Robertson produced HAMLET, also at the Lyceum, and the *Saturday Review* greeted him thus:

The Forbes-Robertson HAMLET at the Lyceum is, very unexpectedly at that address, really not at all unlike Shakespeare's play of the same name. I am quite certain I saw Reynaldo in it for a moment; and possibly I may have seen Voltimand and Cornelius; but just as the time for their scene arrived, my eye fell on the word "Fortin-bras" in the programme, which so amazed me that I hardly know what I saw for the next ten minutes.

Since that time Shakespeare in the theatre has had to undergo a period of heavy upholstery and mountainous realism before the theatre really stripped itself for ac-tion, under the influence of the "expressionist" twenties, and of the vigorous but erratic impulses of that rebellious period. Scenic design has gained enormously in freedom and flexibility, growing steadily nearer to the Eliza-bethan spirit as it grew less representational. The theatre has cast a wide net, from constructivism to modern dress, in its efforts to revitalize plays which, in point of fact, have never lost their vitality.

The course of these theatrical vicissitudes reflected the theatre's reaction to some forty years of scholar-ship and bibliographical research, which has com-pletely changed the face of Shakespearean criticism. The theatre and the scholars continue to show signs of violent maladjustment. In the forefront of the new re-search movement were Dr. A. W. Pollard, with his em-phasis on the value of the neglected Shakespearean Quartos as against the hitherto canonized Folio; Dr. W. W. Greg, whose bibliographical discoveries are of the greatest importance and interest to every theatre student; and Sir E. K. Chambers, whose monumental works com-mend themselves to the plain man by virtue of their pithy and even testy refusal to give way to the fancier theories of the new scholars. In the world of the theatre itself,

William Poel did a series of startling productions in the exact Elizabethan manner, even erecting in London theatres true reproductions of the Elizabethan stages.

Of recent years Prof. E. E. Stoll and Mr. Frayne Williams have exemplified a new trend toward "dramatic" rather than "literary" criticism of the plays. But in the main, professors have still condemned the modern theatre as nothing but a "giant peep-show" and showed no sign of admitting that their bibliographical ingenuity was not an end in itself or that the living theatre had anything valuable to say about Shakespeare. The theatre itself, fearful of choking in library dust, has not extracted from recent research nearly enough of its solid value or even of its more entertaining factors.

It seems to me to be of the highest importance that the theatre and the scholars should learn to appreciate each other. I myself have obtained valuable help and collaboration from such men as Dr. Matthew Black of the University of Pennsylvania, who, during his labors on the preparation of RICHARD II for the Variorum edition of Shakespeare, was deeply interested in the staging of Mr. Evans's production of the play. But, as yet, there have been few liaison officers between the stage and the library. Mr. Granville-Barker, in his series of *Prefaces to Shakespeare*, has proved the most valuable among them. His writing is full of imaginative penetration into Shakespeare's thinking, of considerable scholarship, and of vivid theatre sense. His own production of TWELFTH NIGHT in 1912 inaugurated a new era in Shakespearean production. Yet in his later writings one may detect a tendency toward the bookshelves and away, not from the stage itself, but from the auditorium. The Quarto texts loom larger and larger, and the faces looking down from the second balcony recede into a dim and darkened background.

For the factor which, I think, even Mr. Barker is inclined to underrate is the audience. The modern producer has to be, in some sort, a translator; and he may not translate, as Shakespearean commentators do, for individual readers, one by one. He may not count with the single mind, slowly absorbing the power and beauty of the written word, with the aid of a fire, a lamp, and a comfortable armchair. He has to produce an integrated piece of theatre, carrying as nearly as possible the full intention of the author, and projecting it instantaneously to several hundred people of the most variously assorted character and receptivity.

Given half a chance, Shakespeare at his greatest will still bind an audience with the old irresistible spell. There is much in him that you simply cannot destroy however hard you try. But there is also much which was familiar to an Elizabethan audience but which is strange country to us. The whole background of the listener has changed, even though his emotions answer to the same stimuli. His ears, unfortunately, are nothing like so good as they were. Today the movies have trained our eyes to a high degree of critical expectation. But our ears they have coarsened and made lazy by the continuous ministration of amplifiers. The theatre is practically the only place left where we may hear the unadulterated beauty of speech in the full flood of the English language. And we have, to a great extent, lost our language by neglect, and habitually use no more than a poverty-stricken remnant of its resources.

The whole convention of our theatre has changed. The tacit covenant between actor, author, and audience is on a wholly different basis. How can we preserve Shakespeare's intention in our modern terms? We may, we must, try honestly and devotedly to divine his meaning. We must know, for that purpose, the instruments of staging that he used, for they shaped his craftsmanship, and without a knowledge of them we shall often divine his intention wrongly. But it is not, I think, enough to study the exact way in which he swung his action from inner stage to outer stage, to upper stage and back again; to assess the extent to which the use of boy players influenced his characterization of women's parts; to scan the Quarto texts for signs of his theatre thinking expressed in cuts, additions to, and revisions of his script; least of all to follow the scholars in their passionate disintegration of the texts into "early Shakespeare," "another hand," "a late addition," "a playhouse omission," and so on. Our business is not disintegration, but integrity. For the scholars' "true texts" we are grateful indeed; but it is still our business to transmute them into terms of the living theatre today.

If, however, we were to consider only "audience effect" in its most superficial sense, we should be likely to go as far astray as the great actors of the eighteenth and nineteenth centuries did and to lose as much of the essential Shakespeare. We have yet to produce a dramatist who is more skilled in audience psychology than "the wily William." We shall be foolish to underrate his methods or to disregard his conclusions.

We must know our author and our audience and see to it that the actors interpret justly between them. The resources of the library, the skill of the theatre technicians, the influence of individual creative talent among actors and directors, designers and musicians, all these must be fused into the "two hours' traffic of our stage." It will be the business of this book to suggest some bases from which this fusion may be effected, dealing firstly with the author himself, secondly with the general problems of Shakespearean acting and production as they confront us today, and lastly surveying in broad outline the dramatic values of the plays themselves as we see them more than three hundred years after their author died, from a land of whose existence he never even knew.

CHAPTER TWO

Introducing an Englishman

THE soil which produced Shakespeare and the living and working conditions which molded him are of high importance to us who try to interpret him. We have much more in common than is generally realized, and there is much, a background of the spirit, which it is not beyond our power to recapture. In particular, the study of the Elizabethan stage yields, cleared from a tangled mass of statistical jungle, plain and heart-warming evidence that we of the theatre today may claim with Shakespeare a close and genuine "fellowship in a cry of Players." As an author he was not, as many authors are now, tied by a mere "silken thread" to theatre life and practice. He was soaked in it; it was part of his life, warp and woof; and though theatre conventions have changed very radically in three hundred and fifty years, theatre people seem to have changed remarkably little. An actor's instinct will many times guide him through tangled paths that have caused the literary scholars volumes of perturbation.

When Shakespeare came to London, around the year 1587, from the bosom of the Stratford middle class, the Elizabethan stage, as well as the English way of living, was in an extremely fluid and formative condition. He and his fellows were the most powerful influence of their time in creating a mold for the theatre; what we do on Broadway today comes, artistically at least, in direct succession from the Globe Theatre on the Bankside. As good descendants, we should take the trouble to find out a little about our forefathers.

The theatre which Shakespeare found when he threw up his job as a schoolmaster's assistant in a country grammar school, left his wife flat, and went off to London with Lord Leicester's Men, had already evolved a form of drama as yet fairly rudimentary. It still carried traces of the medieval mystery and morality plays from which, on the paternal side at least, it traced its ancestry. The players themselves were imperfectly disentangled from their own earlier selves. They had started, long before, as small groups of professional entertainers supported by great lords and noblemen as members of their households.

Elizabethan actors inherited, among other things, the variety of skill which their fathers' patrons had required. They could still sing, dance a jig, and give exhibitions of superlative swordsmanship, in an age when every gentleman was an accomplished swordsman, like any singer or wrestler who draws crowds today to the Met. or Madison Square Garden. There were no fumbling, dangerous duels, with heavily blunted points; there was no faking of singers off-stage. If the dramatist could introduce a song, a dance, or a fight, he had a troupe full of experts, panting for the chance to exhibit their skill and assured of an audience passionately eager to applaud them. There is a record of payment in Richmond, Surrey, to the Admiral's Men, for "shewing certaine feats of activitie." Will Kemp, the leading comedian of Shakespeare's early days, danced his famous morris dance all the way to Norwich and toured it through Germany and over the Alps into Italy. It was a more lucrative accomplishment than his ability to play Dogberry and Bottom and Justice Shallow.

But with the fuller way of living inaugurated under the Tudors, the horizon of the old actor-retainers had expanded. They had begun to travel, under the protection of a kind of passport from their masters, and they were available for hire at other private houses of the great, or even at the court itself. They ceased, finally, to be mere retainers and maintained themselves, though they still needed the protection of a master, and were at his service when he so required. But they were beginning to apprehend another market, and another audience. They turned their eyes to London City, growing, prospering, teeming with a new life; London the boom town; a little town, as we look back at it from the top of the Empire State, snuggled along the banks of the Thames River; a little wooden town, never wholly free of the fields and marshes that encircled it and closed in around its straggling outposts; but the heart of a new life, beginning to pump its blood far across the seas, sending its citizens in tiny wooden cockleshells westward to Virginia, northward toward Hudson Bay, and southward through the Straits of Magellan, to a New World.

But Shakespeare's predecessors, Shakespeare himself, found in London the capital of a nation at war, engaged in a protracted life-and-death struggle against the mighty Spanish Empire, which ruled by conquest, by fear, or by alliance almost the whole continent of Europe. The Lowlands of Holland and Flanders were the cockpit of the contest between the great armies of Spain and the little companies of men from countries which had not yet learned to call themselves democracies, Dutch and Flemings and French, and troops of Englishmen. Channel ports were in enemy hands; the danger of invasion was constant and imminent. The crisis came with the assault and destruction of the Invincible Armada in 1588. Shakespeare was already in London, already, perhaps, trying his hand at some tentative play tinkering; and looking back years later he could write, through the mouth of the Queen in CYMBELINE:

> . . . Remember, sir, my liege,
> The kings your ancestors, together with
> The natural bravery of your isle, which stands
> As Neptune's park, ribbed and paled in
> With rocks unscaleable, and roaring waters,
> With sands that will not bear your enemies' boats,
> But suck them up to the topmast. A kind of conquest
> Caesar made here, but made not here his brag
> Of "Came, and saw, and overcame:" with shame
> (The first that ever touched him) he was carried
> From off our coast, twice beaten; and his shipping
> (Poor ignorant baubles!) on our terrible seas,
> Like egg-shells mov'd upon their surges, crack'd
> As easily 'gainst our rocks: for joy whereof
> The famed Cassibelan, who was once at point

(O giglet fortune!) to master Caesar's sword,
Made Lud's town with rejoicing fires bright,
And Britons strut with courage.

But the war dragged on with varying fortunes for many years. In 1596, Calais was besieged by the Spaniards and fell. For many days the sound of cannon was clearly heard in London, and men were afraid. But the fleet struck back at the enemy in a brilliantly successful expedition to Cadiz, which was taken and sacked. In 1598, the French, contrary to their treaty with England, made a secret peace with Spain. There were other expeditions and flaming exploits, and there were muddled, languishing campaigns, both in the Low Countries and in rebellious Ireland, dark with wasted opportunity. Men saw only too clearly the consequence of war:

> The imminent death of twenty thousand men,
> That for a fantasy and trick of fame
> Go to their graves like beds, fight for a plot
> Which is not tomb enough and continent
> To hide the slain.

There were rumors and counter-rumors, "Alarums and Excursions," faint hearts and Fifth Columnists, uneasy crowds of citizens who lived in an unanchored world, and swaggering soldiers of fortune who delighted in:

> Matter deep and dangerous,
> As full of peril and adventurous spirit
> As to o'er walk a current roaring loud,
> On the unsteadfast footing of a spear.

Shakespeare wrote of a nation at war; here, too, his descendants may reach out and touch his hand.

At home, there were further causes for unrest. The uncertainty and turbulence of our world are not without parallel in Shakespeare's. There was bitter religious strife; the Catholics perceived a perilous "divided duty" between the Queen and the Pope; the Puritans were growing in power and were prime enemies of the players; the new Established Church had not as yet grown firm roots. There was an unemployment problem, as the structure of the medieval guilds began to crack under the strain of an expanding economy. There were plots and treason in the highest places, and the great Lord Essex himself, "idol of idiot worshippers" and closest to Elizabeth of all her noblemen, died on the scaffold as a traitor. There was, above all, the great Queen, old, childless, whose throne must shortly stand dangerously, unimaginably empty.

But in spite of all this, the Englishman was becoming conscious of England, of its past and of its future. He wanted to hear about and to see on the stage the glorious wars his ancestors had made in France, very gratuitously, in point of fact, but he didn't care about that. He wanted to feel reassuringly the throbbing pulse of his nation, so that he, the plain man, could stand up and say: "Britain is a world by itself, and we will nothing pay For wearing our own noses." We shall miss something of primary importance in Shakespeare's play if we neglect this surging of the blood behind them.

For him, too, when he came at last to his great business of playwrighting, a world of the mind was opening. The stage derived its maternal ancestry from the university wits and scholars. For source material, there was not only Holinshed's *Chronicles of English History* but North's translation of Plutarch's *Lives*. Florio was translating Montaigne, and numberless Italian and French romances began to find their way into English, bearing the seeds of ROMEO AND JULIET, MEASURE FOR MEASURE, and OTHELLO. Englishmen were trying their hands at embryo novels, naturally unaware of the service they would render posterity through the medium of AS YOU LIKE IT and A WINTER'S TALE. "Little Latin and less Greek," said Ben Jonson of Shakespeare, with a University man's scorn. But there were plenty of translations.

It was little more than a hundred years since Caxton had set up his first printing press at Westminister, and written in his Epilogue to the *Recuyell of Troy* that "in the writing of the same my pen is worn, mine hand weary and not steadfast, mine eyen dimmed with overmuch looking on the white paper, and my courage not so prone and ready to labour as it hath been." But he prayed his readers "not to disdain the simple and rude work" and finished the first printed book from his English press with the sigh of relief, "and say we all Amen for Charity." In that intervening hundred years the riches of the Renaissance culture came pouring from the new English printing presses, and the language itself began to take full and glorious form. Shakespeare found the instruments of immortality ready to his hand.

The first bands of players who came to London were not concerned with such flights as these. They unpacked their wardrobe and props in the innyards of the Saracen's Head, the Red Lion, the Bull, the Boar's Head, the Cross Keys, and the Bel Savage and set to work first to attract and then to entertain their rowdy, fickle audiences. They began a long struggle for their livelihood which seesawed between the opposition of the city authorities and the favor of the court and the nobility.

The city aldermen disapproved of players on principle and feared that the places where they played would become meeting grounds for riotous and disaffected elements in the community, as well as dangerous centers for infection in time of plague. Such outbreaks were frequent, and the plague statutes perpetually forced players to close down and take to the road. The court, however, demanded its players, and an exasperated Privy Council, tired of the tug of war, finally evolved a licensing system primarily controlled by the Master of Revels. This system, long outgrown in utility, persists in England to this day. The Lord Chamberlain, an official functionary of the court, is still censor and licensor of plays.

But even before this, ten years before Shakespeare came to London, the players had taken a most decisive step. Badgered by his reluctant hosts, the landlords of the inns, and harried by the city authorities, one James Burbage, actor and manager of Lord Leicester's Men, had taken himself off to Shoreditch outside the city limits, leased a plot of ground, and erected on it a building which he called, with simple grandiloquence, The Theatre. His example was soon followed, though the center of activity shifted to the south bank of the river. The Theatre became merely a theatre.

The early period of Shakespeare's stage experience in theatrical companies, which had not yet crystallized into permanent units with an unchanging personnel,

must have been immensely valuable to him. It brought
him into contact with the Burbages, with Edward
Alleyn, considered the greatest actor of his time, and
with all the leading playwrights of the day, Marlowe,
Kyd, Peele, Greene, and others. They taught him the
craft which is so nearly related to their own in his early
plays and which he gradually developed into a dramatic
technique infinitely beyond anything they had ever
achieved. Their plays make unutterably dull reading
nowadays; in the very rare stage revivals they acquire
some color, but their characters remain maddeningly
wooden. Occasional lines find startling echoes in our
mind's: Pedro's "We burn daylight" in THE SPANISH
TRAGEDY; Edward II's "Gallop apace, bright Phoebus
through the sky" (indeed this whole play leads us inexorably up toward Shakespeare's deposed Richard);
and a line in the disputed SIR THOMAS MORE, which may
indeed be Shakespeare's own, and he twice uses it later,
"I do owe God a death."

But even Marlowe, to whose name we automatically
tack the addition "mighty line," thunders on the ear
like a dynamo of decasyllables. Kyd's SPANISH TRAGEDY,
the greatest hit of its day, has still the flash of power and
theatre effect; but for us it is too full of darkness and
murder and madness and ghosts and the whole dreary
bag of Elizabethan tricks which Shakespeare alone was
able to galvanize into lasting life. Peele and Greene
manipulate their comic interludes like puppeteers. The
scholars rightly tell us that here are to be found all the
embryonic ingredients of Shakespeare's plays, and we
are more than content to take their word for it.

We do not know for certain what Shakespeare's first job was; his first coming to London is a matter for speculation based on doubtful tradition. He is supposed to have held horses at the theatre door; it seems more than likely that he was some kind of assistant to the stage manager, or "Prompter" as he was then called. At all events he acted, and began the journeyman play tinkering, revising, and odd-job collaboration from which he spasmodically emerges as an independent author in his own right.

By 1592, he was well-known as an actor. There are several contemporary references to him in that capacity, as well as a large number of small personal records, engagingly human. In St. Helen's Ward in Bishopsgate "the petty collectors . . . neither might nor could by any means" get hold of him for the payment of back taxes. It is good to know that a few years later, in a more prosperous time, he offered to lend money to a fellow townsman from Stratford, "which," writes the borrower's brother warily, "I will like of, as I shall hear when, where and how." By 1594, not bad progress for some seven years, Shakespeare is certainly one of the foremost members of the newly formed company of Lord Chamberlain's Men, for there is a court record of a payment to them made in the names of Richard Burbage, Will Kemp, and William Shakespeare.

A study of the history and working habits of this company provides us with a very entertaining chronicle. We realize with surprise that we of the theatre today come extraordinarily close to our predecessors in the pattern of our work and lives in the theatre. The evidence which the scholars have accumulated for us, freed from a dusty mass of deductive addenda, reveals to us people whom we might hail as friends and comrades, whose prototypes are to be found today in every drug-store around Times Square. We can no longer be oppressed by any odor of sanctity, once we have entered this very recognizable workshop where Shakespeare learned and developed his craft.

The basis for Shakespearean study which we may thus establish is sufficiently humdrum. It is no part of the imaginative reach which we shall finally need; but it is possibly a better point of departure than the feeling of remote respect with which many actors approach Shakespeare. We shall at least begin by planting our feet on solid, sawdust-covered ground.

CHAPTER THREE

Backstage in 1600

THE Lord Chamberlain's Men, promoted to King's
Men in 1603 when James I succeeded to the throne,
remained together as a closely cooperative working unit all through Shakespeare's lifetime and for many
years after his death in 1616. In 1598, they decided to
leave The Theatre, which had fallen into a bad state of
disrepair and, after much embittered argument with the
ground landlord, finally took matters literally into their
own hands. The young Burbages and their fellow actors
arrived one morning with picks and axes, pulled the
entire building apart, and transported it, lock, stock, and
barrel, across to the south bank of the Thames, where
they "built the Globe," as the Burbages later testified,
"with more sums of money taken up at interest, which
lay heavy on us many yeeres, and to ourselves wee joined
those deserving men, Shakespere, Hemings, Condall,
Philips and other partners in the profittes of what they
call the House."

It was this theatre which saw the production of Shakespeare's greatest plays. In 1613, during a performance of HENRY VIII, some wadding from one of the stage cannon caught the thatched roof, and the whole theatre was "casually burnt downe and consumed with fier." Sir Henry Wotton describes the incipient fire as being "thought at first an idle smoke, and their eyes more attentive to the show, it kindled inwardly, and ran round like a train, consuming within less than an hour the whole house to the very grounds. This was the fatal period of that virtuous fabric, wherein yet nothing did perish but wood and straw, and a few forsaken cloaks; only one man had his breeches set on fire, that would perhaps have broiled him, if he had not by the benefit of a provident wit, put it out with a bottle of ale."

Shortly afterward, however, the "partners in the said playhowse resolved to reedifie the same," which they did. In 1608, they had already acquired the Blackfriars, an inheritance from James Burbage which had been leased to one of the boys' companies, the children of the Queen's Chapel. It was an indoor theatre, and the new method of staging which it inaugurated has a noticeable effect on the elaborated stagecraft of Shakespeare's later plays, such as CYMBELINE, A WINTER'S TALE, and THE TEMPEST.

The company also played many command performances at court or in private houses, not always under the most ideal circumstances. At a performance of PERICLES in honor of the French ambassadors, it is reported that "after two actes the players ceased till the French all

refreshed them with sweetmeats and . . . wine and ale
in bottells, after the players began anewe." However, the
constant court performances provided not only glory but
a useful income.

The members of the company are well-known to us.
Burbage was the leading man from the time of RICHARD
III until his death at the age of forty-five. He is described
as "wholly transforming himself into his part and putting off himself with his clothes . . . animating his
words with speaking, and speed with action . . . an
excellent actor still, never falling in his part when he
done speaking, but with his looks and gesture main-
taining it to the heighth." Will Kemp is probably the
actor aimed at in Hamlet's "there be of them that will
themselves laugh, to set on some quantity of barren
spectators to laugh too, though in the mean time some
necessary question of the play be then to be considered";
and it may have been his "pitiful ambition" that led
him to leave the company about that time. He was succeeded by Robert Arnim, for whom Shakespeare wrote
the more oblique and delicate fooling of Feste, Touchstone, and the exquisite Fool in KING LEAR.

The kindly Philips is clear to us; Condell and "old
stuttering Hemings," who rendered us the inestimable
service of publishing the 1st Folio edition of the collected plays; Lowin, creator of Henry VIII; and his
predecessor, Thomas Pope, whose method as Falstaff
and Toby is satirized by Ben Jonson in an embittered
reference to his "barren, bold jests with a tremendous
laughter between drunk and dry."

The leading boy-ladies are less richly documented.

Most of them graduated to the status of hired men or even sharers. Among them is a mysterious "Ned," who may have been Shakespeare's young brother Edmund. The dashing Will Sly, who, as Laertes, Hotspur, and Macduff, crossed many swords with Burbage, is conjectured to have started his career as Rosaline; and Richard Robinson graduated so successfully from his apprenticeship that he ended by marrying Burbage's widow.

We have accidental records of the small-part actors in the company from stage directions and speech headings in the texts, where the marginal notation of the actor's name made in the theatre script has inadvertently leaked into the published edition. One John Sinklo, a hired man, is especially persistent. His name crops up over a speech in THE TAMING OF THE SHREW Induction, for a Keeper in HENRY VI, PART III, in company with "Humphrey" for the other Keeper, and as the Officer who comes to arrest Falstaff at the end of HENRY IV, PART II. Jack Wilson is marked as the singer of the lovely "Sigh no more, ladies," in MUCH ADO ABOUT NOTHING; and we know that he afterward became a Doctor of Music and bequeathed a very dignified portrait of himself to the Music School at Oxford University. Kemp and Cowley are used for the speeches of Dogberry and Verges through an entire scene in MUCH ADO, and Kemp appears again for Peter in the Quarto ROMEO AND JULIET. "Harvey," "Rossill," "Will," and others are similarly, by a chance inefficiency, assured of a lasting link with Shakespeare's fame.

The small-part actors were hard worked owing to the

universal practice of doubling parts, and not merely doubling, but tripling and quadrupling them. Up until the 1560's, four had been the standard complement of actors to a troupe. The Players in HAMLET do faithfully represent a theatrical company of the period immediately preceding Shakespeare's own. In SIR THOMAS MORE, there is a dialogue between the visiting Actor-manager and More, his patron for the night. More asks the Player, "How many are ye?" "Four men and a boy, sir," answers the Player.

MORE: But one boy? then I see
There's but few women in the play.

PLAYER: Three, my lord: Dame Science, Lady Vanity,
And Wisdom, she herself.

MORE: And one boy play them all? By'r Lady, he's loden.

Henslowe records that Dick Juby played seven parts in TAMAR CAM; and on a tour, which carried a reduced personnel, Burbage not only played the lead in THE BATTLE OF ALCAZAR but threw in the First Spanish Ambassador and a Moorish Soldier, for good measure.

Even Shakespeare was sometimes compelled to adapt himself to limitations of man power. It is probable that the unaccountable replacement of Poins by the insignificant Peto in HENRY IV, PART I, at the end of Act II, scene 4, enabled Poins to change himself rapidly into Young Mortimer; and that the unfortunate Antigonus in A WINTER'S TALE made his abruptly ignominious final exit "pursued by a bear" (it used to be a real bear) in order to reappear shortly afterward as a different character, conceivably the Clown.

Even though we no longer accept a hasty beard and a cloak as adequate disguise, as did the zestful Elizabethans, modern actors can achieve some doubling too. In fact, Sybil Thorndike's wartime touring company of MACBETH, visiting the villages of South Wales, carried one actress who played Donalbain, the Third Witch, Young Macduff, the Gentlewoman, and an army or two. Why should the modern actress be outfaced by a lot of Elizabethan children?

The Globe Company was in many respects, and important ones from the dramatists' point of view, radically different from the haphazard collection of actors from whom we, today, expect the same results in three or four weeks of work on the isolated problems of a single production. It approximated more nearly to an institution; not to the highly formalized and richly encrusted traditionalism of the old Comédie Française, but more closely to the recent transformation of that great theatre under the invigorating impact of the producers of the Cartel. A closer parallel might well be found in Stanislavsky's Moscow Art Theatre Company. The methods of the two companies are as widely apart as the poles, but it is probable that Chekhov and Shakespeare would have found a common ground of experience in the simultaneous and inseparable evolution of a dramatist and a company of actors.

The hierarchy at the Globe was intricate and exact. Certain members, including Shakespeare, were "Housekeepers," or joint owners of the lease and property, and as such received among them a half share of the takings. They were also, with the other principal actors, actor-sharers and in this capacity divided between them the other half of the gross. The proportion of expenses borne by each category of sharers corresponds roughly to the front-stage and backstage division still prevalent today between theatre owners and the current producing company. The rest of the Lord Chamberlain's Men were made up of "hired men," paid on a salary basis, and boy apprentices for the female parts, who were often ex-members of the children's companies.

When there was a landlord, like Henslowe of the Rose and the Fortune, matters became more complicated. Henslowe, the first of the commercial managers, is an Awful Warning. He received at first half the gallery receipts from his tenant company; then, as they grew more and more deeply indebted to him, he took three quarters, and finally the whole gallery receipts, part of which went to pay off the debts the company had contracted. Sometimes these were as high as £658 6s. 4d. in Elizabethan money, which has been very roughly computed as worth about five times the same amount in sterling today. When his company, the Lord Admiral's Men, were elevated to the position of Prince Henry's Men, also at the accession of the new king, they apparently made a Herculean effort to extricate themselves from the toils of the commercial manager and reduced the debt to £24, "casting all the accounts," Henslowe notes in his diary, "from the beginninge of the world until this daye," March 14, 1604.

Henslowe is undoubtedly a portent. But posterity may be grateful to him, because, ironically enough, it is from his meticulous accounts that we draw much of our

present knowledge of the Elizabethan theatre. One of his
hack authors writes of him:

> Most of the Timber that his state repairs
> He hews out of the bones of foundered Players.

But he himself notes wistfully at the end of a murky
computation of unpaid loans, "When I lent I wasse a
frend, when I asked I was a foe." Many of the loans were
evidently made to the Company for production expenses,
such as:

"For hose for Nick to tumble before the Queen . . . "

"For the mending of Hugh Davies tawney coat that
was eaten with the rats . . . " [£2, this.]

"Pd for the poleyes and worckmanshipp for to hange
Absalom . . . xiiii pence."

Such entries as "lane aperne wraght eaged with
gowlde lace and creamson strings" and a black velvet
cloak which cost as much as £20, so richly was it
decorated, were presumably for theatre wear. But on the
other hand, Dowton borrows £12 10s. to redeem two
cloaks—and Henslowe keeps the cloaks as security!
He has to lend Dekker, the playwright, £2 to "discharge him out of the Counter." Another author borrows for his reckoning at the Sun. Richard Jones gets a
loan of £5, "to be payed me agayne," notes the cagey
Henslowe, "by ten shillings a weake." We may be sure
that 10s. were stopped from Richard's salary until the
debt was discharged. Even the sum of 5s. for the hearten-
ing purpose of "good cheer at the Tavern in Fish street"
is noted as a loan. We can almost hear a young actor's
protesting "Look, Mr. Henslowe, my salary's sixpence

short this week." "Your share of the party, dear boy,
your share of my party." ·

Several of the hired men who were not sharers were
doubly in Henslowe's grip, for, contrary to common
practice, he put them under personal contract to himself.
One was engaged to play for two years at 5s. a week the
first year and 6s. 8d. the second; another signed for 10s.
a week and 5s. on the road; others were bound to him
for three years under penalty of forfeit. Such practices
as these were probably not current in Shakespeare's
company, which was a cooperative joint-stock actor-
managerial affair; but the bases of its financing may be
deduced from Henslowe's accounts.

The authors attached to his companies were paid
something like £4 to £6 for an entire play, which would
seem little enough, judging from the comparative munif-
icence of the sums expended on props for their plays—
£5 13s. for instance, for BEROWNE. The initial payment
bought the play outright, and it became the property
of the company. As prices rose, the author's fee rose also
to an average of £7 or £8. In 1613, Daborn actually ex-
torted £20 from Henslowe, £6 on signing, £4 on the
completion of three acts, and the balance on delivery of
the finished play.

When, as was very frequently the case, a play was
written by several authors in collaboration, they divided
the fee among them. Chettle, Dekker, Heywood, Smith,
and Webster must have done some unsatisfactory arith-
metic over the £8 they jointly received for THE FIRST
PART OF LADY JANE.

Very often, too, an author earned a few shillings by

revising an old play for revival, or adding a scene or two
to someone else's script. The method is startlingly paralleled today in any Hollywood studio. It has caused
commentators endless headaches in their diligent efforts
to disentangle the early Shakespearean hand from that of
his fellows, particularly in the HENRY VI's. Several of the
late ones are unmistakably the product of collaboration,
such as HENRY VIII and PERICLES, and most of his work
bears the mark of addition, revision, or hasty cutting,
either by himself or one of his fellows.

There was no system of continuing royalties. But
Shakespeare was not dependent on them, nor on such
down payments as Henslowe's hack authors received.
He owned his share in the Burbage theatres and properties and his further share as an active member of the
company. He was, in a sense, employer and employee,
and his income was a steady one. The shares were sal-
able and could be left to the owner's heirs. In addition
there were rewards for court performances and other
miscellaneous remuneration. Shakespeare and his fellows were, by the standards of their day, pretty prosperous men.

The plays in all the companies were, of course, played
in repertory. They were seldom performed even twice
consecutively. HENRY VI, PART I, which was a hit on its
first production at the Rose in the season of 1592–1593,
received only sixteen performances. Marlowe's popular
JEW OF MALTA was played thirty-six times, but over a
period of four seasons. His FAUSTUS is recorded by
Henslowe twenty-five times in all. These records are
for playhouse performances only, and do not include

special performances at court or at private houses. But, presumably bearing these in mind, Queen Elizabeth commented furiously that the offensive RICHARD II had been played "over forty times in public streets and houses." Presumably, this was a typical "run" for a successful play, few of which seem to have held their place in the repertory for more than three or four consecutive seasons.

Some unsuccessful ones may literally have been given "not above once." But despite the extensive and rapid changes of bill the players had to be prepared to play practically anything at practically any moment. Hamlet's request to have THE MURDER OF GONZAGO played "tomorrow night" reflects current practice. The court authorities or private patrons might make similar demands at any time, as Essex's friends did for the performance of the already obsolete RICHARD II, which had been produced five years earlier and had completely dropped out of the repertoire. Sir Walter Cope writes to Robert Cecil on one occasion:

I have sent and bene all thys morning huntyng for players Juglers and Such kinde of Creaturs, but fynde them harde to fynde, wherefore Leavinge notes for them to seeke me, Burbage ys come, and Sayes ther ys no new playe that the quene hath not seene, but they have Revyved an olde one, Cawled LOVES LABORE LOST, which for wytt and myrth he sayes will please her excedingly. And Thys ys appointed to be playd to Morowe night . . . Burbage ys my messenger Ready attendyng your pleasure.

All this "attendyng" must have pleased Burbage, with two shows, several rehearsals, and a revival to get ready for the following night.

A stock revival, which would always fill a gap, was

vividly known as a "get-penny." But the repertory
changed very rapidly, and authors were consequently
called upon to turn out new plays like sausages from a
machine. There was no sitting in a vacuum clasping his
domed brow and waiting for the Muse to descend, in
Shakespeare's busy life. Two hundred and eighty-two
plays are mentioned by Henslowe in the records of his
company, during their years at the Rose and the Fortune.
The modern impresario may well stand aghast at such a
feat of continous production.

The living people in the Elizabethan theatre have left
us traces of experience amusingly, and sometimes touch-
ingly, analogous to our own. Burbage and Kemp interview potential apprentices, in the play RETURN FROM
PARNASSUS, and Burbage starts off with some familiar
phrases: "I pray you take some part in this book and act
it, that I may see what will fit you best. I think your
voice would serve for Hieronimo." To another, Kemp
says: "Your face methinks would be good for a foolish
Mayor or a foolish justice of the peace." And Burbage
winds up one audition with the old-new vagueness of
"you may do well, after a while." Ben Jonson gives us a
nervous author on an opening night undergoing an experience with which members of the Dramatists' Guild are
familiar and describes the strain on the actors "to have
his presence in the tiring-house, to prompt us aloud,
stamp at the bookholder, swear for our properties,
curse the poor tireman, rail the music out of tune, and
sweat for every venal trespass we commit." The author
was something of a director too, and seems to have
acquired some directorial habits.

And we have, of course, accounts of Shakespeare and his friends at the Mermaid tavern, or Lambs Club, which are endearing, even if some of them are apocryphal. "Many were the wit-combats between him" (Shakespeare) "and Ben Jonson, which two I behold like a Spanish great Gallion and an English man of War; Master Jonson was built far higher in Learning; Solid, but Slow in his performances. Shakespeare . . . lesser in bulk, but lighter in sailing, could tack about and take advantage of all winds, by the quickness of his wit and invention." If this is fancy, it has the ring of truth, and we do know that Jonson argued Shakespeare into cutting some lines out of JULIUS CAESAR, that he called PERICLES "a mouldy tale," which in parts it is, and assured the author of MACBETH that some of the bombast speeches were simply "horrour."

Although these people are so familiar to us in their ways of thinking and the details of their theatre lives that we can almost stand in the wings and hear them talk, it is hard in some respects to get the "feel" of an Elizabethan performance. We have to think in terms of a stage which used no scenery whatever but simply shifted the action from the curtained alcove of the inner stage to the balcony of the upper stage and out onto the projecting forestage, on three sides of which the audience stood or sat. This sense of playing to three sides at once is difficult for us; the space to be covered by the actors is also greater than ours. The forestage alone was as deep as our deepest sets today, and its width nearly half as great again as our average proscenium opening.

We might feel a little lost without our familiar scenic

background to indicate locality, though of late years producers in New York have proved the complete fluidity of action which such freedom affords. An Elizabethan play was free of interruptions too, in the sense of scene changes or act waits, and gained thereby a flowing unchecked rhythm. Props were used: furniture, usually set up on the inner stage while the curtains of it were closed for the preceding scene, and such things as a caldron, a gibbet, or even "a cloth of the Sun and Moon."

This radical difference in physical production caused Shakespeare to obtain, by methods different from ours, effects at which we too aim, with our picture stage and act curtains. It is essential that we should remember the craft by which he was governed.

Sometimes the scholars, in their invaluable efforts to reconstruct for us the minutiae of Elizabethan performances, come to conclusions which make curious reading to anyone engaged in practical theatre work today. The details of staging, what was placed where, and how who did this or that backstage task, have caused much "throwing about of brains." The available data leave a wide margin for guesswork as to practicalities. Prof. Lawrence, for example, is much exercised as to whether or not the side doors to the stage were fitted with practical locks; he comes to the conclusion that they must have been and instances such scenes as the York family party in RICHARD II, where the Yorks, each in turn, arrive and thunder vigorously on the locked door. I am irresistibly reminded of a production in which I myself played the Duchess of York and held the door closed with a foot and one hand, while I shook it with the other and the stage manager pounded on the floor with a padded stick.

Prof. W. J. Lawrence is further engaged in a valiant attempt to find out what exactly represented such things as the "City Gates," before and through which so much action passes in Shakespeare's plays. He arrives at a complicated conclusion. The back center door could not, it seems, be the gates, but "the leaves of the gate formed the permanent background of the rear stage, and in one of them there was a door through which, when the scene represented something otherwise than outside the City Walls, the characters came in and went out." One cannot believe that the vaunted Elizabethan aptitude for joining wholeheartedly in a game of make-believe really required such intricacy as this.

Authors' stage directions as reproduced in the printed texts and even in extant manuscripts are not especially informative in helping us to arrive at what the author himself really had in his mind's eye in matters of staging. The brief indication "Alarums and Excursions" serves for an entire sequence of marchings and countermarchings, trumpets and drums, victories and defeats. "Alarums and Excursions," says Shakespeare, and we are left with our imaginations and a rather frightening margin for opportunity or error.

His early plays are especially sparse in their directions, despite a few which have slipped into print unintentionally from the playhouse manuscripts. Some of these tiny but vivid touches from the first printed texts are seldom reproduced today in popular editions. In ROMEO

AND JULIET, Sampson and Gregory should make their first entrance "with swords and bucklers," and later the citizens arrive "with clubs." This should be helpful to a harried director trying desperately to evolve some variety of action in the street fights. In the same play, the impossible lamentation scene over Juliet's dead body is at least slightly ameliorated by the Quarto direction: "All *at once* cry out and wring their hands." In the Folio MIDSUMMER NIGHT'S DREAM, a careless corrector has left in the text "Enter Tawyer with a Trumpet" preceding the Clown-actors when they enter to the Duke. Tawyer, of course, was an actor's name; but it is possible that he made quite a funny and usable noise with his trumpet.

Some similar entrance directions, generally left over from an earlier version of the play, give us mysterious characters who never speak at all nor seem to have any purpose in the text as we have it. Such a one is "Innogen" to whom the Quarto of MUCH ADO gives two entrances as Leonato's wife. As Sir E. K. Chambers justly observes: "A lady whose daughter is successively betrothed, defamed, repudiated before the altar, taken for dead and restored to life, ought not to be a mute. It is not motherly."

Wearing apparel is fairly frequently described in printed Elizabethan plays, placing of characters more rarely. In Shakespeare's later plays, besides full descriptions of processions and shows, we have a few such indications. Following a general entrance in CORIOLANUS, Act III, scene 1, "Sicinius and Brutus take their places by themselves"; (Act IV, scene 1) "they all bustle about Coriolanus"; and (Act V, scene 3) "he holds her hand."

THE TEMPEST has "Enter Prospero on the top, invisible"
—*i.e.*, on the upper stage. TIMON OF ATHENS contains an
even rarer type of direction in Act 1, scene 2: "Hautboys
playing loud music. A great banquet is served in; Flavius
and others attending; then enter Lord Timon, Al-
cibiades, Lords, Senators, and Ventidius. Then comes,
dropping after all, Apemantus, discontentedly, like
himself."

But these stage directions which seem to scholars
"extremely full" and "showing the hand of a master"
do not enlighten the modern director much. A modern
author would not appreciate the perhaps salutary process
of having his beautiful dissertations confined to such
notations as "Enter James in a striped lounge-suit" or
"The butler comes on carrying a tray with a bottle of
Ballantine's, some White Rock, and three glasses." We
have to do a lot of careful deduction in order to get a
picture of Shakespeare's plays. The characters, even
their age and appearance, are conveyed by what they say
and what others say of them, and not by pages of
Shavian prefatory comment.

Two sets of contemporary documents yield us more
data as to Elizabethan staging than the printed texts
afford. The first is the dozen or so prompt copies existing
in manuscript and bearing notations by the "prompter"
or "book-holder." Unfortunately, none of these is a
play of Shakespeare's, though it is strongly held that
147 lines in the composite manuscript of SIR THOMAS MORE
are by him and in his handwriting. The prompter's stage
directions in these manuscripts are mostly written in the
left-hand margin and comprise sound cues, underscorings

of actors' entrances, many names of the smaller part actors, full descriptions of props, and occasional illuminating actors' business, such as "shewinge his tongue"! In FRIAR BACON AND FRIAR BUNGAY, opposite a speech of Miles, the soldier, is the direction "You knocke your head." This is of some interest, in view of the fact that the use of the pronoun "you" has entirely died out in English prompt copies today, where such a direction would run "knocks his head." But in America it is still preserved, particularly in actors' parts. The English actor, new to the American stage and habitually self-conscious, is generally a little embarrassed when he first reads such an admonition as: "You pause in the doorway; after a struggle with yourself you overcome your emotion and advance rapidly to your mother."

The prompter's directions, like the authors', get fuller as they get later in date. In MORE and JOHN A KENT, the authors' directions are fairly full, but the prompter has made only insignificant marginal notations. The SECOND MAID'S TRAGEDY, in 1611, carries brief specifications for props and music, a couple of actors' names, the signature of the licensor, Sir George Buc, and a good deal of doodling. A few years later the prompter of SIR JOHN BARNEVELT indicates that he is economizing on the author's optimistic "attendants" and "others" by firmly allotting two actors to do the job. The careful fellow also telescopes two supernumerary characters. Props are noted in the margin.

In later scripts the notes for props, furniture, and actors to be "ready" begin to anticipate the actual cue. "Stet" is used to restore a cut, as it would be today. By

1631, with Massinger's BELIEVE AS YOU LIST, we are in the full stream of the modern prompt-copy tradition. "Table ready and 6 chairs sett out" comes a page ahead of time; "all the swords ready," several pages ahead. It was probably quite a job collecting all the scattered swords. "Harry Wilson and boy ready for song at ye arras" comes thirteen speeches ahead. The "stars" are pampered, too, witness: "Gascoine; and Hubert below: ready to open the Trap Doore for Mr. Taylor." Actors are getting soft. The stage-managerial dog's life is on the way.

Our second set of data comes from the seven extant backstage "plots," some merely fragmentary, preserved among the papers of the invaluable Messrs. Alleyn and Henslowe. These are sheets of cardboard with a hole at the top for the nail on which they hung, pasted over on both sides with a list of successive entrances naming both actors and characters, notes for props, and music cues in the left-hand margin. In up-to-date Hollywood idiom, the musical flourishes are marked simply "Sound." They come pat, simultaneously with the entrances and accompany nearly all the important ones.

Sometimes the prop plot is a callous descent from the sublime to the ridiculous. "A fatal murdering brand" referred to in the text of THE BATTLE OF ALCAZAR becomes succinctly "chopping knife." There are notations of impersonal brevity calling for "3 violls of blood and a sheep's gather" (*i.e.*, liver, heart, and lungs) for "Dead mens heads and bones banquett blood." The principal actors, presumably the "sharers," are respectfully noted as Mr. So-and-so, the others in a variety of abbreviations.

The plots afford exact evidence as to the doubling

business, in which the apparent problems are sometimes capable of quite simple solutions. Dr. Greg, who has edited an admirable facsimile edition of THE BATTLE OF ALCAZAR, is greatly puzzled as to why Richard Alleyn should have had to do a very quick double as the Governor of Lisbon when another actor was doing nothing in that scene. It is possible that Richard was just a better Governor of Lisbon. We gather, however, from Greg's analysis that the small-part actors dashed from one "army" to another, presumably changing helmets as they went, and that page-boys to anyone were page-boys to everyone, occasionally pairing off differently just to make it more difficult.

The use of the plots is not altogether clear. I cannot see, myself, what possible service they could have rendered the prompter, for his own prompt copy gave him all the cues he needed; and the plot sound cues, not being marked ahead of time and having no dialogue beside them, afforded him no guidance for signaling the musicians and "effects" men.

It seems to me more probable that the "plot" hung in the tiring house as a "call board," in a sense more literal than ours. The "Sound" notations should also have been a guide to the actors, who could compare them with whatever "sound" they heard from the stage and so judge how far the play had progressed. I should, however, be amazed if as optimistic a system really resulted in everybody's getting themselves on-stage as the right character at the right moment. Of course they did not. A contemporary description of a man in a high fury runs: "He would swear like an elephant, and stamp and stare (God blesse us) like a play-house book-keeper when the actors missed their entrance."

This personage, "book-keeper," "book-holder," or "prompter" as he is interchangeably described, is, to me, one of the greatest puzzles of the scholars' reconstructed Elizabethan theatre. He is a superman, an Atlas, an everywhere-at-once multiple genius. He is, in fact, our stage manager. But the functions credited to him could not possibly be fulfilled by less than three people, all working twenty-four hours a day.

He is supposed to have been the literal "book-keeper," whose duty it was to take charge of scripts, copy them if and as necessary, take them to the office of the Master of Revels to be licensed, and make any alterations required by that official. One, Knight, did this job for the King's Men in 1633. Before that time Thomas Vincent is described as "book-keeper or prompter" at the Globe; it was probably he to whom Shakespeare was once an assistant. Incidentally, both Knight and Vincent are listed in other documents as "musicians." This is by no means the extent of the symposium. The careful compiler of the BELIEVE AS YOU LIST script, has been identified as John Rhodes, who, in later years, is described as "formerly wardrobe-keeper to the King's Men." Wardrobe-keeper. Well.

We now have a librarian-secretary-copyist-musician-wardrobe-keeper. But he is credited with many other "feats of activity." He fitted the play to the capacity of the small-part actors, casting the small parts himself and probably teaching them their lines if they were unable to read themselves. He was head property man and bought both props and wardrobe for the productions.

This hypothetical prompter is also accredited with keeping his eye on the actors and getting them on at the right place and moment in the midst of all the scuffling, wig changing, and lost-cloak trouble occasioned by the prevalent doubling. He is further responsible for giving "effects" cues (very complicated effects at that) and all music cues, without any warning signals marked ahead of time in his book or plot. The musicians, moreover, are in an inaccessible gallery where he cannot possibly signal to them with a mere flick of the hand. Sir E. K. Chambers does in fact surmise mildly that someone may have been needed to transmit the prompter's orders. But who? Everybody was apparently fully occupied changing hats and getting ready behind the arras and climbing up and down stairs to the upper stage.

The prompter, however, is not through yet. In a contemporary play he is exhorted thus:

> You might have writ in the margent of your play-book, Let there be a few rushes laid in the place where Backwinter shall tumble, for fear of raying his clothes; or set down: Enter Backwinter, with his boy bringing a brush after him, to take off the dust if need require. But you will ne'er have any wardrobe wit while you live. I pray you hold the book well, we be not non plus in the latter end of the play.

For of course, as an afterthought in occasional lucid intervals, the prompter prompts.

Even in this capacity he manages to get himself tinged with the miraculous; for he stands, says one, behind the arras curtains, which, we need hardly be told, he also manipulates. He is also recorded as standing at one or both sides of the stage, for the stage area is wide, and the actors are not "pen-feathered" and must get the prompt when they need it from near at hand. We may assume that, with a daily change of bill, they need it.

Contemporary literature does, as a matter of fact, speak of various individuals loosely described as "stage keepers." In the Induction to BARTHOLOMEW FAIR, there is a conversation between the stage keeper and the prompter. In this play, too, a "tire-man" brings on stools and lights. Perhaps aid is in sight for our over-burdened hero. But no. The Stage Keeper depicted in RETURN FROM PARNASSUS obviously performs a prompter's office. And so Prof. Baldwin, our authority for much invaluable research, decides to brush aside such minions as being no more than terminological inexactitudes and lumps their combined duties back onto the shoulders of our Pooh-Bah prompter. It is not, Prof. Baldwin summarizes judicially, an unimportant position.

By "this kind of chase" we must assume that Shakespeare's picture of the prompting stage manager as poor Quince in A MIDSUMMER NIGHT'S DREAM was the grossest piece of caricature. His real opinion of the prompter must be contained in the famous lines: "How noble in reason! how infinite in faculties! in form and moving how express and admirable! in action how like an angel, in apprehension how like a god!"

O obscure and faithful race of stage managers, drones of the theatre world from that time until this day, hold yourselves immortalized in this tribute, so richly deserved!

CHAPTER FOUR

Old Tools and New Usage

SUCH, then, was Shakespeare's workshop; such were the conditions under which he lived, the people with whom he worked, the conventions and the theatre habits which formed the background of his writing. It is unwise to underestimate their importance. But we must further ask ourselves: what qualities did he draw from his human and physical material? How far did he succeed in reshaping the tools he found to his hand, how far did he transform and how far transcend them? How much, in the plays, may we ascribe to an unwilling submission to conditions imposed upon him, and how much must we respect as dramatic achievement upon which we are extremely unlikely to improve? In other words, what should we, in our staging today, emulate, what can we adapt, and what may we discard?

Our regard for his theatre knowledge must take into account the fact that besides being an actor, a stage

manager, and a business partner in his own theatre he
was also to a great extent the director of his own plays.
A contemporary traveler from Germany relates that in
the English theatre "even the actors have to allow themselves to be instructed by the dramatist." One of the
characters in BARTHOLOMEW FAIR remarks bitterly: "The
Poet . . . has kicked me three or four times about
the Tiring-house for but offering to put in, with my
experience." Here is a familiar accent, indeed! Ben
Jonson also writes, from experiences which Shakespeare
must have shared, as every director that has ever been
in any theatre has also shared them: The actor "does
over-act, and having got the habit of it, will be monstrous still in spite of counsel."

Some of the things which Shakespeare asked of his
fellows must have seemed strange and doubtful novelties
to them; but at least he "knew his stuff," and, if he
comes more and more to rely on the actor, to the exclusion of all adventitious aids, it is a tribute to the com-
prehending and fullhearted cooperation of his fellows,
as well as to his utterly sound theatre instinct. For we
shall find, I think, that this will prove for us also the
only practical solution of our problems.

The physical resources on which he was able to draw
were meager in the extreme; he used their paucity to
stimulate his own dramatic imagination to an overwhelming richness. The simplicity of his stage conventions, their formlessness as to the elements of space and
time, did not lead him back to the classical restrictions
of time and place unity but to a delicately suggested
dramatic dimension of his own, subservient to, and

reflected in the projection of the characters, the people, by whom alone he was inspired.

He wrote, supremely, with his eyes and ears in the theatre; what he saw was not what a modern designer would envisage, but the barest of pictorial elements: ragged banners for the English at Agincourt, flaring colors and burnished golden armor for the French; withered and wild attire, not like the inhabitants of the earth, but yet on it, for the incarnate power of evil; white hairs for age, a "smooth and rubious" lip for unfledged youth. What he heard was not merely trumpets for a battle, leaden weights rolled about on the tiring-house floor with water poured down through a sieve for a storm, hautboys and flourishes and mysterious music "under the stage," but all the infinite variety of speed and splendor and tenderness and brilliance of a language of inexhaustible dramatic potency.

There is, in my view, no value that we may derive from the actual reconstruction of an Elizabethan stage. To me, the experiences both of playing on one, and of directing on an exact, though miniature, reproduction have taught me more about its disadvantages than its advantages. To be able to group actors in the round, working more as a sculptor than as a painter, is an interesting, though difficult, technique. Our modern use of levels, rostra, and steps gives the director in many cases a more effective medium. If it is more two-dimensional, it is at least constant; it may be given approximately the same value for a spectator in any part of the theatre.

The "sight line" in an Elizabethan theatre was ex-

tremely variable and to a large proportion of the
audience extremely bad. The line of sight to the inner
and upper stage is, I have found by experience, such
that the use of these stages is minimized; only a small
triangle of space, sharply angled to vanishing point,
is visible to any but a spectator sitting on a line with the
dead center of the stage. I am led to believe that the inner
stage must have been used largely as a jumping-off-place
for a scene in which standing furniture or props had to be
"discovered," and that the main action must have been
brought forward as soon as possible to the main stage
itself. No intimate scenes can have been played on it
with any degree of effect; they would have been invisible to the spectators sitting at the sides of the theatre,
and between twenty and thirty feet away from the
"front row" of the audience in the center of the "yard,"
or "pit," owing to the projecting forestage. It is, of
course, true that a modern director thinks principally
in terms of the orchestra seats, whereas in Elizabethan
times the "carriage trade" sat in the galleries or on the
stage itself, where they were not troubled by the perpetual "masking" which must often have hidden important actors when the whole cast was ranged around a
flat stage.

The projecting "apron" of an Elizabethan stage did
afford an invaluable degree of intimacy between actors
and audience. An actor could really speak the "To be
or not to be" soliloquy as if it were his thought made
audible; the emotional contact he was able effortlessly
to establish is at the very root of Shakespeare's writing.
His comedian-commentators, like Faulconbridge in

KING JOHN, and nearly all his Fools could get on hail-fellow-well-met terms with his audience so that they voiced, almost as a member of it, what Shakespeare hoped it was itself thinking. The Fool's successful joke was a personal triumph for the audience, each of whose members would have said just that, if only he had thought of it. Mr. Thornton Wilder's Stage Manager in OUR TOWN is no distant relative of Faulconbridge and his fellows.

The relation between actor and audience was not nearly so objective; the actors played with, almost from, the audience, never at it. This is a value we shall be suicidally unwise to neglect. It is often helpful to erect some kind of an apron stage; I do not myself think that it is essential. An actor can get intimacy without it. Alfred Lunt, in THERE SHALL BE NO NIGHT, speaks to us from the little schoolroom on the Finnish front line: he starts very quietly, almost to himself, with the double stress and personal inflection which we know to be Mr. Lunt's; within half a minute we are listening to a voice which comes from inside our own hearts. Helen Hayes as Viola, left alone on the stage, confides her troubles to the audience in the "I left no ring with her" soliloquy in such a way that Viola's problems immediately become their own. You do not need an apron stage to create this power; you do need a great actor and great material.

There are other instances in which our despised "peepshow" stage has compensating advantages over its Shakespearean prototype. The ending of a play can be, generally is, greatly heightened by it. There was no curtain in Shakespeare's playhouse. At the end of a tragedy, it was eternally a case of "Take up the bodies" and everybody march off. There is no sense in pretending that this is not, flatly, an ineffective and clumsy necessity with which Shakespeare did the best he could. But we can leave in an audience's eye and mind an indelible picture which should represent the sum and resolution of our story. Such plays as ROMEO AND JULIET and HAMLET offer us magnificent opportunities in this respect. In the same way, the charming Epilogue farewell of AS YOU LIKE IT is much more graceful if the actors do not subsequently have to turn their backs on the audience and troop sturdily off.

Nevertheless, Shakespeare drew great flexibility from his unrestricted stage and used it to establish conventions of place and time subtly and meticulously fitted to his dramatic purpose. His time rhythm is badly jarred by our scene waits, which in his theatre did not exist. The scenes flowed into each other, often marked by a musical "flourish" or "sennet" to introduce fresh sets of characters, just as the Chinese theatre still uses a gong to punctuate but not separate its changing scenes.

We sometimes, though not always, dislocate his convention further by our act intermissions, for, during the major part of Shakespeare's career, there were no act waits either. After the indoor playhouses began to be used, the practice of having brief pauses filled with music gradually came into being. The five-act division is marked by the Folio for some, though not all, of the plays; it is probably Heminges's salute to the pseudo-classical scheme of play division which Ben Jonson was bringing into fashion; but it certainly does not represent Shakespeare's common practice.

The scene divisions indicated in almost all modern editions are the entirely gratuitous invention of an eighteenth-century editor, Nicholas Rowe. They are the favorite object for the almost emotional invective of modern scholars and critics and, indeed, are now retained in printed texts mainly for purposes of reference. It is important that we should clear our minds of anything which obstructs the unbroken flow of Shakespeare's writing, and that in staging we should eliminate as far as humanly possible the breaks and checks which scene changes impose on it.

We are not likely to be seduced into four act intermissions, though we are forced to allow our audiences at least one. This is often a contrived affair, and in such a play as ROMEO AND JULIET it is impossible to find any point whatever where the controlled swiftness of its momentum will not be disturbed by an intermission. RICHARD II, by contrast, seems to me to invite two entirely legitimate act pauses, one after the scene of Gaunt's death, and another after Richard is taken at Flint Castle. In the first instance, Shakespeare's time emphasis, which is always a matter of the most delicate dramatic suggestion, is actually helped by the break in playing, and there are many similar cases where we gain rather than lose by an act pause.

We need not feel any difficulty with Shakespeare's manipulation of time in the theatre, unless we create it for ourselves by the unskillful placing of intermissions or by unnecessary scene waits. Even in RICHARD

III, when he had not yet evolved his later technique of time reflected by psychological progression, we do not find it hard to accept the more rudimentary formula which he uses to indicate the passing of the night before the battle. First comes Richmond's line "The weary sun hath made a golden set" followed soon after by Catesby's "It's supper time, my lord, it's nine o'clock"; then come the alternating ghost scenes which demonstrate, using the timeless dimension of a dream world, the passing of the night itself; and finally the announcement to Richmond that it is almost dawn, climaxed by Richard's "Who saw the sun today? . . . He should have braved the East an hour ago." We have lights too, if we need them, to help us emphasize the clock.

Shakespeare's later method is a more abstract but no less effective treatment of time's passing. Reading OTHELLO, it is easy to detect the fact that Cassio and Desdemona would simply have had no opportunity to commit the "act of shame" with which they are charged and to feel one's credulity challenged by the circumstance that Ludovico arrives from Venice with the news of Othello's recall on the very heels of Othello's own arrival. But in the theatre we are swept away, as we are intended to be, by the torrent of Othello's mounting agony, an avalanche of passion too powerful to be checked by chop-logic considerations. The play needs momentum and gets it; emotional pressure successfully defies the calendar.

In MACBETH, the action moves remorselessly from the murder of Duncan through a steadily unfolding cycle of blood, of thickening and haunted darkness, to Macbeth's

> . . . my way of life
> Is fall'n into the sear, the yellow leaf,
> And that which should accompany old age,
> As honour, love, obedience, troops of friends,
> I must not look to have; . . .

Macbeth has been established at the play's opening as a man in the full vigor and prime of manhood; there has been no indication of any lengthy passage of time; on the contrary, the play is filled with an increasing sense of pressure. On the very morning following the murder, we are told that Macbeth is "already named, and gone to Scone to be invested." Banquo's "Thou hast it now, king, Cawdor, Glamis, all," follows immediately, and in the same scene Macbeth tells his hired gangsters that Banquo must be murdered "tonight." After the banquet at which the ghost of the newly murdered Banquo appears to him, he says "I will tomorrow, and betimes I will, to the weird sisters," and, at the end of his scene with the "sisters," he resolves upon the immediate murder of Macduff's wife and children:

> Time, thou anticipat'st my dread exploits:
> The flighty purpose never is o'ertook
> Unless the deed go with it: from this moment
> The very firstlings of my heart shall be
> The firstlings of my hand. And even now,
> To crown my thoughts with acts, be it thought and done:

Ross travels immediately to England with the terrible news he must break to Macduff, and Macduff and Malcolm return with as much speed: "Our power is ready, our lack is nothing but our leave."

But it is not a sudden qualm about the fact that the historical Macbeth reigned in Scotland for twenty years which causes Shakespeare to precipitate him into "old age." He, in his single human soul, has passed through the timeless reaches of spiritual darkness. The world today is passing through just such a cycle of evil, which we are too apt to symbolize in the person of the man whose rise to power first unleashed its forces. But its beginnings stretch back through the centuries and down into the fathomless abyss of man's primeval heritage; its end, measured in days and years, none of us can foresee. If Macbeth can invoke for us even a fragmentary consciousness of a force as mighty as this, we shall not question that its concentration upon himself leaves him an "old" man.

Modern thinking is receptive to the treatment of time in terms of relativity. Theatre practice renders us less amenable to a similar flexibility in the treatment of space. For here Shakespeare is equally content to use suggestion and, having no scenery to bother about, shifts the place with the actor instead of laboriously transporting the actor to the place. In the convention of the Chinese theatre, we may still find a close analogy to the accepted place scheme of Shakespeare's day. An actor leaves by one door and comes in by another, thereby moving from one locale to another. He walks from the back of the stage to the front and so leaves the inside of the "house" for the street outside it. He crosses the stage and in doing so accomplishes a journey of many leagues. So it was with the Elizabethans.

Shakespeare uses his inner and upper stages to indicate a shift of locale, but he is not particular about geographic rigidity in his handling of them. Juliet says good-bye to Romeo standing on the upper stage and then, according to the Quarto's specific stage direction, "descends," bringing her bedroom with her so to speak, to play the scene with her parents. Cleopatra's "monument" is placed sometimes above and sometimes below, as the necessity of the action dictates; the battlements of Elsinore swing from level to level.

Space can be telescoped also; Richmond and Richard, Hotspur and Henry IV will pitch their embattled camps within touching distance of each other. Where the actor is, there is the place, concentrated around the magnetic pole of his personality. When necessary, the place will be described in terms of dramatic atmosphere, physical features, and, much more importantly, poetic value. The moon "tips with silver all those fruit-tree tops," shedding a radiance which no arc lamp can emulate, simply for Romeo to swear by. The "morn in russet mantle clad, Walks o'er the dew of yond high Eastward hill," bringing to Horatio the sanity and strength of day.

> This castle hath a pleasant seat, the air
> Nimbly and sweetly recommends itself
> Unto our gentle senses.
>   This guest of summer,
> The temple-haunting martlet, does approve,
> By his loved mansionry, that the heaven's breath
> Smells wooingly here: . . .

These words are not merely a picture in themselves; they fall on ears which still ring with Lady Macbeth's "Come, thick night, And pall thee in the dunnest smoke of hell"; and we know that Duncan will pass through these gates to his death.

With such scene painting as this, Shakespeare is meticulous and unerring. With local color he is more haphazard. Venice is indicated by a few casual references to gondolas and the Rialto; Cyprus has some cliffs and a harbor, which might be those of Dover but most unmistakably are not; CYMBELINE is as frankly Renaissance as a Veronese picture, for all its references to Early Britain; and around Athens grows a wood filled with Warwickshire wild flowers and Stratford artisans, all transfused with magic. But there is no doubt about the stripped savagery of Lear's world, nor about the luxury and dalliance of Cleopatra's Egypt set against the discipline of Rome, nor about the swaggering hot-blooded gallants who carry with them the sun and color of fifteenth-century Verona.

Once or twice Shakespeare apologizes for the visual short-comings, especially in the overquoted Chorus to HENRY V:

> . . . But pardon, gentles all,
> The flat unraised spirits, that hath dared,
> On this unworthy scaffold, to bring forth
> So great an object. Can this cockpit hold
> The vasty fields of France? or may we cram
> Within this wooden O the very casques
> That did affright the air at Agincourt?

This arrogant apology from an author who knew perfectly well that there was going to be nothing flat nor unraised about his HENRY has nothing to do with the specific limitations of his particular stage. We, equally and always, have to beg our audiences to "piece out our imperfections with your thoughts." It is the artist's eternal sense of frustration when he compares his vision with his power to fulfill it. But Shakespeare knew that his audience would accept the challenge to their imagination. He does not appeal primarily to their eyes but to their hearts; and, when, in a later play, he promises them that they shall "see away their shilling Richly in two short hours," he knows that the richness will have nothing to do with the play's physical mounting.

Because he achieved his effects without benefit of scenery, working with words on the "imaginary forces" of his audience, scenic productions of his plays have been continuously at odds with themselves. Long ago Charles Lamb registered his protest against wood and painted cloth: "The elaborate and anxious provision of scenery, which the luxury of the age demands . . . works a quite contrary effect to what is intended . . . In plays which appeal to the higher faculties" it "positively destroys the illusion which it is introduced to aid."

More recently, we have had some very moody designs, particularly for such plays as LEAR and HAMLET and MACBETH, usually consisting of an arrangement of steps and rostra painted a forbidding dark gray, shifting around occasionally to different relative positions, and illuminated by spare but dramatic shafts of light. The characters are dressed in the Early Bathrobe period and end by looking as if they had got themselves unintentionally benighted on the steps of the Lincoln Memorial. Such efforts to solve an extremely difficult problem have indeed achieved their objective, in that they have facilitated fluid and unbroken performances of the play; but their extreme architectural quality has often been, in itself, more of a barrier than a stimulant to the unfettered vision.

Our theatre, however, can provide an element of visual beauty which Shakespeare's lacked, but of which there is no reason to suppose he would disapprove. In the comedies we can add immeasurably to the brilliance and color of the text; in the tragedies we can point the way by suggestion; and we have evolved, thanks to the initiatory essays of Appia and Gordon Craig, and the recent work of such designers as Robert Edmond Jones, a fluidity of staging which need not and does not imprison Shakespeare within a "cloven-pine" of super-realism. Modern use of stage lighting, though a dangerous weapon in the hands of those who fall too deeply in love with it, has probably done more than any other single factor to enable us to concentrate the audience's attention where Shakespeare wants it, *i.e.*, on the actor. This must not mean overlighting the star; but it must mean grading the visibility and importance of the background in careful relation to the importance of the characters and the scenes they are playing.

We shall do well not to compete too strongly with Shakespeare in such matters as the "temple-haunting martlet" and the silvered fruit-tree tops. They will do better in the audience's imagination than in our three-ply and paint. We shall do better still to let Lear raise the storm from the whirling tempest of his spirit and not drown him out with thunder sheets and "twelve-penny hirelings making artificial lightening in the heavens," to the utter distraction of all beholders.

We must remember that the Shakespearean actor needs

space and generally a sense of the sky. Few, if any, of the plays are of the drawing-room variety. Sooner or later they get out and walk the surface of the world; in Shakespeare's day theatres had, until his last years, the open sky always visible overhead; we do not need to tempt the elements that far, but it will usually be helpful to have a good stretch of sky somewhere around. The plays are full of stars, of the cosmic variety. A star dances and under it Beatrice is born; Sebastian's stars shine darkly over him; Helena might love "a bright particular star"; Laertes

> . . . phrase of sorrow
> Conjures the wandering stars and makes them stand
> Like wonder-wounded hearers.

And Lorenzo still catches us by the throat with the matchless beauty of his "pattines of bright gold." The sun blazes from Shakespeare's heavens in an endless glory of imagery dramatically and purposefully used. The moon wields every kind of beautiful and evil magic. The west and the east bear exquisitely and ominously the burdens of the sunset and the dawn.

We need not, again, compete with Shakespeare, but we should spare him more than one corner of wrinkled blue cloth and a couple of spare spots that we happen to have left over, especially in such a play as ROMEO AND JULIET, which is drenched through and through with the imagery and influence of the heavens.

Generalizations on the subject of stage settings for Shakespeare, as on most other subjects, are apt to become dangerously misleading. Each play presents a separate problem; and every broad solution is encompassed with a hundred difficulties of detail. For, as Granville Barker very clearly puts it: "However high, with Shakespeare, the thought or emotion may soar, we shall always find the transcendental set in the familiar . . . Their [the plays'] rooted humanity blossoms in a fertile upspringing of expressive little things."

This is as true for the physical as it is for the emotional and imaginative aspects of a production, and it is in this very fact that our modern difficulties lie. For, although the transcendental qualities remain constant in value, the "familiar" has changed radically since Shakespeare wrote for an audience whose "familiar" background he shared; and here we return, once more, to our neglected partner, the audience. We do not and cannot look or listen with either the eyes or ears of our ancestors, and for the difference in an audience's capacity to look and listen the modern director, designer, and actor must carefully allow.

The Elizabethan audience was, as we have seen, taken into much closer partnership with both dramatist and actor than is its modern successor. It had, further, a hugely voracious appetite for a form of entertainment which was still novel, plastic, and capable of being molded to its will. In the theatre, as in the streets, it was vigorous and uninhibited, and it had an enormous capacity for make-believe. It did not have to be coaxed, lured, teased, and cajoled into accepting the illusions of the theatre; it positively rushed to embrace and further them. Yet there is evidence that when the theatre attempted any visualization of things or people that were known to its audience, these things had to be tangibly and visually accurate; hence the squirts full of red liquid for the blood which a modern audience would far rather not see, Antigonus' real bear from the neighboring bear pit, and the artificial rain contrived on principles still in use today.

The public was, presumably, exacting in the matter of costume, on which the Elizabethan producer spent by far the greater proportion of his budget; but this costume was, whatever the supposed period of the play, predominantly contemporary, with the vaguest of leanings toward the classic or the pagan if the play required. Elizabethan hats and farthingales and ruffs and rapiers are abundantly referred to throughout the whole range of the plays. Food and drink and flowers and games and pastimes are all such as the audience knew, whether in Elsinore, Egypt, or ancient Britain, and must have been so represented. Surrounded by these small, familiar objects, the characters were not strange and distant beings from another world but old acquaintances who had somehow acquired another dimension.

On the other hand, the audience was more than happy to accept Verona and Ephesus at second hand, as indeed Shakespeare himself accepted them. Bohemia was a never-never land in which magical things happened; it almost *had* to have a seacoast, like all self-respecting lands of fantasy, particularly the fantasy of the seagirt English. There were no illustrated travel brochures to familiarize every member of the audience with the exact topographical features of the Rialto, and probably the great majority of Londoners had never even seen the "high wild hills" of Gloucestershire, which conse-

quently loomed far higher and wilder in their mind's
eye than the cozy, precipitous hummocks of the Cots-
wolds actually are.

These values are hard for us to recapture. A much more
knowledgeable public makes demands upon us equal to
its knowledge. Our answer cannot be Hollywood's
superrealism, obviously; and the pageant productions of
thirty or forty years ago sufficiently demonstrated the
futility of any such attempts, even before the cinema
arrived on our horizon. But we must, in each case, consider the demand, and not run flatly counter to it.

This shift of angle and of emphasis goes deeper than
considerations of scenery or physical staging. The very
framework of each play is affected by it, and in balancing
the structure of our productions we must take it into
account from every aspect. Most vitally we must realize
the metamorphosis which has come about in the relation
between our audience and the plot or subject matter of
the plays. They have much too accurate a knowledge of
what is going to happen, right through to the final
curtain. Their angle of vision is distorted because it
lacks the possibility of surprise.

There are cases where, as it seems to me, we shall have
to exchange plot tension for tension of character in
order to compensate for the missing factor. For instance,
it would be wonderful if we could present THE MERCHANT
OF VENICE to a theatre full of people who had never heard
of it before and did not know that it was the leaden
casket which contained Portia's picture or that she
would succeed in rescuing Antonio from Shylock's
clutches by the quibble of "this bond doth give thee here

no jot of blood.'' Obviously, they would assume that Shylock was going to be foiled somehow, but how easy our problem would be if our audience were not, to a man, waiting with smug superiority for the inevitable "Tarry a little! There is something else.''

I would suggest that it is for us to reinterpret the scene by shifting its focus of tension. Suppose that Portia arrives from her interview with Bellario *not* knowing exactly what she is going to do. She has never seen the bond, and neither has he. He has told her that if she can find a flaw in it, she can rescue Antonio and also deliver Shylock over to the provisions of the Aliens Act; but if the bond is legally good, she may have a hard time proving that Shylock has "indirectly and directly too" conspired against the defendant's life.

After all, no one has even told Portia of the detailed "pound of flesh" proviso. All she knows, or all we know she knows, is Jessica's:

> . . . he would rather have Antonio's flesh
> Than twenty times the value of the sum
> That he did owe him,

and Antonio's phrase in his letter: "since in paying it [the bond] it is impossible I should live.'' These are pretty vague data for Bellario. It is true that the Duke's messenger had presumably acquainted Bellario with some further details, but in the theatre, with our attention concentrated on the protagonists, we shall not pay very close attention to what one off-stage character may have told another.

On comes Portia to the trial. In a few seconds she has pulled herself together and measured the antagonists;

Antonio confesses the bond; to Shylock she makes her famous plea for mercy, but it breaks against his implacable resolve. She asks whether Antonio is able to discharge the money, knowing of course that she herself has made it possible and hoping that a "settlement in court" may be effected. More merciful than Shylock, she does not immediately threaten him with possible penalties, nor has she, as yet, the clear power.

But Shylock refuses the settlement. She is really driven back on the hope that there may be some flaw in the bond; she asks to see it, but a hasty glance reveals no loophole. Again and again she delays, while she frantically searches the wording of the bond. Her very repetitions—"You must prepare your bosom for his knife" and "therefore lay bare your bosom"—are a desperate pretext for delay. She asks are there balances ready to weigh the flesh, is there a surgeon in attendance, hoping in each case to secure a respite. She sits down with Nerissa while Antonio makes his last farewells, praying by this time for enlightenment, panic-stricken that she may fail. Her wry little "your wife would give you little thanks for that" to Bassanio, is not a heartless joke while she plays callous cat-and-mouse with Shylock and Antonio, but is wrung irresistibly from her. She makes a last desperate bid for time with her double "The court awards it and the law doth give it" (her eyes still searching the fatal bond), "the law allows it and the court awards it"; and then at the very last second the solution, simple and complete, flashes over her.

"Tarry a little! there is something else."

If these words can blaze from her in an uncontrollable burst of passionate relief, she will have brought into the scene a new element of genuine and thrilling emotion. I do not claim that this can have been the scene's original interpretation; I do believe that it is legitimate interpretation, designed for a present-day audience. In almost every one of the better known plays, there are instances where such factors as these must be taken into consideration.

Many elements in the subject matter of the plays have changed in value for us. Ghosts and witches and feigned madness seem to have had a certain dramatic appeal for the Elizabethans. The closest modern equivalent is probably to be found in psychiatry and the manifestations of mental suggestion. Again, war is no longer to us an exciting pictorial tournament, filled with "pride, pomp and circumstance," in which picked representatives of opposing sides can do battle much in the manner of baseball teams; where even death is glorious and the misery of the vanquished is minimized. Nowadays war is an irredeemable planetary disaster from which not one of us is immune. It has grown hard for us to participate with eagerness or excitement in the "once-upon-a-time" issues of Shakespeare's mimic battles.

To a lesser degree, we are troubled by innumerable topical allusions, some of which elude even the scholars and all of which need a program note for their elucidation. It is possible to wonder just what an audience three hundred years hence could conceivably make of THE MAN WHO CAME TO DINNER. Parts of such plays as LOVE'S LABOUR'S LOST are equally obscure to us. We are apt to think that a blue pencil will remedy our difficulty. But sometimes the line or allusion, however unintelligible in its exact meaning, remains essential to the pattern or sequence of the scene, and we must retain it and grace it as best we can. Sometimes a topical allegory is woven into the design of the play, as the story of Essex supposedly suggests the story of Achilles in TROILUS AND CRESSIDA. But the plays are never dependent on such by-products for their main strength. Shakespeare was too good a dramatist to write a dramatized gossip column filled with allegorical nomenclature.

But there remains one very important barrier between us and the ideal actor-audience collaboration at which we aim. Our public can no longer take the great characters in Shakespeare fresh, newly blazing from the mint of his mind, bursting with an astonishing revelation of undreamed power. Our audience may feel that no Hamlet, no Lear, no Cleopatra can match the individual vision which the printed page has already created for them. This is a hard challenge for the theatre to meet. Moreover, the majority of our adult hearers have actually seen the great plays performed many times. They nurse ecstatic memories of Barrymore's Hamlet, or Forbes-Robertson's, or John Gielgud's, or Maurice Evans's. They remember what So-and-so looked like when he did such-and-such a thing, how a certain scene was staged, what piece of business the "comics" did at some given moment. They yearn for all these things, grown dearer with memory.

It is the actor's task to present an interpretation that is fresh, arresting, genuine, which will not imitate or consciously strive to supersede the performances of his predecessors but claim its own new life. It is the actor alone who can bridge for us all the gulfs between us and Shakespeare. As Shakespeare relied primarily and finally on the power of his characters to hold attention and arouse emotion, to project the play's content to the exclusion of all facilities or shortcomings in its physical production, so we must rely on the actor to do precisely the same thing today.

CHAPTER FIVE

"These Our Actors"

IT has often been said that Lear is unactable. Antony and Cleopatra have resoundingly defeated a continuous array of glittering names—and incidentally provided an equal number of play-stealing successes for the happy portrayers of Enobarbus. Yet RICHARD III, which cannot be placed anywhere near the top of Shakespeare's greatest plays and is indeed definitely among his juvenilia, was the most constant Shakespearean vehicle for all the great actors who dominated the English-speaking theatre for a period of a hundred and fifty years; and Hamlet is to an English or American actor what Phèdre is to a French actress, the final test and hallmark of his stature.

We might as well admit that Shakespeare's continued appearance on the marquees of the world's theatres is largely due to the fact that he provided an array of parts which no actor can resist. By the same token, he wrote no parts which an actor sufficiently equipped cannot

encompass, nor need there ever be the tug of war between the performer and the pattern of the play which
for so many years practically invalidated Shakespearean
productions, and even caused the clumsy butcherings of
Nahum Tate and Colley Cibber to be accepted as better
theatre vehicles than the original dramatist had himself
provided.

After all, he wrote for actors; he even wrote with
specific actors in his mind; he knew their limitations;
and, if his driving genius sometimes led him to stretch
his human material practically to snapping point, his
sound theatre experience never allowed him to render
his fellows ridiculous. There is no valid reason to suppose that he looked upon his work as "going through
the agony" of fitting his genius to the pattern of his
actors, which is how some scholars regard it. Mr.
Robert E. Sherwood cannot have thought that the writing of such diverse plays as REUNION IN VIENNA, IDIOT'S
DELIGHT, and THERE SHALL BE NO NIGHT for the Lunts,
was particularly agonizing. The results have certainly
proved the reverse. It was part of the Elizabethan actor's
business to be flexible and various; a modern actor
seldom has such opportunities to practice the varied
facets of his art as was enjoyed by Shakespeare and his
company. The standard of the "original" productions
seems to have been remarkably high, though it is hard
to judge from contemporary criticism just how a modern
audience would view them.

The standard requirements of a good actor have,
however, never been more succinctly put than by Shakespeare himself in Hamlet's famous speeches to the

Players. They could be learned by heart by every acting student today with profit to everybody concerned. Heywood in 1612 writes a similarly valid discourse on the art of acting, going back to Roman times for his initial authority. He then continues: "A delivery and sweet action is the gloss and beauty of any discourse that belongs to a scholar, and this is the action behoveful in any that profess this quality: not to use any impudent or forced motion in any part of the body, nor rough or other violent gesture, nor on the contrary to stand like a stiff starched man, but to qualify everything according to the nature of the person personated; for in over-reaching tricks, and toying too much in the anticke habit of humours, men of the . . . best reputations may break into the most violent absurdities."

This does not sound very much like the "ham" method with which so many great actors of the past are charged. This fear of being "ham" is the bogey of the modern actor, trained to a tradition of Anglo-Saxon self-consciousness coupled with a reticent "reserve" which is too often barren of anything to reserve. When an actor rises to the greatness of his vision with the full armory of his physical powers, that, if his vision be great enough, is genius. When his physical prowess outruns the fervor and truth of his vision, ceases to be any sort of impersonation, and becomes merely the actor on parade, then we may call him a "ham."

We may accept that the Elizabethan style of acting was much fuller and physically freer than ours. It was an open-air style, deriving at only one remove from the days of the innyard, with all its free-and-easy crudities,

let alone the competition of any and every street noise
or neighboring activity. Shakespeare's company, still,
let us remember, playing in the open air, must have used
a broad and vigorous method. In the plays themselves
are strong hints for us. Regan knits her brows and bites
her lips; Katharine is exhorted by Petruchio not to
"look big, nor stamp nor swear nor fret," a line which
the Shrew of today is apt to observe with some difficulty
and a faintly apologetic overtone. In TROILUS AND
CRESSIDA, there is a reference to the actor who

> . . . thinks it rich
> To hear the wooden dialogue and sound
> Twixt his stretched footing and the scaffoldage;

and Hamlet, putting in his evidence as usual, directs the
Players not to "saw the air too much" with their hands,
and says of the Player King that, given the cue for
passion,

> . . . he would drown the stage with tears,
> And cleave the general ear with horrid speech,
> Make mad the guilty and appal the free,
> Confound the ignorant, and amaze indeed
> The very faculty of eyes and ears.

Vocally, Elizabethan actors were both fuller and faster
than we are; it is not simply the evidence of ROMEO AND
JULIET's "two hours' traffic of our stage" or HENRY
VIII's "two short hours" which leads us to suppose this.
The very medium of Shakespeare's verse commands it;
he uses it, constantly, for speed and force and pressure,
for the shading of comedy, as swift and delicate as shot
silk, for verbal thrust and parry which has no counter-

part today in what has been called ''typewriting dialogue.''

Almost the first thing a modern actor finds about playing Shakespeare is that he hasn't enough breath; he takes refuge, at first, in end-stopping the verse and in splitting the prose clean against the mathematical involution of its phrasing. Later he develops a diaphragm which is the despair of his tailors, and finally makes of his voice the flexible and resonant instrument which Shakespeare's verse and prose absolutely demand. He still cannot, unfortunately, re-create his audiences' ears, dulled and slow hearing from neglect of theatre listening. He has therefore to speak more slowly than would have been necessary with an Elizabethan public.

The evolution of Shakespeare's use of verse for the predominantly dramatic purpose to which he was forging his weapons must have involved a similar progression in his actors' power to use it. When Shakespeare first wrote, or rewrote, HENRY VI for them, there can have been no one in the company who could have made very good sense of his later verse. They were used to such good straightforward cursing as York's:

> She-wolf of France, but worse than wolves of France,
> Whose tongue more poisons than the adder's tooth!
> How ill-beseeming is it in thy sex
> To triumph like an Amazonian trull,
> Upon their woes whom fortune captivates!
> But that thy face is, vizard-like, unchanging,
> Made impudent by use of evil deeds,
> I would assay, proud Queen, to make thee blush!

which he then assays for a further thirty lines straight.

But it is questionable whether Burbage could have then spoken, and certain that Shakespeare could not then have written, the self-tortured frenzy of a jealous man, such as Leontes':

> You my lords,
> Look on her, mark her well; be but about
> To say "she is a goodly lady," and
> The justice of your hearts will thereto add
> "'Tis pity she's not honest, honourable:"
> Praise her but for this, her out-door form,
> (Which on my faith deserves high speech) and straight
> The shrug, the hum or ha (these pretty hands
> That Calumny doth use; O, I am out,
> That mercy does, for calumny will sear
> Virtue itself:) these shrugs, these hums, and ha's,
> When you have said "she's goodly," come between
> Ere you can say "she's honest:" but be't known,
> (From him that has most cause to grieve it should be,)
> She's an adultress.

Shakespeare does not despise Marlowe's thunder. Who could underrate the ringing music of Tamburlaine's lament for Zenocrate, with its recurrent diapason, or the majestic march of:

> Raise cavalieros higher than the clouds,
> Batter the shining palace of the sun,
> And shiver all the starry firmament.

Certainly not the actors, whose voices were trained and accustomed to its orchestral quality. But Shakespeare, for the first time in English, evolves the use of verse as a medium for the delineation of character.

All through the plays he gives the orator his chance; with Henry V's "Once more unto the breach, dear friends," with the earlier Antony's "Friends, Romans, countrymen," right through to Timon and Lear and Coriolanus. And, Heaven help us, the elocutionists have not failed to take advantage of their opportunities.

But what comes to be increasingly important is not so much the lungs and the larynx, as the heart and the head. Actors do not, however, need long pauses in which to do their thinking and feeling, laboriously to drag up an emotion from about knee level, or conscientiously to let us see the workings of a Machiavellian mind. There is such an infinite variety of stress, phrase, pause, and emphasis in Shakespeare's writing that they will find the framework of their thinking exactly planned and provided for. But they do need clear heads to keep the motif, the thought line, of a long speech clearly held through the lavish involution of metaphor and elaboration with which Shakespeare will surround it.

Take Titania's defiance to Oberon which begins:

These are the forgeries of jealousy:
And never, since the middle summer's spring,
Met we on hill, in dale, forest or mead,
By paved fountain, or by rushy brook,
Or in the beached margent of the sea,
To dance our ringlets to the whistling wind,
But with thy brawls thou hast disturbed our sport.
Therefore the winds, piping to us in vain,
As in revenge, have suck'd up, from the sea,
Contagious fogs; . . .

The whole speech, another twenty-five lines of intricate and exquisite imagery, leads to:

And this same progeny of evils comes
From our debate, from our dissension;

The actress must in each case remember the nails of argument from which the web of elaboration hangs: "And never . . . met we . . . but with thy brawls thou hast disturbed our sport. Therefore . . . " nature has been variously uprooted, because of "our debate, our dissension." It is fatal to get so lost in poetic fantasy that the audience is conscious only of a lot of pretty words which do not seem to make much sense.

Speeches such as these will find out for the actor how much breath he needs. Take Portia's speech when Bassanio chooses the leaden casket:

> How all the other passions fleet to air,
> As doubtful thoughts, and rash-embraced despair,
> And shudd'ring fear, and green-eyed jealousy!
> O love! be moderate! allay thy ecstasy!
> In measure rein thy joy, scant this excess!
> I fear too much thy blessing! make it less
> For fear I surfeit.

To linger lovingly and colorfully over "doubtful" and "rash-embraced" and "shudd'ring" and "jealousy," or to pause for breath at every comma, is to destroy entirely the very feel, the rush and wind of ecstasy.

The actor will need more than technical facility when he comes to think, really think, through the King's prayer speech in HAMLET. Seldom has a "villain" been given so lucid a piece of self-revelation, so supple in expression that we are hardly aware until afterward how completely Claudius has laid bare the conflict in his soul, doubts and scruples which are not so very far removed from Hamlet's own, until their bitter resolution at the end of the scene where Claudius finally puts aside compunction and hesitation. This is not an aria; it is the revelation of a subtle mind and of a soul more deeply troubled and afraid than Claudius himself had realized. The force and clarity of an actor's thinking will alone make it clear to an audience.

There are, however, lyric passages in Shakespeare which will be destroyed if clear thinking results in commonplace speaking. Thought takes wings—just as in the Chinese theatre, which provides us with yet another analogy, song is used to replace speech in order to lift the audience to a different, less realistic plane of emotion. Shakespeare's imagery, his wealth of metaphor and word fantasias, often perform a similar function. And there are, one need hardly add, passages in Shakespeare for which the actor needs to be, as Ellen Terry said, "in a state of grace." Prospero's speech, "Our revels now are ended," is such a case. Here a beautiful voice will not do; clear analysis will not suffice either; the actor must match his author in comprehension and vision.

It is difficult, indeed impossible, to deal with verse, the wedded element of music and feeling, in the dry analysis of print. Almost at once we are in the larger realm not only of music but of character and interpretative understanding. Generalizations about verse speaking can be challenged at every point; the method of dry dissection, pulling the lines apart and pinning them down with a laborious and largely incomprehensible system of dots and dashes and hieroglyphs for stress and pause, will get us conscientiously nowhere. One can only make to the actor the initial suggestion that he should think first, take a deep breath next, let Shakespeare have his way, and not fall too deeply in love with his own beautiful chest notes.

The art of speaking Shakespeare's comedy requires from a modern actor a lucid brilliance which, also, he is not completely trained to give. It, too, requires speed of thought, and great precision of enunciation if it is to be easy to hear and understand without falling into the trap of apparent effort. Shakespeare seems to have had trouble with his clowns and, as in his serious plays, came slowly to his own mature ease of touch. He found a tradition of clowning which has been, and still is, the hallmark of all the great mime clowns from the days of Aristophanes to those of Charlie Chaplin. A German stage direction of the period says:

"John Pansser comes in, wondrously clad; not clownishly, but venerably and honorably yet so that there is something to laugh at. He takes his hat off, bows to all four corners of the stage, clears his throat, wanders around a long time, and when that raises a laugh, he laughs too and waves his hands."

Good. Mr. Wynn or Mr. Clark could follow that direction today and still "raise a laugh."

Will Kemp was the Shakespearean exponent of the tradition. He was equipped with a number of sure tricks, allied to the mime method of the Commedia dell' Arte. Like Mr. Chaplin, he wore enormous slippers and had funny feet. All through theatre history there seems to have been something funny about feet. Very soon Shakespeare was to find himself falling over Will Kemp's feet, for, very early in his career, his comic characters round themselves out into a deeper and more gentle humour.

He starts, modestly enough, in HENRY VI, PART II, with the armorer and his apprentice involved in a treason trial to be decided by personal combat:

FIRST NEIGHBOUR: Here, neighbour Horner, I drink to you in a cup of sack; and fear not, neighbour, you shall do well enough.

SECOND NEIGHBOUR: And here, neighbour, here's a cup of charneco.

THIRD NEIGHBOUR: And here's a pot of good double beer, neighbour: drink, and fear not your man.

HORNER: Let it come, i' faith, and I'll pledge you all, and a fig for Peter!

FIRST 'PRENTICE: Here, Peter, I drink to thee, and be not afraid.

SECOND 'PRENTICE: Be merry, Peter, and fear not thy master: fight for the credit of the 'prentices.

PETER: I thank you all: drink, and pray for me, I pray you, for I think I have taken my last draught in this world. Here, Robin, an if I die, I give thee my apron: and, Will, thou shalt have my hammer; and here, Tom, take all the money that I have. O Lord bless me! I pray God! for I am never able to deal with my master, he hath learnt so much fence already.

SALISBURY: Come, leave your drinking, and fall to blows. Sirrah, what's thy name?

PETER: Peter, forsooth.

SALISBURY: Peter? what more?

PETER: Thump.

SALISBURY: Thump? then see thou thump thy master well.

Elementary, but serviceable. Then comes Horner's

last challenge and—here is the meat of the scene—the direction: "They fight, and Peter strikes him down." A good time is had by all, except Horner, who confesses and dies. York comments dryly: "Take away his weapon. Fellow, thank God, and the good wine in thy master's way."

But the tradition of verbal comedy, elegant and witty phrase spinning, was also at work in the Elizabethan theatre, stemming from John Lyly, the author of *Euphues*. Shakespeare, young and feeling his power, determined to be as fashionable as the brightest of the university wits, devotes a whole play to the euphuistic form in LOVE'S LABOUR'S LOST. The characters bandy repartees like tennis players; the grace and precision of it are enchanting in themselves. But he is already writing with his heart, and his "comics," as well as his court ladies and gentlemen, warm constantly into a simpler truth. In the last scene Biron, supreme phrase maker among them all, speaks, perhaps, for Shakespeare:

> Taffeta phrases, silken terms precise,
> Three-piled hyperboles, spruce affectation,
> Figures pedantical, these summer-flies
> Have blown me full of maggot ostentation:
> I do foreswear them, . . .

He confesses, however, that he has yet "a trick of the old rage . . . I'll leave it by degrees."

Shakespeare leaves it by degrees, never entirely. He splits the two traditions into endless fragments, until the "Clown" line of parts, as his contemporaries understood it, is gone, divided among a dozen human elements: folly, stupidity, humble service, bitter jesting with a sword behind the words; high, zestful living, and pathos and pure song. Sometimes, in the period which includes MEASURE FOR MEASURE, TROILUS AND CRESSIDA, TIMON OF ATHENS, and ALL'S WELL THAT ENDS WELL, there is satire and contempt and a savage disgust behind Shakespeare's fooling. He loses, for a time, the sanity and proportion of healthy laughter. But he comes back to it, and with the light-feathered arrows of Autolycus brings us to the unmalicious laughter of Stephano and Ariel's gossamer farewell.

Always the actor must first ask himself what kind of a man this "comic" is. The jokes may, some of them, have grown "pittiful drie, pittiful drie" to us who cannot appreciate what was once their young and daring novelty of technique or apprehend the sting of their topicality. Sometimes the very cadence of the line will still "get the laugh," as in Maria's description of Malvolio smiling his face "into more lines than is in the new map with the augmentation of the Indies." Sometimes the joke has obvious reference to some piece of stage business, which we must conjecture or devise. Probably Sir Andrew's commendation to Feste, "why, this is the best fooling when all's done," was motivated by what Feste did, rather than by what he said.

But more often the humor is dependent on an interplay of personality rather than on a verbal twist or a trick of "business." I have seen even the impossibly complicated "sorel" scene from LOVE'S LABOUR'S LOST warmed into human and understandable comedy through the humanity and lovable quality of the actors who played

Sir Nathaniel and Holofernes. For the richness of comedy inherent in human beings has not changed, and on this we must primarily rely. The elements of great clowning have not changed much either, and sometimes the director will be saved because a smiling heaven delivers into his hands one of those rare actors who can be funny by simply coming on and saying the alphabet. But such great clowns have never been vouchsafed us on a mass-production basis; and there may well come a time when the blue pencil is, after all, our only weapon.

This will bring down on us the wrath of the professors, but it may save our audiences some stretches where lack of understanding would force them into a shuffling inattentiveness that is our greatest dread. We must, of course, be careful not to dislocate the delicate rhythm of a scene or even an individual speech, not to underrate the value of "business," but above all not to overload the scene with an excessive mass of it, which will slow us up and drive a heavy wedge between the interlacing lines.

We shall depend very greatly on the actors themselves. We cannot cut from theory. We must wait to hear how the lines sound and what the actors will make of them. Some cuts which we have considered possible may go back; others will have to be made in order to temper the wind to an actor who simply cannot get over the hurdle in question. It is too optimistic to suppose that any production will find itself armed with a full complement of ideal comedians, and, with respect to the scholars, it is unwise and stubborn to insist on keeping in a joke that the actor cannot make funny, even though the fault be his and not Shakespeare's.

There is, for me, no question but that the "comedies" are much harder to produce today than the "tragedies." The balance between wit, fooling, low comedy, and poetic fantasy is an extraordinarily delicate one. The blue pencil is a two-edged weapon; the effort to substitute a stylized convention for the plainer human elements can be, when it's good, very, very good; but when it's bad, it's horrid, as the old rhyme says. "Simpleness and duty," however, will go a long way, and we had much better not be too self-conscious about it. Let us above all think the comedy, and the people who carry it, freshly, in terms of today, and make them recognizable human beings to our modern public.

There remains one means of dramatic expression which is strange to a modern actor, unless he happens to have played in the later works of Mr. O'Neill—the soliloquy. As with all his dramatic tools, Shakespeare takes it over as a ready-to-wear device by which the plot may be advanced and characters may tell the audience things which everybody else in the play already knows, while loquaciously announcing their own further intentions. As with his development of other technical devices, he soon makes of the soliloquy a far more eloquent weapon than that. The noble figureheads of HENRY VI recite at us, much as they recite at each other. But Richard III uses the freedom of his monologues to much greater dramatic purpose; he takes us into his confidence with such assurance, such gleeful power, that we are his, villainy and all, right through the play. Even his use of the apostrophe

Shine out, fair sun, till I have bought a glass,
That I may see my shadow, as I pass,

emphasizes for us the self-appointed world in which
Richard has his being, where no creature moves except
in reflected light and nothing is absolute but his own
will. We accept that this monstrous superman will
recount to himself aloud his own schemes and celebrate
his own triumphs for us to overhear, because none but
we, in our all-knowing dimension, could possibly comprehend him. His soliloquies are a poetic extension of
what Kipling reduced to the formula of every schoolboy
in Stalky's "I gloat! I gloat! hear me!"

By the time Shakespeare reaches Iago, the formula has
changed, but still it is the villain who most needs the
device of self-revelation, not the hero, who will command our emotional response without any such assistance. And again with Iago, Shakespeare is reveling in
the mastery of such a man; he cannot get himself to hate
Iago, and neither must we. The man has stature, in his
own right; he is no piece of mechanism, part of the
impersonal machinery of malice; if we were to think
that, we should belittle Othello, and the tragedy of the
play would be totally diminished. Iago's fascination for
us lies just in that smooth, flawless functioning of the
mind, which is yet so fatally flawed because it cannot
conceive of a power greater than the power of the
intellect. Edmund, in KING LEAR, is the play's chief
soliloquizer. The dash and daring of his first outburst,
his hand against all the smug conventions of society, his
analysis of them so brilliantly specious, will carry us
most unmorally with him throughout the play.

In RICHARD II, Shakespeare is beginning to feel his way toward a new device: the blending of the true soliloquy with the interwoven reactions of the other characters. Richard has a long series of exquisite cadenza speeches, but only the last, in the solitary confinement of his prison, is a true soliloquy. Each time he turns to his hearers at the end of his lyric self-analyses, the thread of his self-revelation is knotted to the progression of their understanding of him. So, after his salutation to his kingdom's earth, he links the speech to the scene with "Mock not my senseless conjuration, lords"; after the virtual soliloquy of "Let's talk of graves, of worms and epitaphs," he turns again to them with "Cover your heads, and mock not flesh and blood with solemn reverence"; and, after his speech to the looking glass in the deposition scene, he draws Bolingbroke back into the current of his thought with the gravely bitter comment:

> Mark, silent king, the moral of this sport,
> How soon my sorrow hath destroyed my face.

The soliloquy reaches its greatest flexibility and glory in HAMLET, where it is so apparently an integral part of the character Shakespeare was creating that any dissertation on its use would be redundant. He does not subsequently pursue this method of introspection because he is not writing another Hamlet. His later heroes, the men of action, Antony and Coriolanus, are in no need of it; and he has, by now, found twenty other ways of dealing with the establishment of a motive or the advancement of the story. Caliban will need it briefly, grumbling to himself as he sullenly trudges about his work; Autolycus will belong to the long line of liaison-commentators, his "Ha! what a fool Honesty is! and Trust, his sworn brother, a very simple gentleman!" chiming with the echo of Falstaff's soliloquy: "Well, 'tis no matter, honour pricks me on, but how if honour prick me off when I come on?"

In CYMBELINE, almost all of the soliloquies partake of the new artifice and objectivity, the masquelike quality, with which Shakespeare is experimenting in his last plays and which is least resolved in this one. But Iachimo has his long, whispered monologue in Imogen's bedroom, economically revealing and put into words of intricate loveliness; and Imogen herself will take us to her heart, if she is true and tender, as few of the heroines have done since Juliet's day.

It is a curious fact that Shakespeare's women are not nearly so confiding as his men; it is tempting to generalize from their wariness to their author's opinion of womankind; tempting, but probably misleading. Julia, in THE TWO GENTLEMEN OF VERONA, tells us directly a little; Juliet most of all. Afterward we receive occasional confidences from Viola and Helena—a few words only from Beatrice. The rest talk to their waiting maids a great deal, and Cleopatra sets up a hundred mirrors for her infinite variety. But only Lady Macbeth, most particularly herself and akin to no other woman in the plays, reveals herself by soliloquy first, and last by the broken fragments of nightmare.

The actress of today is divided from Shakespeare by a

crevasse of which the scholars have been apt to make too much, and theatre people possibly too little; by the fact that his heroines were originally played not by women but by boys. It is easy to see what Shakespeare refrained from doing because of this limitation, if such he considered it, but not so easy to define what positive effect it had on the great women's parts. He very rarely wrote an "emotional" woman in the maturity of life; the Queen in HAMLET is the only important example. There are some comedy women, of course, who are no longer young, such as Juliet's Nurse, Mistress Ford and Mistress Page. There is a beautifully tender old woman in the Countess of Rossillon, and one of the high, heroic mold in Volumnia. There are Hermione and Paulina in A WINTER'S TALE. None of these lies outside the easy range of the boy actor's power. If, as some scholars conjecture, the older "character" women were played by men and not boys, his scope was slightly wider. But in any case, the Queen is a type that he did not dare pursue or amplify.

The passionate purity of young love is Juliet's, and the boy actor could understand and portray it. Yet even here there is little physical contact between the two lovers; the balcony scene is one of the greatest love scenes ever written, and yet Romeo can do no more than touch her finger tips. When they meet at Laurence's cell to be married, their encounter is touched by a grave and wondering ecstasy, as if the miracle of their love were fragile and enshrined. Their parting, after passion, is all we see of physical contact between them. Shakespeare must have had in mind the weakness of his boy actor, but he derived from it a beauty and a poignant, ephemeral quality which nothing could have bettered.

It was harder for him to write for boys on the lines of:

> Rebellious hell,
> If thou canst mutine in a matron's bones,

and poor Gertrude is given practically no opportunity to show the sensual side of her love for Claudius. Yet what actress could better the image that we shall conjure up for ourselves from the "glass" that Hamlet sets up for her and us, the vivid, unsparing:

> Let the bloat king tempt you again to bed,
> Pinch wanton on your cheek, call you his mouse,
> And let him, for a pair of reechy kisses,
> Or paddling in your neck with his damned fingers,
> Make you to ravel all this matter out . . .

It is in Cleopatra that actresses have been most continually deceived. The very name registers sex appeal. Sex appeal is instantly sought and monotonously pursued in every modern production; and, as Cleopatras only get born once in several generations and, when they do, are, in their own right, people who make history, the actress of today usually fails to measure up to the comparison. But Shakespeare wrote a Cleopatra as quick and gleaming and elusive as a drop of mercury, not in terms of kisses close-up size, but devious as light on the facets of a diamond, flashing and shifting in infinite variety. The boy actor could do all this and bewilder his audience into a fascinated acceptance. They would not notice, they do not notice, that there is not one passionate love scene between Antony and Cleopatra which would be thought worthy of any B picture shipped off to us by M.G.M.

The modern actress could do it too, and better, if she would try to play Shakespeare's Cleopatra instead of a Victorian oleograph of the same character, as flat and gaudy and unbelievable. She would also be helped if producers would remember that the setting has as great value as the stone, and Cleopatra is set in the solid, carved mounting of the conflict between Antony and Octavius, the two disparate pillars of the Roman world. Shakespeare was not simply writing a straightforward love story; we shall wreck the powerful rhythm of the play if we so handle it and wreck the lovers into the bargain.

The memory of the boy actor and his probable achievements will help us to interpret many of Shakespeare's other heroines as he must have thought them. There are no sloppy, boneless, blonde milksops, wistfully bleating out their loves and sorrows. Perhaps this might be regarded as a malicious description of Ophelia; but, if so, she is serving a definite dramatic purpose. If she had been a woman of character and understanding, a Viola or a Portia, there would be no tragedy of Hamlet.

Desdemona is a young woman who has the strength of mind to marry a man from a different race and country, a "black" man, and to brave first her father's fury and then the possible censure of the whole Venetian Senate. Her lie about the handkerchief is not the lie of a spineless little ninny, scared out of her wits. The motive which prompts it is positive, if it is not wise or particularly admirable. She can face Othello and repeat the lie, more strongly, and a few moments later reason her love into forgiveness for his strange behavior and into strength to stand "within the blank of his displeasure" again, for Cassio's sake.

It is regrettable but, I fear, true that every woman will understand very easily just how she is trapped into denying the loss of the handkerchief in the hope of saving Othello's trust and love. The boy actor, as I guess, must have stood up very straight and young, without any whimpering or cringing, and said his "I say it is not lost" clearly to Othello's eyes.

Cordelia, of course, is plain downright obstinate, as obstinate as Lear himself; but she is drawn with a simplicity and firmness that make the tenderness of her last meeting with her father noble in its humility. The heroines of the great comedies are full and clear; the modern actress is in no difficulty, unless she is tempted to put too much sugar in the mixture.

But we have a great tendency to prettify the heroines of the last plays, Perdita and Miranda and Marina. It is true that Miranda shares with some of her predecessors the regrettable tendency to demonstrate her strength by insisting on loving a man her father professes to dislike. Shakespeare's heroines are, from a paternal point of view, most constantly perverse in their affections. But Miranda, fresh and tender as the first curled leaves of spring, is by no means a half-wit. Perdita, delicate as a snowdrop, is no less strong; Marina stands up in the brothel to which she has been sold and talks to its inmates like a mixture of St. Joan and Mrs. Grundy.

She would become almost Shavian if Shakespeare gave her a chance; but he transports her swiftly to the meeting with her lost father and delivers her to a scene of music and dream. There, too, he gives to Pericles a description which may speak for all these "golden girls" of his last plays, who seem to stand forever in the dawn. He seems to see in them the heartbreaking gallantry of youth on the threshold of the world, and to draw from their grave tenderness the comfort that he needs, after the storms and tempests that he, like Pericles, has endured:

> My dearest wife was like this maid, and such a one
> My daughter might have been; my queen's square brows;
> Her stature to an inch; as wand-like straight,
> As silver-voiced, her eyes as jewel-like,
> And cas'd as richly, in pace another Juno;
> Who starves the ears she feeds, and makes them hungry,
> The more she gives them speech . . .
> Falseness cannot come from thee, for thou look'st
> Modest as Justice, and thou seem'st a palace
> For the crown'd Truth to dwell in: I will believe thee.

The frequency with which the heroines disguise themselves as boys does not help us, as it helped Shakespeare's original Violas and Rosalinds. In fact there are a few places where we are in bad trouble. Rosalind's epilogue, her "if I were a woman . . . " is nonsense, because she is; and we are apt to think Orsino and Olivia really remarkably dull of eye and ear in not recognizing our modern Viola's apparent womanhood; whereas Orlando, Proteus, Posthumous, and Bassanio become credulous to the point of absurdity, in the opinion of the literal-minded.

But if we cast the right spell, Shakespeare's spell, in
AS YOU LIKE IT and TWELFTH NIGHT and CYMBELINE, we
should dissipate all tendency to literal-mindedness in the
world of fantasy and music which we shall create, a
world in which a man may thankfully consent to "still
his beating mind" and surrender to a dimension which is
rich and strange. After all, we gratefully agree not to
quarrel with the hypothesis that Lord Fancourt Babberly
could continuously persuade an entire collection of
assorted individuals into the unshaken belief that he is
Charley's Aunt from Brazil where the nuts come from.
Compared with this camel, Cesario and Ganymede are
gnats indeed.

In one instance we are, it seems to me, in a particular
difficulty with our woman heroine, and that is with
Isabella in MEASURE FOR MEASURE, admittedly a difficult
heroine in a difficult but fascinating play. It is hard for a
woman, especially if her personal quality conveys to us a
fulfilled woman, to prevent Isabella's refusal to save her
brother by yielding to Angelo from seeming a piece of
selfish wrong-headedness, arising from a sense of values
so distorted that we lose sympathy with her. The boy
actor must have had, in some sense, an easier time in
conveying Isabella's whole-souled, nearly fanatical, passion of chastity.

As is most usual in Shakespeare, the emotion is positive, not negative. Isabella's outburst in the prison,
when she turns on Claudio and furiously reproaches him
for the suggestion that death is a worse fate for him than
a night with Angelo would be for her, was not, as I
think Shakespeare's boy played it, a pathological in-

hibition; it was the outburst of a young spirit, as passionately in love with chastity as a young knight keeping vigil before the altar before he received the accolade. There should be something forlornly splendid about it, ''her face and will athirst against the light''; there must be no denial, but rather a fervent affirmation. The actress of today can play this and play it with added poignancy because of her womanhood, but only if she can give us the searing purity of flame.

It has been generally accepted that the employment of boy actors must have been a very limiting factor in the Elizabethan theatre. We are perhaps too apt to think of them as coltish choirboys, lacking in style or grace. The evidence is against this view. It is even possible that, if the closing of the theatres during the Cromwellian regime had not interrupted the training of boys for the stage, the convention might have lasted much longer. In China, it has lasted down to the present day, though the great imperial training school of the Pear Orchard is no more, and women are gradually ousting the male actors of female parts.

It is interesting to observe the several respects in which the English theatre at its beginning paralleled the dramatic conventions which have endured in China. We have seen that its freedom in space and time was very similar; and, from the playing of Chinese actors trained to impersonate women, we may glean something of what Shakespeare's boys, apprenticed from childhood to the same task, could accomplish. Those who were privileged to see the performances of Mr. Mei-Lan-Fang in America some ten years ago will remember the

exquisite grace of his playing. Occidental actresses might
well envy the truth of quality which he brought to his
heroines, whether it was in seductiveness, ardor,
simplicity, or passion.

Shakespeare's boys, of course, had no such tradition,
worn smooth by centuries of observance, as lay behind
Mr. Mei. They were a formative part of a theatre still
plastic, still feeling its way. Nor did they continue to
play women after they themselves attained manhood,
and could therefore never have brought to their parts
the mature comprehension of the Chinese actor. But,
if they reflected any part of such perfected art as informed
Mr. Mei's acting, they must have given performances
which fully encompassed the glorious parts which
Shakespeare wrote for them. They were, as he was,
dedicated to the theatre. We should not make the mistake of appraising them as schoolboys forced self-
consciously into long skirts.

The importance of one section of the Shakespearean
company is apt to be much underestimated today,
and that is the silent actors, the "Lords, Officers, Gentlemen and Servants," the "Attendants and others," those
who only stand and wait. Many important scenes are
critically dependent upon them. The end-of-the-play
revelations, the unravelings of the plot which we have
seen worked out before our eyes, will fall very flat
except in so far as we can see them mirrored in the emotions of the listeners. At the beginning of the plays, the
lineless actors must often establish for us the atmosphere
that surrounds our principals, the state of "public
opinion." What elements in the community approved

of Richard II, what sort of people disliked or mistrusted him, and why? Over what kind of court did Lear rule that he should have become the kind of ruler that he was?

In John Barrymore's HAMLET, the curtain rose on the court of Elsinore in blackness. Before the lights came on, the whispering of the courtiers standing grouped around the throne made itself audible; then, gradually, the light grew, picking out Gertrude and Claudius, and Hamlet, coiled in his chair, tense as a spring. The courtiers gradually hushed, and Claudius turned to them with the smooth facility of:

> Though yet of Hamlet, our dear brother's death
> The memory be green . . .

It sounds simple, but it took a lot of rehearsing, because the junior Equity members standing around in the black-out had to register by their whisperings that this was, to use Mr. Barrymore's phrase, "a very lecherous court." Now, that took some acting. It was the harder because it is extremely difficult for modern actors to extemporize in blank verse; and, when they do try, an irresistible tendency to laugh overcomes everybody present. The fervent "Esperance! Take it easy!" with which I once heard my Hotspur cheerleader nerving his men to the fight in HENRY IV was not conducive to the preservation of illusion.

It is of vital importance that the director should provide for every member of his "crowd" a consistent line of individuality, which the actor can follow out in its relation to every situation as it arises while he is on the stage. It then becomes the director's business to see to it that no individual line of extemporaneous dialogue is actually audible to the audience because of the blend of sound which surrounds it. But if there are any blank-minded lookers-on, even one, the tension and excitement of a climactic scene may be fatally destroyed.

It is hard for us to know, to conjure up a true picture of what the great actors of the past were like, because the innermost quality of acting, the emotional relation between actor and audience, defies printed analysis. When we read that to watch Edmund Kean play Lear and Richard III was "to read Shakespeare by flashes of lightning," we get a vivid picture of Kean's quality; but we do not really know to what extent he would move us, or how. The actor's instrument is himself, incommunicable by any alternate medium.

It is easy, in commenting on an actor's performance, to spin destructive phrases that will raise an easy laugh. Sometimes such comments do succeed in teaching us by contraries. When Shaw remarks of a Rosalind that "that dainty, pleading, narrow-lipped little torrent of gabble will not do for Shakespeare," or that a Mercutio "lounges, mumbles and delivers the Queen Mab speech in a raffish patter which takes . . . all beauty of tone and grace of measure out of it," he is not being solely destructive. We get some idea of what *will* do for Mercutio and Rosalind; more, perhaps, than a handful of superlatives would teach us.

We have old prompt copies, and contemporary descriptions from which we can gather the traditional business and tangible framework with which productions of the past were surrounded; but the essence, which is all that matters, escapes us. A tradition sometimes has the hallmark of tested validity; more often it is dead-wood. Those with which we are familiar should not be accepted or rejected wholesale in accordance with a general principle. Many times the powerful influence of time-honored theatre values will lead us to follow our predecessors more closely than we ourselves have realized. Many times, I believe, they may bring us very close indeed to the Globe Theatre of three hundred years ago.

I do not mistrust actors, when their hearts and minds are engaged in their work. I do not accept as valid the commonly received idea that a star actor will auto-matically distort a play unless somebody stops him. Shakespeare has a way of bringing the best out of his fellows if they come to him with fresh and honest minds directly brought to bear on the task of interpreting him with integrity.

Many great scholars, men of letters, and poets have left us the fruits of their study of his people and his plays. Mr. Mark Van Doren has recently written an appraisal of the plays which cannot but light candles in our minds. We shall be unwise to reject, as we so often do, the stimulus which Shakespeare critics can provide for us. But in the last analysis the actor must face his Hamlet, or her Juliet, alone.

There is not one "right" Hamlet, with all the others wrong. Shakespeare allows his actors a greater margin of interpretation than can possibly be pinioned by any single mind. He wrote to be interpreted, not to lay down a system of mathematics. The actor must use his own physical powers, his own mind, and his own personal quality, that essential flavor of the spirit which will insensibly pervade his performance despite miracles of make-up and physical assumption. It is recorded that Mrs. Siddons did not play the Lady Macbeth whom she ideally deduced from Shakespeare's text. She could not; but she absorbed her own physical assets in a totally different Lady Macbeth, not false to the text, but true to another facet of it and so powerful as to become a theatre tradition for a hundred years after she died. There were probably members of the audience who said: "This is not *my* Lady Macbeth"; but it was Mrs. Siddons'; and as she, not they, was playing the part, it was in that instance the "right" Lady Macbeth.

The director of Shakespeare will be foolhardy to evolve in advance a hard and fast, detailed blueprint of his production before he has met and reckoned with his human element, the actors. He will be more than foolish to allow his pattern, Shakespeare's pattern as far as he can divine it, to be thrown out of focus by one actor's personal predilection. The theatre is, we do not need to be told, a fusion of the arts. It is also a fusion of the spirit. There should be no boundaries to its vision, no barrier to the most revolutionary contribution nor to the oldest fragment of an inheritance worn smooth by time.

CHAPTER SIX

"Unwillingly to School"

IT is only of recent years that the theatre has bothered itself at all about fidelity to Shakespeare's scheme. Garrick, professing his determination to "lose no drop of the immortal man" yet omitted, "very properly," as a contemporary critic thought, a great part of MACBETH, including the Porter and the "trifling, superfluous dialogue" between Lady Macduff and Ross. An extant description of Kean's RICHARD II shows how far textual patchwork could go without fear of reproof:

The scenes of Aumerle's conspiracy and the character of the Duchess are cut. In the farewell scene between the King and Queen, some lines are borrowed from the parting scene between Suffolk and Queen Margaret in HENRY VI, PART II. The scene changes to a palace. Bolingbroke speaks a short soliloquy from ANTONY AND CLEOPATRA, TROILUS AND CRESSIDA, TITUS ANDRONICUS and elsewhere. Bolingbroke concludes with a short soliloquy, the sentiments of which are quite unsuitable to his character. The last scene is laid at the Tower, instead of Pomfret castle. After Richard is killed, the Queen enters and speaks a few lines from KING LEAR. She falls on the dead body, and Bolingbroke concludes the play.

It would even seem that Shakespearean pretenders are more numerous than we generally realize, and that the scripts to which they lay claim can stand up to the most drastic treatment, at least if we may trust the testimony of the following playbill from the Theatre Royal, Kilkenny, Ireland, in the year 1793, which announces a performance of

. . . the tragedy of HAMLET, originally written and composed by the celebrated Dan Hayes of Limerick, and inserted in Shakespeare's works. Hamlet, by Mr. Kearns (being his first appearance in that character), who, between the acts, will perform several solos on the patent bag-pipes, which play two tunes at the same time. Ophelia by Mrs. Prior, who will introduce several airs in character, particularly "The Lass of Richmond Hill," and "We'll All Be Happy Together," from the Reverend Mr. Dibdin's Oddities. The parts of the King and Queen, by the direction of the Reverend Mr. O'Callaghan, will be omitted, as too immoral for any stage. Polonius, the comical politician, by a Young Gentleman, being his first appearance in public. The Ghost, the Gravedigger, and Laertes, by Mr. Sampson, the great London comedian. The characters will be dressed in Roman Shapes. To which will be added an interlude of sleight-of-hand tricks, by the celebrated surveyor, Mr. Hunt. The whole will conclude with a farce, MAHOMET THE IMPOSTER, Mahomet by Mr. Kearns . . .

No person will be admitted into the boxes without shoes or stockings.

There is no reason why producers should not use Shakespeare's scripts as bases for fantasies which avow no particular fidelity to Shakespeare. It is extremely unlikely that THE COMEDY OF ERRORS has ever been so popular as it was in Mr. George Abbott's THE BOYS FROM SYRACUSE disguise; and Shakespeare himself used his own source material, or "foundation plays," with as lavish a freedom as Mr. Orson Welles took with the script of JULIUS CAESAR. If the end is as brilliantly achieved as Mr. Welles succeeded in achieving his, no reasons of pedantry can be advanced against it.

If we concern ourselves, however, with the specific interpretation of Shakespeare's texts as we have them, we must consider our author with a good deal more care. We should, at least, take the trouble to find the text which is as nearly authentic as modern scholarship can discover before we decide what deviations we think proper to make from it, if any.

In a book such as this, which can do no more than scratch the surface problems of Shakespearean production, there is no place for extensive textual criticism, nor am I equipped for so exact a science. Producers and directors, however, have been too apt to assume, with a relieved delegation of responsibility, that the study of textual problems merely "refrigerates the mind and diverts the thoughts from the principal study," to use Dr. Johnson's invaluable phrase. On the other hand, it is only too easy to get lost in the commentators' maze, which they can make as exciting as a "whodunit" and as relentlessly absorbing as a jigsaw puzzle.

But, if the theatre is to prove itself worthy of the attention of Shakespearean students, as well as of the general public, it cannot afford completely to ignore the illuminating material which scholars such as Dr. Pollard, Dr. Greg, and Dr. Dover Wilson and their successors have recently brought to light. Their general conclusions may help us too much to be tossed aside with the "what-does-it-matter" attitude generally adopted;

and I believe that we in the theatre have some contribution to make toward testing the validity of their assumptions through our knowledge of theatre practice and our habit of theatre thinking, both of which Shakespeare himself must have shared to a high degree.

Shakespeare's works, as they have been preserved for us still retain "many of the shavings and splinters of the workshop sticking to them," as Prof. Williams puts it. Some of the plays were published in Quarto form soon after their production. The 1st Folio of 1623, published by his old fellow actors, Heminges and Condell, seven years after his death, constitutes all the collected plays now accepted as his, with the single exception of PERICLES, afterward admitted to the 3d Folio as being largely his handiwork. The Folio is our sole authority for seventeen of the plays; but the remainder survive in other texts, none of which is in exact agreement with the Folio version, and many of which differ widely from it. The plays for which we have more than one text may be briefly classified under three generally accepted heads:

1. Those which in the Folio have obviously been printed directly from the earlier Quarto printing, with only minor deviations or printer's errors: TITUS ANDRONICUS, RICHARD II, HENRY VI, PART I, RICHARD III, HENRY IV, PART I, LOVE'S LABOUR'S LOST, A MIDSUMMER NIGHT'S DREAM, THE MERCHANT OF VENICE, MUCH ADO ABOUT NOTHING, and KING LEAR.

2. Those in which the Folio prints evidently from another source, presumably an original manuscript, which, however, agrees substantially with the Quarto version: HENRY IV, PART II, TROILUS AND CRESSIDA, and OTHELLO.

3. Plays for which the earliest Quarto printing is radically different from the Folio and must obviously have been ''pirated'' and published without the authorization of either Shakespeare or the Globe Company: THE TAMING OF THE SHREW, HENRY VI, PART II and PART III, ROMEO AND JULIET, HENRY V, THE MERRY WIVES OF WINDSOR, and, of course, HAMLET.

HAMLET and ROMEO AND JULIET also exist in a ''good'' Quarto, presumably a printing authorized by the Players to replace the garbled version; these two texts are described on their respective title pages as ''Newly imprinted and enlarged to almost as much againe as it was, according to the true and perfect Coppie,'' and ''Newly corrected, augmented and amended.''

It seems that the Players were reluctant to have plays printed which were still an important part of the current repertory. After they became the King's Men and were better able to put their prohibition into effect, very few Quarto printings appeared. They did not intend that the scripts should be used by any but their own company, but once in print they were liable to be appropriated by others, especially in the provinces and on the Continent.

There was no royalty system to protect the authors, though printers were able to register their publications, or intended publications, with the Stationers' Company and thus acquire a kind of copyright. It was natural that printers should try to get hold of Shakespeare's very popular plays, and, when the method of direct negotiation seemed unlikely to succeed, they tried to reproduce the text through notes taken during a performance by a system of shorthand which was even then in existence and also by bribing the actors to lend their individual parts or to help in a memorial reconstruction.

Each of the "bad" Quartos so obtained has been the subject of heated debate as to its degree of correspondence with the performance which the "reporter" saw and the degree to which that performance may be thought to have represented an earlier "tryout" version by Shakespeare of the as yet unfinished play. When Heminges and Condell finally published their Folio of the collected works they avowed their intention of providing, once and for all, a definitive text of the plays as Shakespeare wrote them:

> It had been a thing, we confess, worthie to have been wished, that the Author himself had liv'd to have set forth, and overseen his own writings; But since it hath bin ordain'd otherwise, and he by death departed from that right, we pray you do not envy his Friends, the office of their care, and paine, to have collected and publish'd them; and so to have publish'd them, as where (before) you were abus'd with diverse stol'ne, and surreptitious copies, maimed, and deformed by the frauds and stealths of injurious imposters, that expos'd them; even those, are now offer'd to your view cur'd, and perfect of their limbes; and all the rest, absolute in their numbers, as he conceived them.

Unfortunately, however, the Folio's compositors were unable to live up to the perfection aimed at by their employers: and of late years much weighty argument has been brought to bear in proving that the "good," *i.e.*, authorized, Quartos lie very often closer to Shakespeare's original manuscripts than the later Folio text.

Both sets of texts are subject to considerable confusion in the very process of printing. The science was still young; the art of spelling was in an extremely formative

state, and even among the most highly educated men of
the day was still liable to the most variously individual
fluctuation. The hard-working compositors who tried
so honestly to set up their type from the authors' extremely difficult scripts made valiant attempts at sys-
tematization, and indeed are largely responsible for the
peculiarities of spelling which the English language so
confusingly displays today. Calligraphical confusion
added to the compositors' woes, for handwriting still
varied between the "English" script, deriving from the
Anglo-Saxon, and the "Italian" hand, from which our
own is taken.

Playhouse manuscripts were particularly difficult.
There would generally be alternating hands, due to the
several collaborating playwrights, the stage manager's
notes, and even the licensor's comments. Cuts would
have been made or restored, additional lines written in,
or separately supplied by the author, original material
transposed or deleted in handling the prompt copy for
successive productions, and stage managers' directions
incorporated with the authors' own. Sometimes plays
were abridged for shorter, touring versions, not always
with the author's consent; and, although it is extremely
unlikely that Burbage would want to study a new Hamlet every few years, some refurbishings were probably
thought necessary for revivals. We can also verify, from
modern practices, that certain cuts might be reopened
and other fresh ones made as new actors of greater or less
ability came into the company. The unfortunate compositor was apt to get understandably confused between
these various notations on the manuscripts, unless the

author himself were on the spot to oversee the finished work.

Sometimes the printers were supplied not with the author's own manuscript but with transcripts made by a careless copyist to replace the tattered and dog-eared prompt copy; these were often the work of some theatre underling who was familiar with the play from hearing it on the stage and trusted to his memory of what the actors habitually said, without troubling to check from the official script. This last source of error in the printed texts is possibly even more important than research scholars have realized. In every production, even to this day, actors unconsciously alter small words, substitute synonyms, or transpose the relative position of words and are not always corrected by the stage manager. Or they go to the author themselves and ask if they may not say "warm" instead of "hot," "because surely, my dear William, if it were really a hot afternoon, I'd never come in wearing a tweed jacket;" or they object that "this thin pretext" is a tongue twister, and can't they say "this fine pretext" instead. So the author gives his consent, but it never occurs to anybody to tell the stage manager, and the alteration is never embodied in the prompt copy. But our hypothetical copyist hears it said and embodies it in his transcript.

Theatre practice is regrettably far less scientific or standardized than a scholar's thinking. Some hardy guessing based on a knowledge of its vagaries might often come closer to the truth than the carefully organized theories of the commentators, but unfortunately would not be susceptible of bibliographical proof.

The theory that many of the "bad" Quartos were constructed with the help of actors' parts seems to me especially fallible. Only one actor's "part" has been preserved from Elizabethan times. The fact that there is only one is no surprise to anyone who has ever had to collect actors' parts at the end of a run. As soon as he has learned his "sides" the actor puts them down in any odd corner and forgets about them. Moreover, it seems that some of Shakespeare's actors could not read and learned by ear only, without a written part.

The only part extant belonged to the methodical Alleyn and is the lead in Greene's ORLANDO FURIOSO. It consists of small strips of paper pasted together to form a long roll, and its layout corresponds exactly to modern practice. The speeches are given in full, and the cue words are written on the right-hand side of the paper preceded by a long line. The brevity of the cues would drive a modern actor mad. Five successive ones run as follows: . . . my lord. . . . neither. . . . lord. . . . my lord. . . . lord. There are some very brief stage directions written in Alleyn's hand, usually a single word in Latin, such as "currunt," "decumbit," and, in a fight sequence, two directions spaced over the lines of a speech show at which exact point the losing combatants were to receive the coup de grâce. This would afford little data for a subsequent reconstruction of the script.

Nor is the further evidence any more convincing. For instance, in the 1st Quarto HAMLET, the actor who doubled Marcellus and Voltimand is supposed to have helped the pirate printer, for these parts, and the scenes in which they participate, are exceptionally correct. Yet it seems that this actor never knew his own cues, or the speeches which immediately preceded his entrances and to which he must certainly have listened at every performance, for these are wildly different from the text of the authorized versions. Similarly, this same actor must have been on the stage during all the general scenes, such as the Play scene, the Graveyard, and the last scene of the play, and he has done some incredibly poor reporting here. Yet Prof. Dover Wilson even argues that the Folio texts for THE TWO GENTLEMEN OF VERONA and THE MERRY WIVES OF WINDSOR and parts of A WINTER'S TALE were entirely reconstructed from actors' memories and from a collection of the acting parts, owing to the loss of the complete script.

At this, common sense utterly rebels. THE TWO GENTLE-MEN OF VERONA had first been produced about twenty-eight years earlier, and, although there is evidence for later revision and revival, it seems to me completely incredible that anything approaching a full set of parts could conceivably have survived, and survived in a state clear enough or, judging from Alleyn's part, full enough to allow reconstruction of any scene comprising more than three people.

One wonders whether scholars are not partly deceived by the remarkable state of clarity in which Alleyn's Orlando part has come down to us. On the theory of collaboration between different authors and active participation of the acting company, it would seem probable that this is a fortuitous example of an acting part, not a representative one. We might guess that Alleyn finally got so exasperated with trying to disentangle the various alterations and additions which had been scratched all over the sheets of his part that he handed it over to "his boy, Pig," or to one of the assistant stage managers, with instructions to copy the whole thing out clean, for Heaven's sake, or how could he ever be expected to learn it?

Today plays are possibly less susceptible to alteration, especially in England, where the necessity of submitting the script to the censor, and of adhering in all important respects to the version for which license has been obtained, still parallels Elizabethan practice. Yet even so, we wonder whether research professors have ever seen a set of actors' parts, such as are left, in the state of disorganization which they have reached by the opening night. They might also be disagreeably enlightened by attending rehearsals for a revival, such as took place for Mr. Evans's RICHARD II after a three-month layoff. The difficulty is not that nobody remembers anything, but that everybody remembers, with whole-hearted conviction, totally different and conflicting things.

And, with the Globe Company, we must bear in mind that they were playing daily changes of bill and continuous and extensive changes of repertoire. As the Folio was printed about thirty years after the earliest of its component texts was first produced in the theatre, I cannot believe that the actors' suggestions, or their surviving parts, could result in anything but utter confusion.

In the case of the "good" Quartos, recent scholarship has produced convincing evidence that they were, in fact, honestly purchased from the Globe Company and in many cases were printed direct from Shakespeare's own scripts. Their readings, where they conflict with the Folio texts, have consequently found increasing favor, and no theatre director can afford to neglect a study of them if the play he is handling exists in Quarto form. Even from the pirated "bad" Quartos, we may learn something, often in stage directions, where the reporter's eye was more accurate than his ear. The cuts and omissions in some instances are exactly what any director, conscious of a time limit and not too scrupulous about his author, would in fact strike out today.

We may glean one or two interesting hints from their title pages as to how the play stood in popular regard. For instance, the 1st Quarto of THE MERCHANT OF VENICE is subtitled with "the extreme crueltie of Shylock the Jewe towards the sayd Merchant in cutting a just pound of his flesh, and the obtayning of Portia by the choyse of three chests." It does not mention what some modern producers have translated into the extreme meanness of Portia and the sayd Merchant in cheating the Jewe out of his just deserts. The running titles of HENRY V and THE MERRY WIVES OF WINDSOR mention, respectively, "ancient Pistoll" and "the swaggering vaine of Ancient Pistoll and Corporal Nym," which would seem to accord those worthies a higher place in Elizabethan regard than we are accustomed to afford them.

Poor Heminges and Condell and their devoted labors with the Folio have recently been done considerably less than justice. It is, indeed, probable that many of the Folio texts were not printed from Shakespeare's own manuscripts. It is hard to see how the original prompt copy could always have survived years of theatre handling and never been replaced by a transcript. We have, in a surviving script of BONDUCA, the unfortunate copyist's glum apology for certain missing passages, in his notation that "the booke whereby it was first acted from is lost: and this hath been transcribed from the fowle papers of the Authors which were founde." We may conjecture that trying to reconstruct a transcript from the "fowle" notes of Shakespeare's original draft was a pretty wearing task, also.

It is true that the transcript from which, to take a representative instance, the Folio text of MACBETH is supposedly drawn shows very evident signs of later additions by a hand other than Shakespeare's, notably in the childish Hecate scene. But when the scholars bitterly complain that the play is too short and must have been extensively cut, we are tempted to ask what could usefully be added which would enhance a theatre pattern as exact and nearly perfect as anything Shakespeare ever wrote.

On two other counts, Heminges and Condell have almost certainly been unjustly maligned. In plays where Shakespeare has evidently worked in collaboration, usually very early or very late in his career, critical thinking is based on a subconscious desire to claim for Shakespeare everything that we approve of, and a determination to blame on somebody else everything which shows signs of lazy or second-rate workmanship. For instance, we would like to pull out a plum for him from the midst of a sequence in PERICLES which is widely supposed not to have been his, the isolated lines:

> The blind mole casts
> Copp'd hills towards heaven, to tell the earth is throng'd
> By man's oppression; and the poor worm doth die for't.

On the other hand, MEASURE FOR MEASURE, a corrupt text but Shakespearean to its very fiber, has been split up into the most exact fragments of "Shakespeare's," "partly based on Shakespeare's original," "added by another hand," and so forth, because there are portions of it which the commentators would prefer Shakespeare not to have written.

But Shakespeare was far from writing always in his own best manner. He worked fast, hurriedly, sometimes quite apparently lashing himself to get the thing finished in time, often scamping the end once he was in sight of it and had got bored by the necessary machinery of tying up the loose threads. He stuffed in topical jokes to raise an easy, sometimes a dirty, laugh; he cut and altered, sometimes with the perfunctory method of a writer forced to go against his own better judgment. He passed through a period when his own emotional balance was so greatly disturbed that his workmanship shows plain signs of impatience and disgust, greatly to the detriment of its lucidity and poise. In the plays so produced he fits his people to a theatrical design with an almost savage disbelief that life could produce any such conclusion and writes shoddily through his own lack of conviction. Even in his best periods he gets led away from his line of thought into a web of verbal intricacy. He is by no means free of what Ben Jonson roundly told him was "bombast"; and, finally, as Dr. Johnson judicially remarked: "It does not appear that he thought his works worthy of their posterity . . . or had any further prospects than of present popularity and present profit. When his plays had been acted his hope was at an end: he solicited no addition of honour from the reader."

We cannot blame all the roughnesses of the Folio texts onto its editors. It is as foolish to insist on divorcing Shakespeare from all traces of bad workmanship in the plays as it would be overreverent for us to preserve all such blemishes in our theatre performances.

In one minor respect Heminges and Condell have been absolved for the differences between their texts and the earlier Quartos, for after the earlier set of publications Parliament passed an "Act to Restrain the Abuses of Players," which had involved the Globe Company in certain necessary revisions of lines and phrases which fell under its ban. One of its provisions forbade the "profane or jesting use of sacred names upon the stage," under penalty of a £10 fine. We are apt to be impatient of this, regarding it as a puritanical archaism. And yet, during the 1941 tour of the Theatre Guild's production of TWELFTH NIGHT—which is, incidentally, a purged Folio text—a member of the company received the following communication from a citizen of Cincinnati: "TWELFTH NIGHT would be so much better without the unnecessary and irreverent expressions, for example: "By the Lord," "By Heaven' . . . Irreverence always spoils a play for some people, and, what is much more important, you do not want the responsibility of having the actors use it, or of accustoming people to hearing God's Name used lightly." Heminges

and Condell would have felt justified in their obedience
to the Puritans' way of thought.

The second important accusation, however, which
has been brought against them, and upon which they
have been widely condemned, is that they did, in fact,
accept and print what may be called the "Globe Company Acting Versions" of the plays. These were not
identical with the script Shakespeare had originally
read to the assembled Company. Yet these versions had
been tested over and over again before audiences, and so
had been subjected to cuts and alterations. No doubt
some passages were lost which we would think most
worthy of preservation, and no doubt some inferior
material was added, especially after Shakespeare's re-
tirement, and subsequent death, when the additions
were necessarily made by another playwright. The error
lies, I believe, in the automatic assumption that each
and every one of these alterations must have been for
the worse. From the standpoint of the current theatre,
we cannot, I think, accept that assumption without
strong reservations.

The texts of HAMLET provide as clear a test case as
any. Let us leave aside the question of the "bad" 1st
Quarto and the debate as to how and from what original
material it was put together. Not that this corrupt and
mysterious text is devoid of interest for us, for it is
obviously drawn from some early draft by Shakespeare
of his material. How he could allow the play to be performed in so crude a state, even allowing for the mis-
reporting incorporated in the printed version, is extremely mysterious. But it does contain valuable pointers

for us. For instance, in the Closet scene the Queen says to Hamlet:

> But as I have a soul, I swear by Heaven
> I never knew of this most horrid murder,

and further agrees to aid him in his plans against the King. Later there is an entire scene between her and Horatio, in which she ranges herself still more firmly on Hamlet's side against Claudius. Such must have been Shakespeare's original conception of the Queen's attitude, and, though he saw fit to modify it subsequently, I see no reason to suppose that he reversed it.

But it is behind the other two texts, the corrected and augmented 2d Quarto of 1604 and the Folio of 1623, that commentators have ranged themselves during three hundred years of doughty battle. Q2 and F1 become protagonists as vivid and personal as Hamlet himself. The Folio is the shorter text, omitting 229 lines which appear in the Quarto and yet including 85 which the Quarto lacks. The Folio is much the more carefully printed, punctuated, and spelled, despite the usual and obvious compositor's errors; but it differs from the Quarto in innumerable matters of words, phrasing, spelling, punctuation, line division, stage direction, and speech heading.

Until the researches of Dr. Pollard in 1915, most editors had viewed both texts with profound mistrust, holding the balance according to their individual preferences and brilliantly guessing their way out of the murkier tangles in either. But the Folio was definitely the favorite. On such a basis, numberless classroom and

popular editions were built, and, for most of us, the
Folio readings are the ones which ring so familiarly in
our ears. This, in my opinion, must be taken into account in stage versions. For instance, it is the Folio
which has the famous "O that this too, too solid flesh
would melt . . . " Instead of "solid" both the Quartos
read "sallied," which modern editors guess as a mis-
reading of "sullied," and this adjective they accordingly
support with passion. I cannot myself see quite why
they are so greatly disturbed by "solid."

When Mr. Evans played Hamlet, he also felt, as I did,
that the substitution of "sullied" would lead the audience either to suppose that he meant "solid" but was
simply being rather Oxford English in his pronunciation
of it, or would start an automatic debate in their minds
as to what had become of their tried and trusted friend
"solid." We accordingly kept the Folio reading.

Dr. Dover Wilson's fascinating book, *The Manuscript
of Shakespeare's Hamlet*, unfolds the gripping human
drama which lies behind the modern editors' Quarto
preference, to which text they incline with increasing
determination. His conclusions, in brief, are these: that
the Folio was printed from the prompt copy in use at
the Globe Theatre and therefore represents the text as
actually played by Burbage and his colleagues, whereas
the Quarto was printed direct from Shakespeare's
original manuscript. Any modern author will confirm
from his experience how divergent any two such texts
are likely to be.

Dr. Wilson, however, postulates two "Villains" in
each case, between us and Shakespeare. In the Folio,

they are "Scribe P" and "Scribe C." Scribe P is the prompter, or stage manager, at the Globe. He is responsible for the cutting and pruning of the original text and also for several "actors' additions," such as Burbage's dying groans, which incongruously occur in the form of "O, o, o, o!" after "The rest is silence." Up to a point, Dr. Wilson respects Scribe P, and even admits that he sometimes introduced "technical improvements and clarifications." He was "a business-like fellow," and where he had to shorten the play, or cut away what seemed to him—or to Burbage—extraneous matter, did so with skill and with a due regard for meter and meaning.

Some of the cuts were forced on the Players by the altered circumstances owing to the accession of James I and his Danish Queen Anne; long descriptions of the Danes' habitual drunkenness became inadvisable. There is the usual Folio crop of "Heavens" for "God's," and other similar ameliorations. But the Folio cuts have been incorporated in almost all subsequent stage versions; the most inexcusable of them is the omission of the "How all occasions do inform against me" soliloquy. Apparently Burbage did not know when he was well off, or else had not the power to rise to its demands after the long, tiring sequence of the Play scene and the intervening scenes of unremitting strain on Hamlet.

Unfortunately, however, there are many smaller errors both of omission and commission for which Scribe P cannot be held responsible; and it is to explain these that Dr. Wilson postulates his Second Villain, Scribe C, or Scribe Copyist, for whom he has nothing but withering scorn. Scribe C is supposed to have made a transcript of the prompt copy, which naturally could not be spared from the theatre, for delivery to Jaggard, the printer. "He was," says Dr. Wilson, "thoroughly familiar with the play upon the stage, but, confident of his acquaintance with the various parts, he often allowed his pen to run straight on without checking what he wrote from what he was copying." Dr. Wilson accuses him of "irresponsible self-confidence" and "slovenliness," which he was cunning enough to realize would probably escape detection.

Poor Scribe C. I prefer to see him as a stage-struck, rather illiterate youth, a fervent Burbage fan who sat, hour after hour, his tongue stuck in the corner of his mouth, laboriously copying out this inordinately long play, his master's greatest "vehicle," in the happy confidence that he knew every word of it. He wasn't, of course, any too sure of what a great deal of it meant and wrote down what he supposed he heard without bothering much as to whether it made sense. Thus he produced "His beard was grisly," for "grizzl'd," and "each in his particular sect and force" for "act and place." Often he "misremembered," as the children say, and probably at least as often he faithfully wrote down the lines the actors were, in fact, in the habit of speaking, whether or not these were "true text." It was laborious work for him, who was readier at learning words than at writing them; but, because of his idol, Burbage, and all his hopes and dreams of success in following his master's footsteps, he plodded away at the allotted task. He little knew that his future fame would rest upon just this, and that three centuries later he would be dragged into anonymous notoriety to play a minor villain for Dr. Dover Wilson.

With the Quarto, supposedly printed from Shakespeare's own manuscript, it is a different story. Shakespeare himself seems to have been the First Villain, owing to his vagaries of spelling and more than usually illegible handwriting. One would judge from the variety of conjectural emendation of obviously corrupt words that he formed the letters of the alphabet in such a way that they were all practically identical. Among the "fowle papers of Authors," Shakespeare's must have held pride of place. The Quarto Villains are: first, the compositor, another plodder, but inexpert and not very good at deciphering; Dr. Wilson even deduces from some of his fancier flights of orthography that he was a Welshman; second, the press corrector, whose emendations of the compositor's efforts, although "not wholly wanton," were made very much at random; and, last, Roberts the printer himself, who so harried and drove the compositor that the wretched man can hardly ever have had time to stop for a "stoup of ale" and was forced to skip through the interminable manuscript at a speed which led him to omit numberless small stage directions and other apparent trivia.

Given a cast like this, and the apparatus of modern bibliographical research, it is possible to ascribe almost anything to almost anybody and to "prove" almost everything, just as two French critics once argued themselves into a duel as to whether Hamlet was fat or thin. But in the Maurice Evans production of HAMLET, we dutifully set out to follow the Quarto lead in disputed

readings. Dr. Wilson tells us that we ought to start
with the Quarto readings, preferring the Folio only
when the Quarto is obviously incorrect or unmistakably
inferior. Dr. M. R. Ridley, whose admirable New Temple edition the actors used, is a declared Quarto cham-
pion. But over and over again we found ourselves driven
back to the Folio text by the fact that it provided much
the clearer spoken, as against written, word; arrangements of speech headings which seemed to us dramatically more cogent, and sometimes stage directions which
provided valuable theatre hints.

Let me give a few examples. In some cases the Quarto
reading involves quite simply a clumsy duplication of
sound, which the Folio avoids. It has "Therefore, for
brevity is the soul of wit . . . " and "Wilt thou hear
now how I did proceed . . . " In each case we chose
the Folio's "Therefore since brevity is the soul of wit,"
and "Wilt thou hear me how I did proceed."

In other cases the sound suggestion of the Quarto
reading seemed to us a false one, and I feel sure was
altered by Burbage for that reason. A clear example is to
be found in the Queen's description of Ophelia borne up
by her garments in the "weeping brook," "which time
she chanted snatches of old lauds," says the Quarto,
followed by the modern editors. One wishes they had
tried saying the line aloud to an audience. "Look,"
one hears the Elizabethan actor expostulating, "if you
talk to an audience about old 'lauds' their ears instinctively hear 'lords,' and it's going to take them several
seconds figuring that you can't mean that, and finally
getting to 'lauds.' Can't you find another word?" So

Shapespeare found "tunes," and the Folio keeps it, and so did we.

For reasons relating to the indefinable rhythmic counterpoise which can only be judged by speaking the lines, we kept the Folio arrangement of Hamlet's last exhortation to Horatio and Marcellus in Act 1, scene 5:

> . . . this not to do,
> So grace and mercy at your most need help you,
> Swear.

The Quarto has the, to me, theatrically ineffective:

> . . . this do swear
> So grace and mercy at your most need help you.

There are several similar passages in HAMLET, and many more are to be found in the other plays for which both Folio and Quarto are extant. Dr. Ridley's New Temple ROMEO AND JULIET prints astonishing variants on the Folio text, which it is impossible to believe he can ever have tested by the ear.

As an instance of the Folio's more theatrically valid speech-heading arrangements, let us take the exit of Polonius after he tells Hamlet that the Queen would speak with him in her closet, Act III, scene 2. The Quarto finishes the scene thus:

> HAMLET: Then I will come to my mother by and by. (*aside*) They
> fool me to the top of my bent. I will come by and by.
> Leave me, friends. I will, say so.
> [*here, we presume, "Exeunt all but Hamlet"*]
> "By and by" is easily said,
> Tis now the very witching time of night . . .

The Folio rendering runs:

HAMLET: Then I will come to my mother by and by. (*aside*) They fool me to the top of my bent. I will come by and by.

POLONIUS: I will say so.   (*Exit*)

HAMLET: By and by is easily said. Leave me, friends.

I think it is apparent that the breaking up of Hamlet's speech lends it point and decision, besides providing Polonius with a definite exit, instead of a mere drifting off.

In another instance, the Quarto heads the line "In that and all things will we show our duty" (Act 1, scene 2) "Cornelius and Voltimand." The Folio has "Voltimand" only, which I thought preferable, because ambassadors do not habitually indulge in community speaking. My guess is that Shakespeare did not care which of them said it, and that the point was cleared in rehearsal. On the other hand, at the climax of the Play scene, after the King rises, the Quarto gives the line "Lights, lights, lights!" to Polonius only, while the Folio has "All." It is very evident that in practice the cry for lights might well be started by Polonius but must be taken up by "All."

The stage directions of either text are, because our methods of staging have changed so much, to be regarded by the modern director more as indications of what was wanted or what was done than as specific injunctions which he must actually follow. The Folio is more detailed, I think very definitely the stage manager's reduction to actual theatre terms of what Shake-

speare had more vaguely asked for. Both are valuable in
their respective indications. Judging from the Quarto,
Shakespeare evidently wanted a "Counsaile" for the
first Court scene, and I think we should give it to him,
even though it appears by the Folio direction that the
Globe Company's proceedings were more informal and
allowed the presence of Ophelia. The Folio's "A Saylor"
for the Quarto's "Saylers," in Act IV, scene 6, may very
well have been due to the Globe Company's scarcity of
man power.

The Folio's readings at the very end of the play are
illuminating. It has "Enter Fortinbras and English
Ambassador" (again only one) "with Drumme, Colours
and Attendants." Before the final two lines it gives
Fortinbras the command "Take up the body:" and
finishes up with "Exeunt marching: after the which, a
Peale of Ordenance are shot off." The Quarto's version
of the same sequence starts with "Enter Fortinbrasse
with the Ambassadors," gives him "Take up the
bodies:", and ends simply "Exeunt." This seems to me
to reveal clearly the stage manager's usual definition of
the author, which could be exactly paralleled in any
manuscript and prompt copy today, and also the interesting information that the company had contrived
to dispose of all the bodies but Hamlet's, either on the
inner stage or in some place where they did not have to
be taken up and removed. The avoidance of this plethora
of corpses draped around the set seems to me an excellent
idea, which I personally followed with the utmost
alacrity.

These examples could be endlessly multiplied. I do

not, however, pretend that in Mr. Evans's production
we were entirely won over to the Folio text; the Quarto
is manifestly superior in many places; and there were
others where our choice between the two readings was
frankly a personal one. I do feel, however, that, whatever the play, theatre people today will be unwise to
let the scholars deter them from careful consideration
of what Mr. Heminges and Mr. Condell have made of it.
Whatever their faults, or the degree of deviation from
the probable original which their text shows, they were
theatre men; they had worked with Shakespeare; they
and their colleagues had handled his scripts for almost
thirty years; the evidence that may be gleaned from their
edition of his works is in no case negligible.

The textual problem varies with every play, and its
solution with every editor. But the main lines of textual
derivation are fairly well established and are worthy of
more study than we usually afford them. When it comes
to the commentators' business of disintegration, with
the texts that are not wholly by Shakespeare, we may
well beg to be at least partially excused. If "another
hand" did write certain passages, there they now are
in the texts we must play. Sometimes the knowledge
will fortify our wavering blue pencils, but in the main
it is our business to produce a unity of impression which
will diminish as far as possible any textual disparities.
For, having decided upon our text, it now becomes our
business to produce it.

In the following chapters I shall not attempt to offer
anything approaching a detailed production scheme for

the thirty-seven plays, which would be an evident impossibility. In the theatre we work with highly flexible material, and it is, in my view, only the director of great mental poverty, or the temperament of the most unimaginative schoolmaster, who rings up the curtain at the opening night on precisely the same edifice as he had blueprinted in his script before rehearsals began. Shakespeare's plays offer an unequaled latitude of interpretation; the greatest of them, especially HAMLET, are inexhaustible. The standards by which a production may be adjudged good or bad are similarly subject to change. There is no book of rules. There are, as I have said, the actors, the audience, and Shakespeare; and it is the director's business to bring them into harmony, with justice to all parties. It is not his business to offer a set of showy directorial stunts based on an evasion of this issue, still less to lay down the law as to the right and wrong as applied to any production but his own.

I shall, however, review in outline the Shakespearean canon as it forms part of our modern theatre inheritance and in some cases offer possible solutions for the difficulties which confront us, or the fallacies which beset us, in presenting the plays today. What can we show of the real Mr. Shakespeare under the cloud-capp'd towers of Manhattan and over the breadth of the forty-eight states so far removed in time and place from the little wooden playhouse by the river Thames? We may certainly suppose that Mr. Shakespeare was always stimulated by the prospect of a new audience; what can he offer this one?

In quotations from the plays, scene and line references,

I shall use the New Temple edition edited by Dr. Ridley, because it is complete and easy of access to the casual reader. The reader who desires to follow the labyrinth of modern comment cannot better do so than in Dr. Dover Wilson's enormously stimulating New Cambridge texts, as yet only partially complete. The Furness Variorum series is a complete mine of almost overpowering information on every point and will furnish the necessary ammunition for any controversy whatsoever.

Part Two

CHAPTER SEVEN

The Early Plays

THE "early" plays I have here grouped together are those written between the years 1590 and 1595. The earliest of all are probably HENRY VI, PART II and PART III, PART I being preponderantly due to other hands than Shakespeare's. This trilogy, however, together with RICHARD II and RICHARD III, which also fall within the early period, may be more conveniently considered in conjunction with the other histories. The remaining plays show Shakespeare's full development from a 'prentice dramatist with a poet's gift for words and a youthful zest for the beauty and passion of living, to assured knowledge and dramatic skill. They are, in the chronological order given by Sir. E. K. Chambers, TITUS ANDRONICUS, THE COMEDY OF ERRORS, THE TAMING OF THE SHREW, THE TWO GENTLEMEN OF VERONA, LOVE'S LABOUR'S LOST, ROMEO AND JULIET, and A MIDSUMMER NIGHT'S DREAM.

TITUS ANDRONICUS need hardly be considered seriously

by the modern theatrical producer, unless he wishes to present an archaeological curiosity, interesting for its faint foreshadowing of things to come, and an object lesson to those who are so ready to inform potential dramatists that they have no gift for the theatre and had better stick to minor verse or else go to Hollywood. Both these courses would surely be urged on the author of a modern TITUS. The poet in Shakespeare, who was writing "Lucrece" and "Venus and Adonis," perpetually breaks through:

> The hunt is up, the morn is bright and grey,
> The fields are fragrant and the woods are green.
>
> II, 2, 1

> Now, by the burning tapers of the sky . . .
>
> IV, 2, 90

> What fool hath added water to the sea,
> Or brought a faggot to bright-burning Troy?
>
> III, 1, 69

And Titus' funeral oration at the burial of his sons:

> Rome's readiest champions, repose you here in rest,
> Secure from worldly chances and mishaps.
> Here lurks no treason, here no envy swells,
> Here grow no damned drugs, here are no storms,
> But peace and silence and eternal rest.   I, I, 151

At the end of his life, in CYMBELINE, the poet will bring the wheel full circle with the lovely song beginning:

> Fear no more the heat o' the sun,
>   Nor the furious winter's rages,
> Thou thy worldly work hast done,
>   Home art gone, and ta'en thy wages;

Golden lads and girls all must,
Like chimney-sweepers, come to dust.

But in TITUS the characters, with the exception of
Aaron the Moor, are wooden puppets only, and the plot
is hopelessly melodramatic by modern standards. We
really cannot do with a young woman who is careless
enough to get herself quite gratuitously raped and have
her hands and her tongue cut off to boot; who wanders
through the rest of the play gesticulating with the
stumps, and at one point is told by her father, whose
hand has also been cut off: "Bear thou my hand, sweet
wench, between thy teeth." The last part of the plot,
though Grand Guignol to a high degree, does not lack
a certain melodramatic tension. But the play as a whole
is irretrievable for modern audiences.

THE COMEDY OF ERRORS is better, but not, I think, much
better. Mr. Mark Van Doren classes it among the three
"unfeeling" farces, the others being THE TAMING OF
THE SHREW and THE MERRY WIVES OF WINDSOR. Its
mistaken-identity theme has gone entirely out of
fashion; we might possibly be prepared to take one set
of twins, but two are really excessive, especially when
one pair is so relentlessly funny as the two Dromios,
with their everlasting puns. It is one of the few plays
which may be stylized to the limit of a director's invention and with all the extended artifice of music, ballet,
and comedy tricks. So trimmed and graced, and mercilessly cut, it may still serve as an hors d'oeuvre for the
less sophisticated, especially if the actors saddled with
the Dromios can contrive to bring a real, and personal,
comic quality to our aid.

Shakespeare the poet is still with us, and to a slight degree a sense of character is allowed to creep in. One has the feeling that he has deliberately made up his mind not to try and graft too much humanity onto an entirely artificial slapstick situation, not that he was unable to do so had he tried. The Syracusan twins are just distinguishable from their Ephesian brethren. The actors will do well to emphasize the distinction. Dromio of Syracuse is not quite so brash as his namesake, and Antipholus seems spiritually younger and fresher than his brother of Ephesus; besides, he is given the advantage of being in love and therefore entitled to the lyric

> O train me not, sweet mermaid, with thy note,
> To drown me in thy sister's flood of tears;
> Sing, siren, for thyself, and I will dote:
> Spread o'er the silver waves thy golden hairs;
> And as a bed I'll take them, and there lie;
> And in that glorious supposition think
> He gains by death that hath such means to die.
>
> III, 2, 45

and

> It is thyself, mine own self's better part;
> Mine eye's clear eye, my dear heart's dearer heart;
> My food, my fortune, and my sweet hope's aim;
> My sole earth's heaven, and my heaven's claim.
>
> III, 2, 61

This is the early Romeo to his Rosaline; the later Romeo will soon come into view. Adriana has some vigor, aside from her foreshadowing of Katharine and even Beatrice. Dromio of Syracuse's description of his kitchen wench, his "mountain of mad flesh," shares her

capacity to warm things up. The play is not bad vaudeville. Perhaps we are a little spoiled for it because we
expect something more than vaudeville from the Shakespeare we have learned to know.

With THE TAMING OF THE SHREW, he bridges the gap
which lies between us and THE COMEDY OF ERRORS, by
virtue of the full-strength, flaunting, undimmed vitality
of his two protagonists, Katharine and Petruchio. Here
are people, people we can care about, and parts, moreover, in which actors may, have, do, and will "go to
town." There is no lack of vigorous brutality in the
horseplay of the plot; there is some juvenile artifice in
the involutions of the subplot, with its inevitable tangle
of everybody disguising themselves as somebody else
and nobody having the elementary common sense to
discover any of the deceptions. All of this is fair game
for the high spirits of actors and director, and Shakespeare would, I am sure, be the last to object to anything
they may chose to do with it, using any and every means
to beguile the eye and ear. We have seen the Lunts
brilliantly successful by such a method.

The Induction, however, points us to a different kind
of writing, even if the basis of its plot is no less artificial
than the Bianca-Lucentio-Tranio goings on. Christopher
Sly is from a new and different vintage. Shakespeare will
go to the taverns and the highroads many times again
to meet and talk with him. He is

Christopher Sly, old Sly's son of Burton Heath, by birth a pedlar,
by education a card-maker, by transmutation a bear-herd, and now
by present profession a tinker. Ask Marion Hacket, the fat ale-wife
of Wincot, if she know me not.

We have never been to Burton Heath or Wincot, and
Marion Hacket was before our time. But we have no
difficulty in recognizing Christopher Sly.

The grafting of the Induction onto the play proper is
more difficult for us than it was for Shakespeare, who
worked in a theatre where lords and their entourage did
actually sit at the side of his stage; he therefore had no
trouble in introducing the Sly party amongst them.
Their presence is apt to become too obstrusive for us,
because Shakespeare loses interest in them and only once
remembers their presence. If they get between us and the
Shrew herself we shall be enraged, and rightly; for
Katharine and Petruchio are what we come to see.

In the strange Quarto THE TAMING OF A SHREW, which
is variously supposed to be a pirating of Shakespeare's
early THE SHREW or, alternatively, the foundation play
on which he worked, there is more work for Sly and his
Hellzapoppin' gang; and the director will be forced to
have recourse to this if he wants to keep the Induction
characters in the audience's view. But even so, once the
play itself gets under way, it is hard to keep them in just
proportion to it.

The "brutality" and "coarseness" of the main plot
have been much criticized. Audiences do not seem to be
so squeamish. Nevertheless, Katharine and Petruchio
should not be played simply as an "irksome, brawling
scold" and a "mad-brained rudesby, full of spleen," nor
the progress of their relation interpreted solely as the
taming of intolerable bad temper by equally intolerable
physical violence. There is more wit inherent in it than
that, and much more humanity.

Suppose that the two of them do actually fall head-long in love at their very first encounter; in his heart, each knows it of himself, but not of the other. This will take a little more ingenuity in the handling of the woo-ing scene than the set of variations on kicking, scuffling, raging, ramping, and all-in wrestling with which it is usually provided. But a few pauses, a few inflections will do it; the very moments of physical contact between the two of them, when Katharine is in Petruchio's arms, can be made to help.

If this is established, the whole play takes on a differ-ent tone. The contest will be one which we shall wish resolved. We shall know that Katharine, in her heart, wishes it just as deeply. It will be her pride that is broken, not her spirit. We shall enjoy watching the antagonists dealing blow and counterblow, not without zest, matching each other in a duel which is not based on a thorough mutual dislike, as it has sometimes appeared, but increasingly informed with love and finally overwhelmed in laughter.

Katharine has the harder task, for Petruchio scarcely lets her get a word in edgewise; but she is amply re-warded in the ironic wit of her final surrender. Agreeing, with deceptive docility, to call Vincentio "fair, lovely maid," and to accept the sun and the moon as inter-changeable planets, she contrives triumphantly to better Petruchio's instruction. Here at last is a "marriage of true minds." It is not the destruction of one by the brutality of the other. Petruchio could never have endured a tame wife.

Katharine has not become a cipher; she has merged

her brilliance and masked her strength. This is not the woman to deliver the final speech as a groveling creature, fatuously exalting the male sex in general. Her lines are filled with a delicious irony, by no means lost on Petruchio, in their delicate overpraising of a husband's virtues. Katharine has changed her technique.

> I am ashamed that women are so simple,
> [*a wealth of meaning in this "simple"*]
> To offer war where they should kneel for peace;
> And seek for rule supremacy and sway
> Where they are bound to—
> [*"quote" says Katharine for Petruchio's ears and ours*]
> —serve, love and obey. [*"unquote"*]

And a few lines further on:

> But now I see our lances are but straws,
> Our strength as weak, our weakness—[*with a beatific smile*]—past compare,
> That seeming to be most which we indeed least are.
>
> v, 2, 173

At the finish the two come together in a beautifully negotiated, not an imposed, peace.

THE TWO GENTLEMEN OF VERONA has its own grace, some lyric beauty, the enchanting "Who is Sylvia?" song, two heroines, one of whom has wit and the other valiance, and the immortally endearing Launce, with his mangy, mongrel, adored dog. ROMEO AND JULIET is quick in the depths of Shakespeare's heart; tiny fragments of the mine from which he was to draw it, samples of the golden ore, gleam continuously in the sand. Proteus, an intolerable youth by any standards of heroic

behavior, disarms us completely from time to time by
such Orphean music as:

> Say that upon the altar of her beauty
> You sacrifice your tears, your sighs, your heart:
> Write till your ink be dry, and with your tears
> Moist it again; and frame some feeling line
> That may discover such integrity:
> For Orpheus' lute was strung with poets' sinews,
> Whose golden touch could soften steel and stones,
> Make tigers tame, and huge leviathans
> Forsake uncounted deeps to dance on sands.
> After your dire-lamenting elegies,
> Visit by night your lady's chamber-window
> With some sweet consort; to their instruments
> Tune a deploring dump; the night's dead silence
> Will well become such sweet complaining grievance.
>
> III, 2, 73

But he cannot melt us long with this "golden touch,"
for the exigencies of the plot require of him faithlessness
to his lady, attempted seduction of his friend's beloved,
betrayal of that friend to banishment and probable
death, and the most perfunctory repentance when
nothing is left of his other schemes, accompanied, moreover, by some nauseatingly banal moralizing in his own
excuse. We simply cannot deal with this stuffed shirt.
Valentine, who might rescue the play for us, is more
amiable but not much more lively; he is burdened by
perpetual conversations with his loquaciously wooden
servant, Speed, a puppet full of wisecracks. On the stage
we may do something with music, costumes by Botti-
celli, a fine clown for Launce, and the deceptive warmth
of personality which emerges from the stage presentation

of Shakespeare's most improbable plays. But we may as well accept the fact that but for Shakespeare's name on the title page we should never dream of bothering. The fireside, and the anthologists, seem to be entitled to this piece.

We should, however, claim, or reclaim, LOVE's LABOUR's LOST; for here Shakespeare wears his youth like a bright cloak, his mastery like a plume of feathers, and his wit like a silver-hilted sword. The play has been condemned from the classrooms as no more than a brilliant exercise in parody, outdoing the verbal intricacies and studied efflorescence of the euphuistic school; but it becomes far more than that; for in the end, Shakespeare falls in love with his characters.

Take Armado, the Spaniard,

> A man in all the world's new fashion planted,
> That hath a mint of phrases in his brain:
> One whom the music of his own vain tongue
> Doth ravish like enchanting harmony,

whom the King has hired to entertain his little court with tales of "many a knight from tawny Spain." Shakespeare may have started out to make him ridiculous. This intention barely lasts out the first scene; for at the end of it, before we have seen Armado, comes a letter from him. It starts with a flourish of grandiloquence, endearing in its very absurdity, and progresses through a minuet of phrases to its accusation against the rustic Costard, "that low-spirited Swain, that base Minnow of thy mirth, that unlettered small-knowing soul, that shallow vassal . . . " We are more than half won already to a man who can sauce accusation with such sublime disdain. At last he comes, with Moth, his page, trailing his tattered finery, his molting feathers, and his threadbare cloak, like the greatest grandee among them all; "his humour is lofty, his eye ambitious, his gait majestical." He sits, we suppose, with studied hauteur. He sighs. "Boy," he at last addresses the page, as one affectionately condescending to a very small insect, "what sign is it when a man of great spirit grows melancholy?"

He is, of course, in love, most reluctantly in love, and "with a base wench" too, the very same wench with whom he had seen Costard dallying, and the unfortunate progress of this humiliating but delicious passion constitutes his part in the play. From his "mint of phrases" he scatters pearls of largess: "Warble, child; make passionate my sense of hearing." "Define, define, well-educated infant." "Now, by the salt wave of the Mediterraneum, a sweet touch, a quick venue of wit,—a snip, snap, quick and home! it rejoiceth my intellect, true wit!" and his majestic yielding to Cupid, saluting him like a vanquished but not inglorious duelist:

Adieu valour, rust rapier, be still drum, for your manager is in love; yea, he loveth. Assist me some extemporal god of rhyme, for I am sure I shall turn sonnet. Devise wit, write pen, for I am for whole volumes in folio.

In the pageant played at the end before the King and Princess, a scene, incidentally, capable of being made much more delicately funny than its famous counterpart in A MIDSUMMER NIGHT'S DREAM, his humiliation begins.

He plays Hector, and gets mercilessly heckled by the flippant audience; he is incensed, not for himself, but for Hector. "Sweet Lord Longaville, rein thy tongue." he protests, "The sweet war-man is dead and rotten; sweet chucks, beat not the bones of the buried; when he breathed he was a man."

But worse is to come. He is accused by the base Costard; Jacquenetta, it seems, is with child by him. He is challenged to fight "in his shirt." He refuses, with passion. Pressed further, he is forced to the last humiliation: "The naked truth of it is, I have no shirt." But he redeems himself, with simplicity and honor. "For mine own part, I breathe free breath. I have seen the day of wrong through the little hole of discretion, and I will right myself like a soldier." Shakespeare rewards him for his reformation by letting him introduce the lovely song with which this intricate play so simply ends:

> When daisies pied and violets blue,
>   And lady-smocks all silver-white,
> And cuckoo-buds so fair of hue
>   Do paint the meadows with delight . . .

and gives him the final line: "The words of Mercury are harsh after the songs of Apollo. You that way, we this way," and so the gleaming bubble of a play floats up out of our sight.

If an actor cannot warm Armado into our love and living memory, it is no fault of Shakespeare's. Mr. Barrymore would give him greatness. Nor is he the only living figure in the play. Biron has been much discussed and praised. He has, probably, the glibbest honey tongue among them all and a good share of fine common sense. He thinks the vow he and his three companions have taken, "to fast, to study and to see no woman," the merest nonsense and says so. And when the four of them all fall in love, as they inevitably and symmetrically do, with the visiting Princess of France and her three Ladies, his ringing lyric on the virtues of love would win a saint from his vows:

> A lover's eye will gaze an eagle blind,
> A lover's ear will hear the lowest sound
> When the suspicious head of theft is stopp'd;
> Love's feeling is more soft and sensible
> Than are the tender horns of cockled snails;
> Love's tongue proves dainty Bacchus gross in taste:
> For valour is not Love a Hercules,
> Still climbing trees in the Hesperides?
> Subtle as Sphinx, as sweet and musical
> As bright Apollo's lute strung with his hair;
> And when love speaks, the voice of all the gods
> Makes heaven drowsy with the harmony.   IV, 3, 332

His counterpart, more lightly sketched, is Rosaline, an early Beatrice; and the two exchange some light, swift sallies, "snip, snap, quick and home!" The Princess has dignity and a gentler wit; the sonorous King, though more stilted, can be humanized too. Costard is juicy and round, if a trifle heavy. A good comedian can save him very easily for our liking, because he, too, partakes of the human compassion which students have so signally failed to discern in the play; witness his apology for the shy, stammering little curate, Sir Nathaniel, who has ignominiously gone up in his lines as Alexander the Great, in the masque:

There, an't shall please you, a foolish mild man, an honest man, look you, and soon dash'd. He is a marvellous good neighbour, faith, and a very good bowler: but, for Alisander, alas, you see how 'tis, a little o'erparted.

The whole play needs a gloss of style and brilliant speaking; unfortunately it also needs pretty quick listening. Whole passages in it are too long, too wordy, and too pun-ridden for our ears. If we are to redeem it, we shall have to be very drastic with the blue pencil, even though we protest that it hurts us as much as it hurts Shakespeare. The formalized passages should be handled with all the richest visual and aural trappings of formality. The setting should remain unchanged, so that the flow and movement of the characters can move through its spacious and decorated greenness with the rhythm of a pageant. But, above all, if we can love these people as their creator did and revel in their feast of language as we do in a brilliant piece of orchestration, we should be able to provide an opulent return for any audience.

The remaining plays numbered among this early group have been so long a part of the practicing theatre and have been so copiously commentated upon, their potentialities so amply translated into actuality, that there seems little to be added by theorizing. ROMEO AND JULIET, in particular, will prove a staple item in any theatre repertory so long as there is an actress left in the world, for she will surely want to play Juliet. An actor does not feel the same yearning for Romeo; he usually spends days of troubled debate as to whether Mercutio is not the showier part; while "Mercutio" will be con-

templating his death half way through the play with
almost as keen a sense of waste as did that high and
lusty Veronese gentleman, feeling the quick, sharp
pain of a random thrust and suddenly confronting
nothingness.

The productions of this play have provided a continuous commentary on the progress and divagations of the
theatre, especially in its physical aspects. It is a play
which makes us realize most clearly the crossroads at
which we stand today. The scenes are exactly set, without vagueness: A Veronese Street, A Hall in Capulet's
House, A Friar's Cell, An Orchard, A Tomb. But we
have at last come to realize that we must not split the
pattern of the play by dividing it up into little sets of
small, gaudy, Veronese bricks, with constant lowerings
of the curtain in order to rearrange our self-imposed
limitations. Two main factors have led us to apprehend,
though not as yet to solve, this problem.

Firstly, Shakespeare was deliberately following a
schedule of the headlong pressure of events in a strictly
limited space of time, so that their power is canalized
into a dynamic force; and to achieve this, he is using his
ungeographical stage with almost undisciplined freedom. The scenes following the Capulet Ball are marked
by the older editors as Act II, scenes 1 and 2, but they
are indivisible spatially. While Benvolio and Mercutio
exchange their callous jests, Romeo presumably hides
somewhere on the stage, smarting under this pro-
fanation of all that he deems holy until they go, at last,
with the words: "For 'tis but vain To seek him here that
means not to be found." He steps forward, completing

the couplet with "He jests at scars that never felt a wound." Then, it is as if he did no more than turn and stop short with a catching of the heart,

> But soft! what light through yonder window breaks?
> It is the East, and Juliet is the sun!

And we are straight away in the enchanted orchard, Mercutio and Benvolio a thousand miles distant, poor beings from a lesser world.

But somewhere in this sequence, Romeo must have climbed the orchard wall, and we, with our realistic minds, fussily demand just where and how, and can't we see him do it? If so, we must have an open "suggested" set, in which we can see the outside of the wall, for Mercutio, the wall itself in whose shadow Romeo hides, and the orchard with Juliet's balcony beyond. Here we are getting into some heavy carpentry. We can fall back on the old "front-scene" convention, let Romeo hide between the curtains, and have the curtains part behind him, melting into the orchard scene. Or perhaps we may, in time, evolve a setting addressed not to "the outer eye that observes," but to "the inner eye which sees," as Mr. Robert Edmond Jones puts it.

Later in the play we shall again need this method. In Act III, scene 4, we see Capulet, that lusty, gusty, unimaginative old gentleman, dismissing the tragic events of Tybalt's death with a commonsensible "well, we were born to die," and arranging for Juliet to marry Paris in three days' time. It is "very, very late" on Monday night. We know that this is to be Romeo's first, and last, night with his new-made wife. We know that even as Capulet is talking, exhorting Lady Capulet "Go you to Juliet e'er you go to bed," Romeo must be with her; and in the same visual breath we see them.

> JULIET: Wilt thou be gone? it is not yet near day:
> It was the nightingale, and not the lark,
> That pierc'd the fearful hollow of thine ear;
> Nightly she sings on yon pomegranate tree;
> Believe me, love, it was the nightingale.
> ROMEO: It was the lark, the herald of the morn,
> No nightingale: look, love, what envious streaks
> Do lace the severing clouds in yonder east:
> Night's candles are burnt out, and jocund day
> Stands tip-toe on the misty mountain tops.
> I must begone and live, or stay and die.   III, 5, 1

We are again in another world, the heartbreakingly fragile world of the lovers.

The outer world breaks through, relentlessly, with the Nurse's announcement that Lady Capulet is indeed coming; Romeo climbs down from the balcony; he goes; almost before he is out of sight comes Lady Capulet, with her "Ho, daughter, are you up?" There follows the scene between the desperate Juliet and her enraged, oblivious father, working himself into a pretty passion at her refusal of the Paris match and the imminent wedding. Briefly we leave the stormy Capulet house for the scene at Laurence's cell, where he gives Juliet the sleeping potion which may save her. Then back to Capulet, fussing and fuming over the wedding preparations; Juliet returns, and makes her submission to him. He instantly siezes the opportunity to advance the wedding to "tomorrow" and starts an even gayer commotion. Juliet goes up to her closet; she bids farewell to her mother and the Nurse; she drinks the potion, daring all the nightmares of the unknown with the childlike gallantry of "Romeo, I come! this do I drink to thee," and—it is an authentic stage direction—"falls upon her bed within the curtains."

The curtains are barely stilled around her, our eyes deeply filled with them, when we are back with the frantic household preparations simultaneously going forward:

LADY CAPULET: Hold, take these keys and fetch more spices, Nurse.

NURSE: They call for dates and quinces in the pantry.

CAPULET: Come, stir, stir, stir! the second cock hath crow'd,
The curfew bell hath rung, 'tis three o'clock.

A merry thirty lines of this, ending with Capulet's "Go waken Juliet, go and trim her up . . . Make haste, I say," and we are instantly back in Juliet's silent, shadowed room, with no more than a cold, pure, knife-blade of light slanting in between the shutters, and those still, unforgotten curtains. With the Nurse's drawing of them and discovery of Juliet apparently dead within, the outer world at last engulfs the oasis of sanctity which she has hitherto preserved for us, and the household lamentations complete the pattern; not without a wry little coda from the musicians engaged to play at the wedding, for whom there is nothing to do, but "tarry for the mourners and stay dinner."

It is only very recently that producers have realized the poignant heightening of tragedy which this counter-point of domestic activity provides. But it is only effective if the juxtaposition between them is unbroken and visually so knit that we never lose consciousness of it. Mr. John Gielgud in London and Mr. Lawrence Olivier in New York, both assisted by some ingenious and decorative sets by the firm of Motley, have recently attempted the solution by showing a scenic cross section of the Capulet house. Mr. Gielgud's version held the Capulets below and the lovers above simultaneously in the eye, to very considerable effect. But the danger of this method lies in reducing the whole sequence to doll's house proportions and forcing the lovers to play the exquisite closeness and intimacy of the parting scene somewhere suspended between the floor and the top of the proscenium arch. Here, again, we may be forced from our persistent realism and may turn with advantage to localization by means of lights and the merest suggestion of surrounding walls.

The second element in the play which will also drive us in this direction is its extreme preoccupation with the influence of the heavens, the sun, the moon, and the stars, dawn and high noon and night. The brief, ecstatic, tragic days turn to the rhythm of the turning globe of the world, defined with a procession of lovely metaphors and phrases. The lovers are "star-crossed" from the very opening lines; it is as if the wings of their passion lifted them too near to the tremendous candles of the planets. Romeo, in particular, is aware of them with his eyes and his soul. The director and designer will need what Mr. Robert Edmond Jones calls an "overwhelming sense of the livingness of light . . . Lucidity, penetration, awareness, discovery, inwardness, wonder . . . These are the qualities we should try to achieve in our lighting

. . . a quality of lustre, a shine and a gleam that befits the exceptional occasion."

This is the quality which the theatre must strive to recapture in ROMEO AND JULIET. The lovers themselves may do a great deal toward it, with a soaring of the spirit. The play is filled with flesh-and-blood smaller characters, which, if they are fully played, will amply give us the swift-moving life around them; Mercutio, of course, irresistible in almost any hands; Capulet and the Nurse, strongly, surely painted in with rich, warm color; the fiery, overbearing Tybalt; Friar Laurence, so full of wise precepts, so lamentably inadequate with worldly intrigue; Benvolio, dependable and sane in his own right; Peter, and even Sampson and Gregory, who start the play at a tempo which befits it; a gallery of portraits done with the opulence of Titian and the clarity of Piero della Francesca. No actor or director is in danger of underrating them. We can hardly miss the drama of Mercutio's death or the feast of theatrical opportunity at Capulet's banquet or the overwhelming music of the lovers. Indeed, our temptation is to get drunk with one or other of these elements. Let us remember what Shakespeare himself must have had as the theme nearest his heart:

> When I consider everything that grows
> Holds in perfection but a little moment,
> That this huge stage presenteth naught but shows
> Whereon the stars in secret influence comment . . .
>   Sonnet 11

Let us try to invoke the secret influence of the stars.

A MIDSUMMER NIGHT'S DREAM is as moon drenched as ROMEO AND JULIET is shot with stars. The moon is not in a malignant phase, but her radiance sheds a disturbing magic this midsummer night, holding all the play in an opalescent enchantment, where everything seems "translated." Only with Theseus' hunting horns at dawn and the music of his hounds does the thin, silver mist dissolve, and a world emerge in which lovers are mortal men, trees are trees merely, and Bottom can scratch his ear without the inexplicable feeling that it has grown long and hairy. Not until THE TEMPEST will Shakespeare write a play with elements as delicately ethereal as these.

Our scenic problem is thereby the more complicated. We can so easily crush the flowerlike fragility of Titania by requiring her to sleep upon a bumpy bank, a little grayed with honest theatre dust, amid a laborious forest, with real rabbits, as in Sir Herbert Tree's production, to keep her company and "add a touch of verisimilitude to an otherwise bald and unconvincing narrative." We need, once more, a mood, an atmosphere, in which anything may happen, a setting which suggests but does not specify. Enchanted woods have been with us from the earliest fairy stories we learned as children; if we can persuade our audience to accept enchantment, we shall not need identifiable oaks, nor raucous green stylizations.

There is nothing difficult for the actors in this play. We are apt to discount the lovers, with a secret fear that they are a bore, and to let the clowns loose with free, galumphing feet. The lovers need not be wearisome. As usual, when Shakespeare is writing lovers in sets, the women are better than the men. Both Helena and Hermia are vivid enough and tartly contrasted. If Helena will play a rather silly girl in love as a rather silly girl in love, and not moan for our sympathy all the time, she will be fully rewarded by our surprised delight when the worm turns, and upbraids her dearest friend with all the armory of feminine cattiness assured of male support. There is some very elegant fooling in the quarrel scene between the quartet.

Nor need Demetrius and Lysander lugubriously accept the usual fate of stooges, if they will play for the enchantment of the wood and make us realize the depths of bemused and driveling sentimentality to which its magic has reduced two ordinarily upstanding and normal young men. In the play's first and last scenes they are both drawn lightly but quite firmly; what they establish in these scenes will govern the degree of comedy to be extracted from their moonlit aberrations. Even so percipient a critic as Mr. Van Doren has condemned them as "dolls"; but any actor with imagination knows better, and the play will lose if he cannot establish their humanity.

For the lovers, more clearly even than Theseus and Hippolyta, form the link between the honest, tangible, homespun craftsman's world, peopled by the so-called clowns, and the airy dimension which Oberon and Titania inhabit. Puck knows both worlds and partakes of them. But to him the mortal world represents every reasonable idea standing idiotically on its head; whereas, to the lovers and clowns, Titania's domain dissolves all reliable and stable values in fluidity and bewilderment. Bottom, of course, is the most deeply entangled, and in him the most solid of the earthy elements is emmeshed by the most delicate fabric of the fairy world.

For Titania's attendants, Shakespeare adopts the conventional ideas of his time concerning fairies, and it is hard to see what different idiom we can use on our stage. We shall probably have to use children as he did, and see to it that no brash precocity or excess of song and dance jars against the musical burden of the play which Oberon and Titania so delicately carry.

The clowns are straightforward stuff. They are apt to emerge a trifle encrusted with tradition, which has gathered as thick as barnacles around them. One piece of business has come down from Shakespeare's own time, from a contemporary reference to the fact that Thisbe, in killing herself, falls on the scabbard instead of the sword. Since that time every possible change has been rung on the comic possibilities of the Pyramus-Thisbe interlude; these variations have persisted in actors' minds, and have been preserved and added to from generation to generation.

Many of them remain genuinely, if not very subtly, funny. The director must select judiciously, and above all, keep the fooling spontaneous and not allow it to stretch out interminably in order to meet the contribution of every actor in the play. "Simpleness and duty" are accredited to the amateur actors, and the fun can be heightened if they do remember that they are supposedly playing to the Duke and his companions, and do not too freely caricature the traditions of village-hall theatricals. The scene offers limitless possibilities. We may treat it with temperance and do nobody any harm.

In other scenes than this the Clowns are dogged with tradition. Starveling is supposedly deaf. When he is told that he is to play Thisbe's mother, he has for generations interpolated: "Thisbe's brother?" "*Mother!*" replies the united troupe. Flute has immemorially protested that he has "a beard—" "Huh?" from his companions, "—coming!" But the Clowns are genuine, human, and indestructible. We fall for them today as they did in Elizabethan London. This is a lighthearted, irresponsible piece of mischief and magic; let us lend our best ears to its melodies and warm our hearts at its humanity. The moonlit Shakespearean heavens will not often be so beautifully cloudless, nor his lyric gift of song so purely melodious.

CHAPTER EIGHT

The Histories.

THE problems raised for a modern producer dealing
with any of Shakespeare's historical plays have
a general similarity, though they are by no means
identical. For the purposes of this necessarily generalized
discussion, I shall leave aside HENRY VIII, which is of a
totally different vintage from the main cycle and was
written, probably in collaboration with John Fletcher,
at the end of Shakespeare's career. The rest of the series,
with the exception of KING JOHN, covers in unbroken
continuity the turbulent period of English history from
1398, two years before the deposition of Richard II, to
1485, when Henry VII succeeded to the throne, recon-
ciled the dynastic quarrels which had so long torn the
nation with civil war, and established the Tudor
dynasty, whose last representative, Queen Elizabeth,
still reigned when Shakespeare wrote the plays. These
were not, however, written in order of historical chronology. The HENRY VI trilogy and RICHARD III come
close together; then, after about three years, RICHARD II;

after a further two years, HENRY IV, PARTS I and II; and finally HENRY V.

The plays are, in the main, faithful to Holinshed's *Chronicles*, from which they are drawn, but they cannot be taken as a history book of impeccable accuracy. From the very beginning, with his HENRY VI collaborations, Shakespeare reserved the dramatist's right of selection, and, as he wrote them, he became increasingly absorbed in the presentation of character. By the time he reached the mature writing of the HENRY IV's, he had realized that one Falstaff was worth much more than a king's ransom, and that the Boar's Head tavern in Eastcheap was a more fruitful sphere of action than any field of battle he had yet encountered. By this time, he was in the high meridian of his comedy power; he had already written THE MERCHANT OF VENICE; and MUCH ADO ABOUT NOTHING, AS YOU LIKE IT, and TWELFTH NIGHT were swelling in his heart.

After the completion of HENRY V, he laid Holinshed aside, and from henceforth his dukes are from Illyria and Messina and a Chaucerian Ruritania, which he calls the Forest of Arden, not from the courts of Westminster and Windsor. When he returns again to history, it will be with Plutarch, not Holinshed, in his pocket, and the scene will range throughout the Roman world. But he will have long outgrown his earlier pageant-plus-oratory manner. His stage will have become a frame for living men; there will be no puppets, indistinguishable from one another save by the reds and blues and golds, the lions rampant and leopards couchant of their varying escutcheons.

If the internal politics of England in the fifteenth century are apt to fill an American audience with anticipatory dismay, the English themselves are not, and certainly were not in Shakespeare's day, much clearer about the period. Despite the fact that Shakespeare firmly leaves out characters irrelevant to his purpose, whatever their historical importance, he finds it hard to free himself of such entanglements as Edmund Mortimer, and Edward IV's excessive progeny, and remains helplessly cluttered with amorphous peers.

It is recorded that in a fairly recent production of HENRY V by a modern Shakespearean repertory company, every man, woman, and child available was pressed into double and triple service in order to cope with the procession of English and French nobility with which the play is thronged. During one general scene the stage-manager-prompter suddenly became aware of a horrible silence on the stage. Somebody, he realized, was "off"; he glanced wildly at the book, saw that the character due to speak was Westmoreland, and immediately rushed toward the dressing rooms, yelling vainly for the absentee nobleman, until finally the "Princess of France" stopped him in mid-career by inquiring mildly, "Hey! Peter! aren't you playing 'Westmoreland'?" "My God! I believe I am!" said he, and hurtled back to the field of Agincourt.

The mishap is understandable. It illustrates one of the director's problems, the differentiation of the smaller parts. In RICHARD II, for instance, the "haught, insulting" Northumberland and the poor, well-meaning, befuddled Duke of York are clear enough. But "Ross-

and-Willoughby" can easily degenerate into a pair of cardboard twins; Bushy, Bagot, and Green, "the caterpillars of the commonwealth," become merely "The Caterpillars," a conglomerate species. A little diligent search will reveal distinguishing marks. Green seems to be the executive caterpillar. He brings up questions of finance and is the first to receive the official tidings of Bolingbroke's return; Bushy appears to be the dandy, talking to the Queen in language of precious affectation; Bagot turns king's evidence and tries to save his own skin by framing an accusation against his former confederate, Aumerle. Around such indications as these the director must build a complete scaffolding for the actor, in dress, in characterization of voice and movement, in supplementary "business" and coherent reaction to the events of any scene of which the character is a silent witness.

If we are troubled, throughout the early histories, with this plethora of peers, we are even more perplexed by a problem of staging which pursues us throughout the cycle. What on earth are we to do about the battles? Even Shakespeare grew at last dissatisfied with the inadequacies of his stage to reproduce a conflict of any significance, and our audiences are harder to satisfy than were his. He relied frankly on the method of his period.

> Into a thousand parts divide one man,
> And make imaginary puissance.
> Think, when we talk of horses, that you see them,
> Printing their proud hoofs i' the receiving earth.
>
> HENRY V, Prologue

We, too, will be unable to succeed without the aid of our audience's imagination and good will. We have tried stylization, a ballet effect, a pattern of spears which we fondly hope may recall to the erudite the pictures of Uccello; we have tried impressionism, the method of turning off all the lights but for one slanting beam, through which a few figures pass as menacingly as their numbers will allow. This expedient has served pretty sturdily; but it is apt to lead the literal-minded to suppose that in the Middle Ages all conflicts were fought out at midnight.

We can make a great noise with drums and guns and significant music and muddle things nicely with a few smoke pots and a couple of gauzes; a few very large banners will replace a troop or so. But it is simply no good trying to be realistic in the Cecil B. De Mille manner; we have not the resources; nor had Shakespeare, and he did not write for them. He gave us the isolated duels and conflicts which were necessary to his plot; and he gave us in verse, which we can supplement with heraldic trappings, the sense of a chivalric tournament. If the audience will not help us out, if we have not brought them to the frame of mind in which they are willing to do so, we shall not save ourselves by shouting in the dark.

From the very beginning, Shakespeare seems more at home with the common people than with the confused politics of dynastic wars, the grand monotony of feudal barons, or the pageantry of inadequate armies. Even in the early HENRY VI, PART II, the Jack Cade scenes come to life, crudely but unmistakably. Dick Butcher,

Smith the Weaver, the two anonymous "rebels," for whom we have nothing but the names of the actors, Bevis and John Holland, are much more lively than the nobility. These scenes, too, are vigorously informed with that mistrust and contempt for mob emotion and mob rule which Shakespeare reiterates throughout his life.

> The blunt monster with uncounted heads,
> The still discordant wav'ring multitude,

whom he is to show so terribly in JULIUS CAESAR and CORIOLANUS is here bitterly satirized. Nor is Jack Cade's form of communism so very archaic. "When I am king, as king I will be, . . . there shall be no more money, all shall eat and drink on my score, and I will apparel them all in one livery, that they may agree like brothers, and worship me their lord." His hearers seem unaware of the sting in the tail. But Jack Cade is no fool, and he dies with a prophetic word: "Iden, farewell, and be proud of thy victory. Tell Kent from me, she hath lost her best man, and exhort all the world to be cowards; for I, that never feared any, am vanquished by famine, not by valour."

These scenes are probably the liveliest thing in the HENRY VI cycle, despite the brilliant flashes of poetry and pregnant phrase. Henry VI himself shows originality of thought, and his creator's mind is already too independent to write him off as a weakling and a fool among his hot-blooded, wolfish, power-drunken subjects. He has a mild vision to which we listen more attentively than to his nobles.

My crown is in my heart, not on my head;
Not decked with diamonds, and Indian stones;
Nor to be seen: my crown is called content.

III-III, 1, 62

. . . the shepherd's homely curds,
His cold, thin drink out of his leather bottle,
His wonted sleep under a fresh tree's shade,
All which secure and sweetly he enjoys, III-II, 5, 47

these things are to be envied by all of Shakespeare's
high and mighty ones, his "packs and sets of great ones,
that ebb and flow by the moon."

There are other passages which leap at us from the
cycle: the macabre horror of Duke Humphrey's death,
and the whole scene of Suffolk's execution by the pirates,
from its opening lines:

The gaudy, blabbing and remorseful day
Is crept into the bosom of the sea. II-IV, 1, 1

There are also lines which, because they have become
fortuitously topical for us, should make us realize how
often Shakespeare must have caught his hearers' throats
with allusions of studied topicality which no longer
stir our changed pulses:

HASTINGS: Why, knows not Montague that of itself
England is safe, if true within itself?

MONTAGUE: But the safer when 'tis backed with France.

HASTINGS: 'Tis better using France than trusting France:
Let us be back'd with God, and with the seas,
Which he hath given for fence impregnable,
And with their helps only defend ourselves;
In them and in ourselves, our safety lies.

III-IV, 1, 39

Here is another theme to which Shakespeare will triumphantly return, for the famous lines which conclude KING JOHN, for Gaunt's "royal throne of kings" speech, and for Henry V's speeches at Harfleur and Agincourt. To this extent the HENRY VI trilogy shares the still-vital qualities of its successors.

Possibly a bearable play might be made by compression of the three parts into one. PART I would yield very little but introductory material, the other two are richer. Their fatal defect, from the standpoint of a modern audience, is that we find it almost impossible to care for any of these shouting, swearing, flourishing gangster-nobles. Their flashes of humanity cannot redeem them for us; their strength is the stone strength of a memorial effigy beside the chancel steps. And they are so very much given to speechifying.

The "leading" woman of the plays is unbearably addicted to endless iambic talk, and indeed her stature and power are consequently almost nullified for us. Even in the more entertaining surroundings of RICHARD III, into which play she continues her vindictive vocatives, she plainly bores us with endless repetition, the more so because she is contrasted with Richard's twisting, gleaming mind. Margaret may be a part for an actress "to tear a cat in, to make all split"; her love scenes with Suffolk have passion and very occasionally simplicity; her vocabulary is a god-send to any injured victim who wants a good verbal workout; but long before we have seen the last of her, her cadenzas have reduced us to a state of nervous exhaustion, and few actresses now carry the guns for this pounding rage.

We wish that Shakespeare had returned to his common men, his artisans and tavern brawlers, who had neither the wind nor the wit for decasyllables. But we are to wait for several years yet before he will do more than give the man in the street a fleeting glance. For the next two plays are each centered on a single focus; they swing like a wheel around its axle. Shakespeare has already brought to birth in HENRY VI the miraculous monster who is to become Richard III, and he will turn next to another Richard, who will dominate his play, as Richard III does, to the exclusion of lesser characters.

The intensification of his vision on RICHARD II and RICHARD III saves these plays from the processional quality which makes HENRY VI so hard to bring into sharp dramatic valuation. Nevertheless, his second protagonist, Richard II, does not really "get going," in the sense of being able to carry the play and the audience along, until his return from Ireland, nearly halfway through it. After a deceptively facile first act, he is absent from the stage for four full scenes. The actor will have done all the groundwork on which he is to build; Shakespeare will have established the prefatory character from whom will emerge the lyric Richard, the stricken Richard, the Richard who must pass, before our eyes, through all the ordeals of suffering.

But the play must be carried along for much of this time by the impetus supplied from its lesser characters. The director's problem is to tap the source of power in each of them, use them in their just proportion, blend and balance their component contributions so that they carry Richard himself lightly upon their shoulders and never seem to be doing so. Shakespeare, by now a dramatist with nine or ten productions behind him, was not unaware of the danger and supplied the means for circumventing it.

The play has started, right from the beginning, with everybody at fever heat, except Richard himself and the entourage who mirror him. Bolingbroke and Mowbray swing immediately into the thrust and lunge of conflict, and behind them, we must feel, are ranged the whole strength of the kingdom, ready to back their differing opinions with all the force at their command. We must realize the power of these men; for, once united against Richard, they are to destroy him; and we are to watch them do it.

It is likely that we shall be unable to "put over" the intricacies of Bolingbroke's accusation that Mowbray has contrived the Duke of Gloucester's death; but we can achieve a sense that the country has, indeed, been shocked by this murder, that Mowbray, innocent or guilty, is in some way bound up with the King himself, and that, in accusing Mowbray, Bolingbroke is, in fact, accusing the King. The issues, therefore, which lie on their warring spears when they meet in the lists at Coventry must have raised every spectator to the highest point of tension.

At the critical moment, Richard forbids the fight; he banishes both the combatants, his cousin Bolingbroke, and Mowbray, his partisan and possible confederate. Was he afraid of the issue? Did he fear that whoever won, he would lose? Whatever the motive, we must feel that by this single action he has converted two rival

factions into a unity, mistrusting himself. Both combatants underscore the growing feeling against him;
and their protests are based on the agony of banishment
from England, denial of their right to breathe the
English air and speak the English tongue. Their last
words, each of them, are a farewell to England.

Two scenes later, the dying John of Gaunt nails for
all the play, for all time, the banner of England; and it
is not Richard's flag but the standard of those who for
England's sake, must wish his downfall. We may not
take very much to Bolingbroke, the coldly determined;
we may feel that Mowbray is a man of fierce words and
easy blows, no very reliable guide for us to follow; but
old Lancaster sets the issue beyond mistaking, and, in
flouting him, Richard scorns England itself.

With the little scene between Northumberland, Ross,
and Willoughby, we see the lion of England rouse and
stir. We know that Richard is not for England, nor we
for Richard as England's king. We are left only with the
question: What of Richard for himself? Shakespeare has
split a very pretty issue and left us Richard, the man, not
Richard the King, whose doom is already certain.

Four more scenes will serve to heighten the unsolved
question in our minds. In all of them we see Richard by
indirection: first through his Queen, who cannot still
the misgivings of her heart or her grief and longing for
him; through his shallow friends, who run at the first
hint of danger; through his bemused old uncle, York,
who knows that Bolingbroke is morally in the right,
should prevail, and will, but yet cannot bring himself to
more than a reluctant and wavering acquiescence in

something he is powerless to prevent; through Bolingbroke himself, purposeful where Richard was volatile,
smooth where Richard was impatient, politicly ruthless
where Richard was suicidally highhanded; last, through
one of the few loyal nobles, who will set the emotional
key and sound the very melody for Richard's return with
his:

> Ah, Richard, with the eye of heavy mind
> I see thy glory like a shooting star
> Fall to the base earth from the firmament.
> Thy sun sets weeping in the lowly west,
> Witnessing storms to come, woe and unrest:
> Thy friends are fled to wait upon thy foes,
> And crossly to thy good all fortune goes.   iii, i, 18

Without once bringing Richard on the stage, Shakespeare has entirely shifted the weight of our sympathy;
his friends are ours, his enemies we cannot warm to; it is
now for Richard alone to capture our hearts and the
play; and he does so, with the armory of weakness, the
gentleness of defeat, and the pure gold of the poetry in
which he speaks. The hardest part of the director's job
is over; from now on the solo instrument will lead, and
he will do no more than regulate the tempo of the
orchestral accompaniment.

Shakespeare, then, has written a concerto for the
villain-king, in RICHARD III, and enriched it with all the
brass and percussion of theatre melodrama; in RICHARD
II, he has written a concerto for the poet who happens
to be a king and sweetened it with exquisite melodies
for his solo violin. He is to write one more historical
concerto, for the hero-king, in HENRY V; and, though

this would seem the simplest of the three problems, both for him and us, we cannot feel that his heart was ever quite so fully engaged with it.

HENRY V is psychologically and emotionally plain sailing, or it should be. Henry himself satisfies all the standard requirements. He is given some of the most magnificent passages of rhetoric ever written for any-body, a wooing scene which is delicious comedy, and, probably the most moving thing about him, a scene where he talks anonymously with his soldiers on the night before the battle and knows the humility and infinite responsibility of the man who must throw a thousand lives within the imminent reach of death.

This is the human value which we must stress, as Henry V goes his glamorous, not very deeply explored, progress through the play. Before the walls of Harfleur, he has inspired his men to victory with a magnificent fanfare of words, but little reckoning of the cost in human lives.

> Once more unto the breach, dear friends, once more,
> Or close the wall up with our English dead.   III, I, I

Facing the terrible odds of Agincourt, he will move us much more deeply, more gently, with a new and more poignant awareness of the heroism of man against death:

> . . . he which hath no stomach to this feast,
> Let him depart, his passport shall be drawn,
> And crowns for convoy put into his purse:
> We would not die in that man's company
> That fears his fellowship, to die with us.
> This day is call'd the feast of Crispian:

He that outlives this day, and comes safe home,
Will stand a tip-toe when this day is named.

. . . .

And Crispin Crispian shall ne'er go by,
From this day to the ending of the world,
But we in it shall be remembered;
We few, we happy few, we band of brothers;
For he to-day that sheds his blood with me
Shall be my brother; be he ne'er so base,
This day shall gentle his condition:
And gentlemen in England, now a-bed,
Shall think themselves accurs'd they were not here;
And hold their manhoods cheap, whiles any speaks
That fought with us upon Saint Crispin's day.   iv, 3, 35

Our failure to capitulate may be due to the fact that
we have lost our taste for the pageantry of war; it may
be that we see so little of Henry, the man, as against
Henry the King, and the Prince Hal we used to know
seems to bear little relation to this fighting monarch.
But actor and producer will have to use every device they
can jointly evolve to save our hero from his own glory.

The minor characters are scattered with a liberal hand
and vividly portrayed. Shakespeare is once more moving
freely among the soldiers and men-at-arms whom he met
in the taverns of Thames-side. The French Princess is
delicate, precise, filled with gaiety and grace; the fiery,
loyal Welshman, Captain Fluellen, is instantly endearing; Bates and Williams are the eternal English Tommy,
almost unbearably up-to-date. In fact, the wealth of
minor characters, following a track of their own, sometimes threaten to overwhelm the play, unless they are
kept very skillfully within its pattern. This will be a
large part of our problem. Shakespeare must have known

it. For he had promised, in the Epilogue to HENRY IV, PART II, to put another character into this sequel and must subsequently have realized that, if he did so, both the English victors and the French vanquished would fade like mist from the field of Agincourt, and, between the wraithlike armies, Falstaff would stand alone.

The two plays which come between RICHARD II and HENRY V, both historically and in the order in which Shakespeare wrote them, constitute a special problem and are radiant with a particular glory. HENRY IV is no more than a label. They are FALSTAFF, PARTS I and II; and the difference between the two parts is notable. In PART I, Shakespeare still has his colossal Galatea in hand; he holds the balance between the Boar's Head and the scenes of politics and war by throwing into the scale against Falstaff the magnificence of Hotspur and by setting Prince Hal pretty squarely between the two of them. But in PART II he cannot stop Falstaff. The Tavern scenes are richer than ever and amplified by the gaudily vital creation of Doll Tearsheet, the fuller treatment of Mistress Quickly, and the subsidiary help of Ancient Pistol and Falstaff's new page. Even when the reluctant warrior leaves for the wars, he gets little further than Justice Shallow's orchard, and there conjures up another world of the most entertaining civilian companions to keep himself and us from the military history of the play's original design.

Of this ingredient, Shakespeare uses as little as he can, and that is a good deal too much for us. The remnants of the Hotspur rebels are a tame, colorless lot; as one of them says, describing Hotspur's death:

In few, his death, whose spirit lent a fire
Even to the dullest spirit in the camp,
Being bruited once, took fire and heat away.

I, I, 112

The King's side finally overcomes the last flicker of rebellion by a mean and shabby piece of trickery, and this poor business Shakespeare turns over to Hal's younger brother, Prince John of Lancaster, of whom Falstaff says: "Good faith, this same young sober-blooded boy doth not love me, nor a man cannot make him laugh, but that's no marvel, he drinks no wine."

The scenes are dead wood in the play. Hal cannot be mixed up in them; and Shakespeare is in a great difficulty with Hal. Henry V is already in his mind. At the end of the play, Hal is to disown Falstaff utterly, and the ties between them are already so loosened that they appear together only in one scene, of which Hal has a very minor share. To bridge the gap, Shakespeare gives Hal the moving scene with his dying father; but Henry IV himself has preserved no more than a melancholy sonority, in our remembrance, and, though we are moved, we are still Falstaff's, heart and soul; so that when Hal, at his coronation, utterly rejects his old companion, we are not at all appeased by the high-minded moral precepts which father and son have interchanged to prepare us for this denouement.

We are left, therefore, with two-thirds of the play Falstaff's, incredibly rich, brimming over with life and gusto. Of the remainder, the rebellion scenes are a plain weariness, and the King's scenes a dignified interlude from laughter, whereas the final curtain is bound to leave us with a sense of frustration and dissatisfaction.

It is hard to see what a modern producer can make of the puzzle. Perhaps lift a couple of Falstaff scenes from PART I, add an Epilogue consisting of the beautiful description of Falstaff's death from HENRY V, and make a Falstaff play of it. This has, in fact, been tried. It is not without dangers; Shakespeare knew that it would be perilous to give us too much Fat Knight at a stretch, without any variation of diet. But it is tragic that the wealth of the Falstaff scenes in PART II should so long have been lost to the stage.

It would seem that Falstaff is like Hamlet in that a very great deal of scholarly toil, amateur psychology, and printer's ink have been expended on him; and the two characters are certainly equal in the towering superiority they enjoy in their respective spheres. Many commentators have been at great pains to analyze just why the world should have taken Falstaff to its heart. "Why," asks one of them, "should we laugh at an old man with a huge belly and corresponding appetites," a coward, a boaster, a thief, a liar, a man untroubled by the smallest moral principle or scruple? Falstaff himself gives the best answer:

> The brain of this foolish compounded clay-man is not able to invent anything that tends to laughter more than I invent, or is invented on me; I am not only witty in myself, but the cause that wit is in other men.   II-I, 2, 5

Perhaps it is partly his refreshing freedom from all the limitations of conventional behavior, from the tyranny of "honor," from the load of moral obligations under which the lesser man staggers, together with his unquenchable zest for life, which gives him such unequaled power in raising our fullhearted laughter. When Shakespeare balances him with Hotspur, the embodiment of all the high romance of medieval chivalry, with its daredevil fearlessness and its pursuit of personal honor as the most glittering of all the world's prizes, he gives us what is perhaps the fullest and richest of all the histories, HENRY IV, PART I.

This play has never received in the theatre the popularity that has been accorded the "star vehicles," RICHARD III, HENRY V, and, more recently, RICHARD II, simply because it has no single leading part. Honors are fairly equally divided between Falstaff and Hotspur, with Hal a very close third, and star actors have appeared in all three of the parts. But the ten-week run it received in New York in 1939 with Mr. Maurice Evans as Falstaff, Mr. Wesley Addy as Hotspur, and Mr. Edmond O'Brien as Hal proved its power to hold modern audiences. A fraction of the problem which the play presents was eased in this production because Mr. Evans's RICHARD II was still a recent memory to the audiences who saw it, and the political background supplied by the events of the earlier play was therefore familiar to them.

As always, Shakespeare gets the necessary political groundwork done with as quickly as possible and settles down, as we do, to the fascination of watching character in action. Again, however, according to his habit, he besprinkles the political scenes liberally with the names of off-stage personages, a complication which once caused an absent-minded "King Henry" to declare in perfect pentameters that

> The Earl of Whatsisname, Lord Something Else,
> Some kind of Bishop and two other guys
> Capitulate against us, and are up.

But in this play the balance between military and civilian activity is much more evenly held than in most of the other histories. Even the Hotspur scenes are packed with comedy, from Harry Percy's opening speech about the "certain lord, neat and trimly dressed," who came with such elegant insolence to demand the prisoners after the battle of Holmedon, to the warmth and mischief of his scene with his wife, and the impish caricature of Glendower. Hotspur is always kept alive and burning; he is no puppet warrior. On the other side of the picture, Falstaff and Hal, whose story at the outset is far removed from any theme of war, seldom stray for long from the sound of the distant trumpets. At the close of the second Boar's Head scene they too are for the wars. Hal strides off with a martial flourish. Says Falstaff wryly:

> Rare words! Brave world! Hostess, my breakfast come!
> O, I could wish this tavern were my drum!   III, 3, 205

The minor characters, all richly painted, complement the strength of their leaders in the two halves of the play. The satellites of the Falstaff scenes need some help from their actors, especially Peto and Gadshill, who seem to be sketches for an actor's personality to amplify.

The tiny portraits of the two Carriers who are robbed
by Falstaff's gang come instantly alive, however, with
their "gammon of bacon and two razes of ginger to be
delivered as far as Charing Cross," and their comment
on the lately deceased ostler: "Poor fellow never joyed
since the price of oats rose, it was the death of him."
To the Hotspur side come the lively wit and grace of
Lady Percy, the fiery Glendower, and, late in the play,
Sir Richard Vernon, who bursts upon us with a blazing
description of Hal and his companions:

> Glittering in golden coats like images,
> As full of spirit as the month of May,
> And gorgeous as the sun at midsummer. iv, i, 100

The balance is the more remarkable in that Falstaff
and Hotspur hold credos as opposite as the poles, and
yet, in voicing them, they complement each other and
bind the play as indivisibly as the two sides of a shield.
Says Hotspur:

> By heaven, methinks it were an easy leap,
> To pluck bright honour from the pale-fac'd moon,
> Or dive into the bottom of the deep,
> Where fathom line could never touch the ground,
> And pluck up drowned honour by the locks,
> So he that doth redeem her thence might wear
> Without corrival all her dignities.   i, iii, 201

Says Falstaff:

> Can honour set to a leg? no: or an arm? no: or take away the grief
> of a wound? no. Honour hath no skill in surgery, then? no.
> What is honour? a word; what is in that word honour? what
> is that honour? air. A trim reckoning! Who hath it? he that

died o' Wednesday. Doth he feel it? no. Doth he hear it? no.
'Tis insensible then? yea, to the dead. But will it not live with
the living? no. Why? detraction will not suffer it, therefore
I'll none of it, honour is a mere scutcheon, and so ends my
catechism.   v, 1, 131

Hotspur is killed, dying with bitterness on his lips:

> But thoughts the slaves of life, and life time's fool,

and Hal, his conqueror, speaks for him a bitter epitaph:

> When that this body did contain a spirit,
> A kingdom for it was too small a bound,
> But now two paces of the vilest earth
> Is room enough.   v, 5, 89

But Falstaff, having politicly saved his own life by
counterfeiting death, survives to take up Hotspur's
body and drag it ingloriously from the field; a bitter
conclusion, which we must suppose Shakespeare fully
intended. He has given us life, at its fullest and most
red-blooded, and he gives us death like a sudden blow
between the eyes. He gives us all the panoply of war,
but he is not finding much to commend the spurious
glamor of battle. We shall miss the play's meaning if we
lose ourselves among the banners.

As we have seen, in the following play, PART II, he
turns entirely away from war to follow Falstaff, and in
HENRY V he cannot go back to his fighting scenes until
he has disposed of the figure who might so easily make
them seem ridiculous and pitiful. So Falstaff, too, must
die, Shakespeare's loving tenderness for the broken old
rascal flowing through every word of Mrs. Quickly's
description of his passing:

He's in Arthur's bosom, if ever a man went to Arthur's bosom. A' made a finer end, and went away an it had been any Christom child: a' parted e'en just between twelve and one, e'en at the turning of the tide: for after I saw him fumble with the sheets, and play with flowers, and smile upon his fingers' ends, I knew there was no way but one; for his nose was as sharp as a pen and a' babbled of green fields. "How now, Sir John?" quoth I: "what, man? be o' good cheer:" so a' cried out, "God, God, God!" three or four times: now I, to comfort him, bid him a' should not think of God; I hop'd there was no need to trouble himself with any such thoughts yet; so a' bad me lay more clothes on his feet: I put my hand into the bed, and felt them, and they were as cold as any stone: then I felt his knees, and they were as cold as any stone, and so upward and upward, and all was as cold as any stone.

II, 3, II

No wonder we have a hard time, after this, in working up an interest in the men of war.

There remains one play, isolated in historical position, which was written before Shakespeare started on the HENRY IV's; he had already turned from his single-character focus, and he had not yet arrived at the superb triple-protagonist achievement which was to follow. KING JOHN, therefore, presents some special difficulties, and its merits have been theatrically subject to un-deserved neglect. It shares, with the other plays which have dropped out of stage use, the lack of any focal point. It is significant that both KING JOHN and RICHARD II were revived, after lengthy periods of oblivion, on the English stage around the turn of the last century by Sir Herbert Tree; but while RICHARD has held its own ever since, KING JOHN has once more disappeared, despite a fine revival by Robert Mantell in New York shortly afterward.

For King John himself falls, so to speak, between two Richards. He is a "villain," but an uncertain one, liable to panic when the tide turns against him; he is a weak monarch, but there is little we can discern of the man behind the façade. From the beginning he seems to have a fever in his veins; he grasps at the stronger wills of his mother and his illegitimate brother, Faulconbridge. He can rant with the best of Shakespeare's early reciting monarchs, but these tirades, though richer, are not more revealing than theirs. Shakespeare is still clinging to something of the pageant method. But his doubts about the dramatic potency of the war theme are stronger. He had begged the question in RICHARD II. Through John's mouth he voices disillusion:

> There is no sure foundation built on blood,
> No certain life achiev'd by others' death. v, 2, 104

In two scenes, John comes fully alive: first in the devious fascination he exercises over the blunt-minded Hubert in order to incite him to the murder of young Arthur; when he suddenly breaks the oily, inferential speech he has so far used with the single command, "Death," the effect is as startling as a flash of forked lightning from a heavy sky. But, like the Thane of Cawdor, ' nothing in his life became him like the leaving it." It is a great death scene. The fever rages through his veins, the poison he has eaten brings him to a tortured, writhing, ugly end:

> There is so hot a summer in my bosom,
> That all my bowels crumble up to dust:
> I am a scribbled form drawn with a pen

Upon a parchment, and against this fire
Do I shrink up . . .
And none of you will bid the winter come
To thrust his icy fingers in my maw;
Nor let my kingdom's rivers take their course
Through my burn'd bosom; nor entreat the north
To make his bleak winds kiss my parched lips
And comfort me with cold. I do not ask you much,
I beg cold comfort; and you are so strait
And so ingrateful, you deny me that.   v, 7, 30

Here is fine material for an actor, but still we have no pattern for a play.

Shakespeare seems curiously ill at ease. Perhaps it is that he is being forced to adapt and telescope an old play, THE TROUBLESOME REIGN OF KING JOHN, without his heart in the work. He does not transform his material with his usual freedom. Perhaps he has grown weary of the old iteration of defiance and lament, without as yet discerning the way of freedom which Falstaff, and even the "little men" of HENRY V, were to bring him.

The play looks backward, with its high, heroic, over-embroidered verse; with the verbose peerage; and with the character of Constance, another Margaret, with a mellower tone and some strain of moving nobility, but an equal tendency to dull our ears and hearts with repetition of her griefs. It looks forward with the character of Faulconbridge, who has independence, humor, stature, and a dimension all his own.

He steps out of the play like a flesh-and-blood actor from a puppet stage; he interprets to us and for us; he is most particularly ours. Falstaff would know him; their minds would meet. Hotspur would know him by the

flash of his sword, and the resounding clarion of his con-
cluding lines:

> This England never did nor never shall
> Lie at the proud foot of a conqueror,
> But when it first did help to wound itself.
> Now these her princes are come home again,
> Come the three corners of the world in arms,
> And we shall shock them. Nought shall make us rue,
> If England to itself do rest but true.   v, 7, 112

KING JOHN is one of the plays which should be revived;
there is a turbid power in it. It is also one of the plays
which, as the theatre stands today, could only repay
revival as part of a repertoire, perhaps then only "on
Saturday nights," proverbially reserved by the old actor-
managers for the plays which could never draw an
audience on a Monday. There are half a dozen other plays
like it. They are too dangerous a gamble for the commercial manager of today; and we have succeeded in
evolving no substitute for him, no answer to the question of how to be daring yet solvent. There is an audience
for KING JOHN, but not one which will repay us an investment of $35,000; it will therefore probably remain
unproduced for many years to come. Something seems
to be wrong somewhere.

CHAPTER NINE

The Comedies

BY the time Shakespeare came to write the HENRY IV's, he had already produced the first of the group of comedies with which he gloriously rounds out his first ten years as a playwright. Indeed HENRY IV, PART II is perhaps more purely a comedy than THE MERCHANT OF VENICE, which preceded it. Next comes MUCH ADO ABOUT NOTHING, probably in the same year as HENRY V, and, in 1599–1600, AS YOU LIKE IT and TWELFTH NIGHT. The date of THE MERRY WIVES OF WINDSOR, like everything else about the source, plot, and textual aspects of that play, is the subject of much discussion. General agreement assigns it to the period immediately following the other Falstaff plays, but Sir E. K. Chambers, whose chronology I have elsewhere accepted, puts it three years later, contemporaneously with HAMLET, on evidence which I think inconclusive.

At all events, by the time Shakespeare brings the fantasy of Illyria to its golden close, he is already wrestling with the stern realities of ancient Rome; and, from the intermediary form of JULIUS CAESAR, he will take the leap straight into the finished greatness of tragedy. Not the least astounding feature of his career is that he must have made for himself four distinct and separate reputations as a dramatist: first, as a writer of chronicle histories, with some deviations to romantic comedy and one poetic tragedy to grace his poet's reputation; then, as a writer of comedies, and an extremely successful one. Suddenly, when his fellows must have thought the bent of his genius fully settled, came HAMLET, and for six or seven years they settled down to being tragic actors when Shakespeare's work was in rehearsal. But from Stratford in the evening of his days came scripts which were not tragedies at all; he had come back to a form of romantic comedy, but of a mood and design so different from THE MERRY WIVES that the new actors in the Globe Company, who had never known Mr. Shakespeare, must have thought it barely conceivable that the same man could have written them.

All of the comedies have held the stage continuously. As with his other theatrically successful plays, they contain wonderful acting parts and must have rejoiced the hearts of the boy actors of the Globe, who as yet had had nothing except Juliet to compare with the plums which had fallen to the leading men. But the full-length SHREW, and many slighter sketches, had shown what Shakespeare could do for women in comedy, and now came, in swift succession, Portia, Beatrice, Rosalind, and Viola, with Mrs. Ford and Mrs. Page thrown in for good measure. The boy actors must have prayed that Bill would stick to writing comedies; and leading actresses ever since have kept his radiant, witty, gracious heroines continually before the public.

THE MERRY WIVES OF WINDSOR is, of course, another Falstaff play. Long-established tradition has it that Elizabeth, reflecting the popular taste as usual, was a Falstaff fan and demanded another play about the Fat Knight in love. Possibly the Globe Company felt it had disappointed its public in giving them a HENRY V without Falstaff and knew he was still excellent box office. At all events, the text as we have it, from the evidently patched-up Folio printing and a pirated "Bad" Quarto, shows distinct signs of having been written in a hurry and without very much heart. Falstaff has fallen from his former high estate: the penetration, the ironic understanding, the rapier thrusts of philosophy are gone; he is a butt and a dupe, an old, fat fool in love.

But this declension is of more moment to the fireside critic than to the occupant of a balcony seat at THE MERRY WIVES; for the play is a farce, and pretends to be nothing else; it has gusto and facility and momentum; and, if we had not known the earlier Sir John, we should not grumble about this one. The actor, however, who has the good fortune to play both will find the clay on which he works changing curiously under his hands to a softer, spongier texture. He will not be able to mold from it a second figure of a stature equal to the first.

Shakespeare, turning out the play in two weeks, according to the tradition, sits down to his task and starts it off with a sufficient flourish and the impetus of a writer to whom the humors of the English middle class come easily. He has some old friends whom he had by no means exhausted at their earlier appearances: Justice Shallow, Nym and Pistol, Bardolph, who he doesn't apparently think will be of much use to him, and Mistress Quickly, younger, fresher, and sprucer than her namesake. He creates some new friends immediately: the Justice's ineffably foolish cousin, Slender; Sir Hugh Evans, the Welsh parson; and Dr. Caius, the French doctor. Wales and France are always good for comedy.

Mine Host of the Garter Inn is a breezy, beery, hail-fellow-well-met kind of a figure, who can be relied upon to kick the plot into action if it threatens to languish; Page is an honest, worthy, sufficient yeoman who will give the piece ballast, and Ford the usual jealous husband, who will be used for the comic possibilities of jealousy and perhaps will touch a chord in the depths of Shakespeare's subconscious mind which, years later, will provide the thematic base for Leontes. The Merry Wives themselves are new figures in his gallery; they are coarser in grain than the heroines who will follow, near in blood to Emilia and Paulina of the later plays, but more independent and set in quite different surroundings. They will never quite recur; and Shakespeare takes pleasure in them from the beginning and treats them to a brilliant duologue scene together.

So far he is not disliking his enforced task; but he is shirking the Falstaff business, which is just what he has been commanded to write, and dallies with these new creatures as if he would really like to explore them further and see what happens. When he at last buckles down to Falstaff in love he seems to put aside Sir Hugh, Dr. Caius, Shallow, and, to a certain degree, Slender with an apologetic shrug to them and an irritated bow toward the royal command.

His invention does not fail him for the incidents of plot, which are hilarious enough in their kind, and his dialogue does not lose its salt; but the richness of enjoyment is no longer present. Final proof of the mechanical nature of his labor may perhaps be found in the young lovers, Fenton and Anne Page, to whom, alone among all his romantic youth, he does not give one line to stir or lift the heart with music. Fenton is amiable cardboard, Anne has spirit, especially in her comment on the suggestion of Dr. Caius for a prospective husband, the flashing:

> Alas, I had rather be set quick i' the earth
> And bowled to death with turnips.   III, 4, 84

The romance between them, and the consequent confounding of Caius and Slender are necessary to the plot, but the poet in him does not once rise in their defence.

Finally he winds up the play rather like the writer of a musical-comedy book when he finds that it is nearly eleven o'clock; in honor of the royal performance that is to be given for the court at Windsor he puts in a masque, gracefully salutes the Knights of the Order of the Garter, and sends his characters thankfully home to "laugh this sport o'er by a country fire, Sir John and all." He slams the manuscript down on Burbage's table with an enormous sigh of relief and rushes back to the unfinished script which all this time has been waiting in his heart;

we cannot tell for certain which it is; perhaps MUCH ADO, perhaps JULIUS CAESAR, perhaps HAMLET.

Our main difficulty in producing the play lies exactly parallel to Shakespeare's in writing it. We have to supply all the warmth, humanity, and mellowness of which the script runs short. There is plenty of pace in the action; we have only to keep up with it. There are endless possibilities for comic business, some of them so obvious in the script that we cannot miss them, some more subtly implicit in a turn of phrase. We shall have to accept a few editorial emendations where the text, though conceivably correct, is too obscure to make immediate auditory sense. There are some problems of staging where the concurrent plots have to be kept going simultaneously, and Shakespeare has been in too much of a hurry to do more than make one set of characters "retire" to discuss one plan in private while another set discusses the other plan in full hearing.

There are many instances, especially in the middle of the play, where one or more characters are left carelessly standing around while the subject of the scene swings away from them, and we shall have to fill in the gaps for them as unostentatiously as possible. Sometimes their presence is fruitful of comedy even though they have not a line to speak. At the end of Act III, scene 3, after Falstaff has been rescued under the very eyes of the jealous Ford by being carried off in a buck basket, Mrs. Ford, the injured wife, is left during thirty lines of general commotion without a word to say, and Mrs. Page, "a very tattling woman," is similarly silent; but there are indications that the sobs of the one, apparently heartbroken, and the righteously indignant ministrations of the other form a continuous part of the general confusion which swirls around the bewildered Ford. We must read with our eyes in all the general scenes, and play for the comedy of speed and high spirits.

THE MERCHANT OF VENICE, the earliest of the comedy group, ranks among the most continuously performed of all the plays; the elements of successful theatre are felicitously present, contrasted and combined with almost arrogant skill, and their dramatic potentialities and relative importance have been treated by producers in every imaginable way. The Venetian world which Shakespeare created with such opulent facility has remained fairly stable, though variously taken for granted, enhanced, or overlaid with scenic interpretation according to the resources of the producer and the convention of the time. We have had three-ply Bridges of Sighs and painted-drop Grand Canals faithfully reproducing everything but the well-known Venetian odors; and we have had expressionistic treatments, with the Senators of the Doge's Council represented by red-robed figures in sheeplike masks.

Fortunately the theatre has produced a regular supply of magnificent Shylocks and Portias, but it has seldom realized the necessity for producing magnificent Salanios and Salerinos, and has generally thrown onto the stage two callow and underpaid young men in wrinkled tights to deal as best they know how with this supposed pair of notorious bores. Lorenzo has fared a little better, for the exquisite poetry of his last-act speeches at least rates a fine speaker of verse; Gratiano, whom Shakespeare himself has allowed to degenerate as the play proceeds in the quality both of his social status and of his wit, has been pretty handsomely cast; Antonio is frequently treated with insufficient imagination. The actor is prone to take a dangerous cue from the opening lines:

> In sooth I know not why I am so sad,
> It wearies me, you say it wearies you;

and to neglect the dignity, courtesy, and courage implicit in Bassanio's description of:

> The dearest friend to me, the kindest man,
> The best-condition'd and unwearied spirit
> In doing courtesies; and one in whom
> The ancient Roman honour more appears
> Than any that draws breath in Italy.   III, 2, 292

His behavior at the Trial scene has a quiet truth and steadfastness which are not unworthy of the finest actor's service.

Bassanio, being the romantic lead, has been more generally justified by the theatre than by the critics, who analyze him into an ineffectual fortune hunter. Shakespeare, if he did not take much trouble to deepen the character, is not so foolish as to bother with this academic interpretation of plot exigencies. He gives his juvenile lead noble verse from the outset and knows he will have the services of an actor whose appearance will justify Nerissa's "he, of all the men that ever my foolish eyes look'd upon, was the best deserving a fair lady."

These characters between them will carry the Venetian scene, and not least the easy, carelessly arrogant Salanio and Salerino, with their lavish richness of phrase and gilded metaphor. They are lords of the European metropolis, masterfully at home in a city of legendary glamor, endowed with all the wealth of the Italian Renaissance civilization. At the play's first beginning, they anatomize Antonio's sadness into a fantasy of dream-world misfortune:

> I should not see the sandy hour-glass run
> But I should think of shallows and of flats,
> And see my wealthy Andrew dock'd in sand
> Vailing her high-top lower than her ribs
> To kiss her burial. Should I go to church
> And see the holy edifice of stone,
> And not bethink me straight of dangerous rocks,
> Which touching but my gentle vessel's side
> Would scatter all her spices on the stream,
> Enrobe the roaring waters with my silks,
> And in a word, but even now worth this,
> And now worth nothing?   I, I, 25

We should think again of this metaphor of "enrobe the roaring waters with my silks" when the two elegant young men stand aghast and helpless before the torrent of Shylock's outpoured hatred and, sobered by this contact with an unbelievably harsh reality, go, not without dignity, one to stay by the doomed Antonio and the other to fetch Bassanio from Belmont.

They form part of the delicate, invisible links forged by Shakespeare between the fabulous atmosphere of Venice and the fairy world of Belmont; for the story of the three caskets is pure fairy tale, and the encircling air must not blow too roughly upon it. Belmont is the eternal Xanadu of the poet's imagining, from its first foreshadowing in Bassanio's

In Belmont is a lady, richly left,
And she is fair and, fairer than that word,
Of wondrous virtues . . .
Nor is the wide world ignorant of her worth,
For the four winds blow in from every coast
Renowned suitors, and her sunny locks
Hang on her temples like a golden fleece,
Which makes her seat of Belmont Colchos' strand,
And many Jasons come in quest of her.   I, I, 161

The enchanted Princess, at her first appearance, will prove, however, that a fresh, light wind of wit breathes through the scented gardens; the breeze must be kept gentle; Nerissa, if she is brash or labored, may shake the heavy blossoms from the trees.

Only when we have done with the dusky, sonorous Morocco and the fantasticated Aragon will the Princess ripen into full, sure womanhood with the grave beauty of her surrender to Bassanio. The shadow which immediately falls on the lovers with the news of Antonio's danger, matures her to authority, understanding, and deep tenderness. For Belmont must be guided back toward the Venetian dimension, where its Princess is to meet Shylock on his own plane and vanquish him. She who plays Portia will be unwise to neglect this steady deepening of strength in the development of the character in order to skip too skittishly after the easy comedy of the scene with Nerissa where she plans her boy's disguise.

At the play's finish, with Venice once more in the distance, Shakespeare will bring back the enchantment of Belmont, this time through Lorenzo and Jessica's famous antiphonal lyric, through the "still" music which is commanded for them, and through the quiet, spellbound duet of peace which Portia and Nerissa play at their first entrance, broken so delicately when Portia sees the two lovers:

> Peace, ho! the moon sleeps with Endymion,
> And would not be awaked.   v, 1, 108

"Music ceases," says the stage direction, and Portia's very next line,

> He knows me as the blind man knows the cuckoo,
> By the bad voice,

swings the scene to the mood of gay comedy, one might almost call it comedy of relief, after the tension of the trial, in which the rest of the action is to be played. For the whole play is smoothly and beautifully locked together, reconciling apparent irreconcilables with matchless skill and precision. It is our business to preserve this unity of texture by weaving personal color of high contrasting value into an undisturbed harmony.

The black figure in the picture is, of course, Shylock, the alien in these linked worlds, the "outsider" in every spiritual sense, whose single-purposed force nearly shatters them both. The storms of controversy have swept Shylock to the crest of the popular wave, and kept him there. Actors and critics have contributed alike.

His stage history is marked with epoch-making performances breaking through a supposedly established tradition, to become traditional in their turn. Dogget, at the beginning of the eighteenth century, made a comic figure out of him, with the aid of an appalling "adaptation" by Lord Lansdowne. Macklin restored him to a forceful reality, and was so afraid of his own daring that he never rehearsed the interpretation he intended to give, but sprang it as a complete surprise on his thunderstruck fellows at the opening performance. Edmund Kean, penniless and starving, got his first chance in the part in 1814 and electrified London, not only by the savagery of his reading, but by wearing, for the first time in recorded history, a black wig. Even Burbage, according to extant memoirs, had worn a red one. Edwin Booth later made the interesting suggestion that Kean wore the black wig simply because a "black-bald" was part of every stock actor's essential equipment, and he had no money to buy a new "red." Sir Henry Irving played Shylock for all the pathos of the despised and downtrodden Jew, with the dragging, broken exit from the Trial scene which is so enormously effective, and so great a distortion of Shakespeare's intention.

For Shakespeare saw Shylock under a brilliant light; he realized to the full what the pressure of the Venetian world would do to a man of Shylock's race and trade, and did not soft-pedal the issue. But the celebrated "hath not a Jew eyes" tirade has tended to falsify our vision of Shylock, the individual, with generalized partisanship; for there is little that is sympathetic about this particular Jew. He loved his wife, Leah; he loves his daughter, Jessica, though Heaven knows why, for she is a little baggage. But he loves them as his, his possessions, like his turquoise and his ducats and his race and his revenge. His, his, his. It is the keynote of the man; the passion of possession raised to demonic power, driven by the circumstance of his world to the snarling, merciless defence of the cornered rat. His very speeches choke with suppression, with poison. There is tragedy in the stripping from him of everything that is his, daughter, ducats, revenge, religion, everything but the burden of continued, unvalued life. But it is not a "sympathetic" tragedy, and there is more terror than pity in it.

There are no rules for Shylocks; we can hope that traditions will be made and broken as many times as there arise great actors to play the part. There is, I think, a rule for directors, which is, in this as in many other cases, to realize the individual characters first, as vitally close as may be divined to Shakespeare's intention regarding them, and to deduce the moral, social, or philosophical intention of the play from the sum total of their combined power. To postulate a social theory, generally more pertinent to the director's own period than to Shakespeare's, and stretch the characters to fit the formula may result in a brilliant piece of special pleading. It seldom results in Shakespeare.

The remaining comedies contain no Shylock to rock their equilibrium, and, though their balance is thereby more easily obtained, they lack, perhaps, the same thrill of tension. MUCH ADO has a villain, Don John, whose machinations will provide the intricacies of the plot; he is a monosyllabic fellow, whose brief lines strike like single harsh notes through the first half of the play, leaving a faint dissonance in the air. His work done, and Hero delivered to shame and dishonor, he disappears with the sardonic:

> Thus pretty lady,
> I am sorry for thy much misgovernment.

But Shakespeare, in this case, is not mainly interested in the plot. He uses it like an outlined setting, an atmosphere, a frame before which he places the people in whom he and we are really interested: Benedick, Beatrice, Don Pedro, and the humble, solemn, pompous little constables whose simplicity is the means whereby intrigue is brought to destruction.

Dogberry and Verges have been among the most misused of Shakespeare's comics. They have been provided with layers of "character" make-up, and Dogberry has made much ado indeed at forcing his verbal mistakings over the footlights as if they had to be spelled out before the audience would get the point. He and Verges have frequently played with a ruthless determination to be funny or die and have consequently met the latter fate. But the constables are quiet, fearfully earnest, proud of their office, stubborn in its defence, and, in the arrest of Conrade and Borachio, they obstinately pursue the right people for the wrong reasons until truth is brought to light. Dogberry's first exhortation to the citizens of the "Watch," those volunteer keepers of their neighbors' peace, sets the tone for all of them, if it be played simply and fervently, without caricature:

DOGBERRY: [to "*George Seacoal*"] You are thought here to be the most senseless and fit man for the constable of the watch;

therefore bear you the lantern. This is your charge: you shall comprehend all vagrom men; you are to bid any man stand, in the prince's name.

SECOND WATCH: How if a' will not stand?

DOGBERRY: Why, then, take no note of him, but let him go, and presently call the rest of the watch together, and thank God you are rid of a knave.

VERGES: If he will not stand when he is bidden, he is none of the prince's subjects.

DOGBERRY: True, and they are to meddle with none but the prince's subjects. You shall make no noise in the streets; for the watch to babble and to talk is most tolerable and not to be endured.

SECOND WATCH: We will rather sleep than talk, for we know what belongs to a watch.

DOGBERRY: Why, you speak like an ancient and most quiet watchman, for I cannot see how sleeping should offend: only, have a care your bills be not stolen . . .   III, 3, 21

It is much more important that the audience should love Dogberry, and little Verges, "honest as the skin between his brows," than that the actor should concentrate on extorting a forced laugh with his celebrated "comparisons are odorous."

Beatrice and Benedick are, of course, the glory of the play, and on their two actors its success will largely depend. The flexibility and brilliance of their prose gave the English language a new dramatic weapon; Shakespeare himself never surpassed it, and perhaps only Congreve and Sheridan at his height were ever to set a greater luster upon the form. It needs brilliant speaking, extreme lucidity of analytic thought, and phrasing which will exactly correspond to this analysis, precise enunciation, and, above all, speed. Even Ellen Terry, the happiest and most irresistible of Beatrices, said of herself that she was never swift enough. For if Beatrice's railing against husbands in general and Benedick in particular does not bubble as lightly as champagne, it may become tedious and sententious. The following extract may exemplify the danger, and the opportunity:

BEATRICE: Lord, I could not endure a husband with a beard on his face. I had rather lie in the woollen.

LEONATO: You may light on a husband that hath no beard.

BEATRICE: What should I do with him? Dress him in my apparel, and make him my waiting-gentlewoman? . . . he that is less than a man, I am not for him: therefore I will even take six-pence in earnest of the bear-herd, and lead his apes into hell.

LEONATO: Well, then, go you into hell?

BEATRICE: No, but to the gate, and there will the devil meet me, like an old cuckold, with horns on his head, and say "Get you to heaven, Beatrice, get you to heaven, here's no place for you maids:" so deliver I up my apes, and away to Saint Peter for the heavens; he shows me where the bachelors sit, and there live we as merry as the day is long.   II, I, 26

Shakespeare uses a new and daring device when she has overheard Hero and Ursula discussing Benedick's love for her; the little soliloquy which follows is not merely in verse, but in rhymed verse, as formal and simple as the earliest of the heroines. But its apparent stiffness provides the actress with a golden opportunity to show the flashing, self-sufficient Beatrice as humbly, softly, sentimentally in love as any milkmaid; and from here on the softness must never be lost. All through the play Beatrice must remember that she was "born in a merry hour," not a quarrelsome one, so that her interchanges of wit never become rasping. Beatrice has "dancing feet"; she runs "like a lapwing"; a star danced at her birth; the part is featherweight.

Benedick is of rougher stuff; his speeches have a broader sweep, if his speed in repartee is half a jump behind Beatrice. He is gifted with an inexhaustible wealth of metaphor and imagery: "Hang me up in a bottle like a cat," "an oak with but one green leaf on it would have answered her," "I will fetch you a toothpicker now from the furthest inch of Asia." Love does not reduce Benedick to verse, for he "was not born under a rhyming planet." But the surge of love does somehow simplify his speech to a greater directness; his finest declaration to his lady has an accent inescapably his own; it is not merely the language of love, but the language of Benedick in love. "Will you go hear this news, signior?" says Beatrice; and he answers, "I will live in thy heart, die in thy lap, and be buried in thine eyes; and moreover I will go with thee to thine uncle's." Exit. For, among other things, he has a masterly talent for the exit line, until he finishes the play with the impudent "Prince . . . get thee a wife, get thee a wife!" to Don Pedro, the promise to "devise brave punishments" for Don John, and the flourish "strike up, pipers!"

So Shakespeare disposes of a plot which he has never taken very seriously. It has never been merely silly, and we must see that it never becomes so. None of the characters in it, especially Hero, lacks validity. Claudio is rather shabbily treated, unlike Bassanio, and we feel angry with him for being taken in to begin with, and angrier at his wooden repentance afterward. We feel a little mollified by the fact that Don Pedro, one of Shakespeare's most gorgeous Renaissance princes, is equally deceived. But we have known that it must all come out right in the end; and even while the drama of the Church scene holds us, mainly through the way in which it brings out unsuspected qualities in its participants, we know that the little constables are blindly plodding along the road which will lead us all to a happy ending.

The plot has held the shadow which gives depth to the whole picture; no one in the play is left untouched by it; no one is quite the same at the end as he was at the beginning, and we must emphasize this line of personal development. Shakespeare is drawing closer, perhaps unconsciously, to the theme of man under the pressure of circumstance; this undertone, barely audible, gives a depth we must not lose to the gaiety and swinging merriment of MUCH ADO.

AS YOU LIKE IT, however, is the most cloudless of the comedies. It has been described as the most English, but I do not feel this to be true. The yokels of the wood near Athens, its very flowers and trees, are more English than the Forest of Arden, where the pastoral life conducted by the banished courtiers has a quality of playing at rusticity, like a Fête Champêtre by Watteau. There are no dangers in this Forest and not the mildest inconvenience to the progress of mellow thoughts, sweet speech, and gay, fullhearted loving, predestinate to happiness. Danger is the mere painting of itself; the ''green and

gilded snake" glides into a bush at the hero's approach;
the lioness has a "royal disposition" and can do no more
than scratch his arm; one generous action will win the
implacable Oliver to unstinted response, and even the
blackhearted Frederick will meet "an old religious
man," and, "after some question with him," be "converted both from his enterprise and from the world."

There is magic in this wood too, but the magic of the
sun, and it is a more constantly effulgent planet than
ever shone in the uncertain English summer. The very
prose of the play is shot with poetry, as the shade is
checkered with sunlight. The irony of Touchstone's
shafts is nowhere tipped with malice, and Jacques, the
philosopher whose blood is as cold as his mind is clear,
arouses not cynicism but compassion. This is the play of
harmony. It is not England, nor any part of the known
world; it is a part of the happy man's dream, the man
who trusts and loves mankind.

If we can reproduce this quality in the theatre, we
shall have succeeded. The problem is as simple and as
difficult as that. The actors will need a gaiety of soul
more even than they will need technical equipment.
The play must be lovingly performed. Even Audrey and
William, who have so often gaped and yammered
through their scenes, are in love, and it is the most
important thing about them. Even Touchstone decides,
with a wholly conscious dissection of his motives, to
submit to the prevalent emotion. Only Jacques disdains
it, so off he goes to the Duke's "abandoned cave," an
appropriate refuge. It seems to be the people of the outside world, Duke Frederick and Charles the Wrestler

and the Oliver of the early scenes, who are bemused among false perspectives. The little timeserver Le Beau betrays a wistful sense of it, when he takes leave of Orlando with:

> Hereafter, in a better world than this,
> I shall desire more love and knowledge of you.
>
> I, 3, 296

The comedy is so simple, so straightforward, and also so well-known, that we are tempted to think it will necessarily need embellishment. This fear probably accounted for the confusion of inventiveness with which Mr. Rosen overelaborated his New York production a few seasons ago. But at the World's Fair performances in 1939 we found, slightly to our surprise, that AS YOU LIKE IT proved far stronger in the warm regard of our audiences than did THE SHREW and THE DREAM, though it was the least embellished with directorial invention. We had not even the assistance of any scenic background; and the designer may help us greatly in this play if he can devise a background that will fill the eye with peaceful pleasure.

Rosalind, setting the pace and pitch for the whole, is subject to similar temptations. She has probably more "sides," and possibly more puns, than any of Shakespeare's women; sometimes the actress affects a "swashing and a martial outside" to an extent that gives a brassy quality to her scenes. But all the way through there is tenderness as well as ardor in her loving. Miss Edith Evans, in a recent production at the Old Vic, managed to discover moments of a melting sweetness which no one who saw them will forget. She proved that, if Shakespeare's boys had an easier task in the matter of disguise, the modern actress has a chance to achieve a modulation which can be immeasurably valuable.

Like Beatrice, Rosalind demands great swiftness; she must also use much more subtle interplay of thought behind, in contradiction to, the spoken word. Rosalinds do not grow on every theatre bush, nor are they manufactured in drama schools; for Rosalind must put the audience in love with all the gaiety and sweetness of life. If they leave the theatre with sour faces, we shall have failed to translate Shakespeare's intention. If we are merely "bright" about it, we shall be simply unbearable.

TWELFTH NIGHT is the last of the great comedies; the sun of AS YOU LIKE IT shines more softly in the Illyrian air, the beams growing long and level toward sunset. Even the music with which the two plays are saturated has a different note. In AS YOU LIKE IT, everybody sings, men and women and boys, and the play harmonizes like a madrigal or a rondo. But Orsino's musicians play him melodies with a "dying fall," and even Feste's love song ends:

> What is love? 'tis not hereafter;
> Present mirth hath present laughter;
> What's to come is still unsure:
> In delay there lies no plenty;
> Then come kiss me, sweet and twenty,
> Youth's a stuff will not endure.

We feel that the world of AS YOU LIKE IT will abide our

return. But TWELFTH NIGHT is filled with impermanence, fragile, imponderable.

Yet it has in it a set of characters and a sequence of plot more robust and coarser in grain than anything in the other play; our theatre problem becomes, in consequence, the blend and balance of disparate elements.

These elements are not portioned out into watertight compartments of character or class. Sir Toby carries the broadest of the comedy; but he is more than a drunken roisterer; he is a gentleman, Olivia's cousin, not so far removed in rank from the Duke. He is the younger son, the professionless gentleman who hunts and shoots and trades smoking-room stories at his club and lives shamelessly on his relatives and, a little, by his wits. Sir Tobys have supplied a steady counterpoint to English history; until September, 1940, you could have walked into any club on Pall Mall and found him sitting in a leather armchair.

His associates are not boors or rustics either. Maria, though she carries more than a little of the "soubrette" tradition along with her, is Olivia's gentlewoman and confidante; and in the great households of Shakespeare's day such positions were filled by girls and women who were themselves of the lesser nobility. It will, further, be a mistake to cast Sir Andrew as several feet of lank, dank dolt. He is a figure of some importance in his own home town, "the glass of fashion and the mould of form" to some Illyrian Podunk; he is simply out of key with the manners of the great world, overzealous in everything, from his clothes to his French tags, his eager little mind hopelessly outdistanced by Toby's broad and easy jests. Fabian is a superior servant, and a clever one, not much more. He is one of the characters to whom we must be especially careful to give some distinguishing mark by which a modern audience may place him recognizably in the hierarchy. It is a little puzzling to decide why Shakespeare put him in at all, unless he felt the need of another note in the comic chord.

Olivia and Orsino are at the other end of the scale. They live in an unreal world of their own imagining; they are in love with love and with all the trappings of love, phrases and pictures and music. Orsino is brought to a sense of real values before he himself knows it; the presence of "Cesario" has an astringent effect which he would be the last to admit; but, when, in the last scene, he comes to suspect and to receive apparent proof of the love between Olivia and his page-boy, a psychologist might find his furious jealousy to be caused as much by the faithlessness of "Cesario" as by the cruelty of Olivia. If he plays the scene too heavily, he may upset the balance of comedy and romance which it is to resolve.

Olivia will similarly put the play out of gear unless she is willing to play the spoiled young girl, flattered and pampered all her life long, kept from every contact with reality, thinking in terms of the legendary "Fairy Prince" in humble disguise, confident that every love story will have a happy ending, and that she, in particular, could not possibly be denied the love of her capricious choice. A staid and dignified matron, playing earnestly, and unwilling to be affectionately laughed at, will, again, rend the delicate fabric of fantasy, by causing us to interpret the mistaken-identity plot in terms of a realism which will immediately nullify its charm.

The links between the earthy comedy of Sir Toby and Co. and the lovelorn picture-book world of Olivia and Orsino are Viola herself and Feste. Both bring a highly realistic sense of values to the artifice of their masters; both can readily appreciate a good joke, and Viola can even be made the dupe of one without any lessening of our regard for her; both can spin a web of music in song and speech to catch the very essence of loving, and hold the reflection of man's evanescence; both have the gift to soften laughter with compassion. These seem to be the reasons for which Fabian is substituted for Feste in the more ruthless part of the Malvolio plot, for Feste is not to be identified with any single faction in the play but is part of the alchemy which blends them all. For the same purpose, Viola will be involved in the rich clowning of the duel, for she is to be no lovesick Victorian maiden but an inhabitant of all the play's imagined dimensions.

Malvolio is the solitary figure of the comedy; as alone in this fantasy of artifice and song and cakes and ale as Shylock has been in Venice. Illyria is hostile to Malvolio, and he is perpetually at odds with it, because he cannot make it make sense. And to Malvolio everything must make sense; literal sense, pettifogging sense, hierarchic sense, the sense of moral justice and the rewards of virtue. But life itself perpetually conspires to dupe and disillusion its Malvolios through their very adherence to arithmetical values, and brutally tears down the edifices of convention. So, Toby and his fellows embody for this Malvolio the Nemesis of ridicule which awaits those who are strong in principles but weak in tolerance and imagination. Whether we shall pity the man, hate him, despise him, or all three together, and in what proportionate degree, depends on the actor and, to an equal degree, on the balance of all the other actors.

For here is a play which illustrates beyond all the rest the importance of the human element to our theatre pattern. No two TWELFTH NIGHT's could ever be exactly alike, even if they were produced from identical prompt copies. The delicate adjustments between the component elements in the play must necessarily vary with every set of actors; here, the comics will tend to be preponderant; there, the Viola-Olivia scenes will embody our acting high lights. The director will have to balance and combine his ingredients in carefully graded proportions, compensating for weaknesses, keeping a moderating hand on excessive strength. This play, above all, he must treat with a light touch and a flexible mind, keeping the final goal clearly in sight. He must be prepared to reach it by devious paths, around obstacles he had not foreseen, and through short cuts he had not anticipated. For there are no frontiers to Illyria, and its inhabitants will forever elude the totalitarian method of theoretical regimentation.

"A great while ago the world begun," and few things in it have remained immutable but the wind and the rain and the sighing echo of a song. If you do not like the

title TWELFTH NIGHT, you may call the play WHAT YOU
WILL; and, if, striving to please you, we fail of our
purpose, we will lift the curtain another day, upon a
different world. "Man, proud man" will be our theme,
if we are to follow Shakespeare; man, and the immortal
gods; men set against each other; the single man's soul
set against itself. The conflict will never be resolved;
its progress will be labeled "tragedy."

CHAPTER TEN

The Tragic Essence

NORTH's translation of Plutarch's *Lives* exercised, perhaps, a greater influence over Shakespeare than any of his other source material. He never respected Holinshed as he respects Plutarch, who opens to him a new world and a new race of characters. He is not, at first, wholly at ease among the Romans, and he relies greatly on Plutarch's reports of their actions and even their words; his imagination is not confined, but it is disciplined. In this discipline he feels his way to a new style, firmer and more muscular than before; and in the men who move among the streets of Rome he finds a new type of conflict and a new way of thinking. JULIUS CAESAR is his transition to the tragedies, and Brutus the first of his new tragic heroes.

Like most pioneers, Brutus is not, in himself, fully successful. Shakespeare dissects him and puts together the component parts again—nobility, integrity, Stoicism, sensitivity of mind; he gives us the mental conflict, the confusion of personal and public loyalties, the high intention and the disparate deed; but somewhere the fire is lacking. Antony is freer and far showier; the mixture of warmth and shrewdness, impulsiveness and opportunism, directness and demagogy are admirably done. Every scene of Brutus is a hard one for the actor, for Brutus is not a man who reveals himself easily; every word of Antony, and they are magnificent words, is a showpiece in itself.

Cassius is no less successful; the twisted, indriven bitterness of the beginning, resentment raised to the status of a social cause, blends to the loneliness and yearning of the end so inexorably that we are touched to compassion. This man "thinks too much," dangerously to others, destructively also to himself. This is the man who once braved tyranny with the fearless brag:

> Nor stony tower, nor walls of beaten brass,
> Nor airless dungeon, nor strong links of iron
> Can be retentive to the strength of spirit;
> But life, being weary of these worldly bars,
> Never lacks power to dismiss itself   I, 3, 93

and who will, indeed, dismiss his own life at the last with the very sword which had killed Caesar, because his fears are greater than his courage to abide the issue of the battle. Brutus is not the only tragic hero in JULIUS CAESAR.

The play is more a conflict between these three contrasted men than it is an onslaught on dictatorship. The dictator himself is a question brilliantly begged; and the new order which is to succeed his fall is to be governed not by the enfranchised people, nor by the confused liberalism of such men as Brutus, nor even, in the final event of which ANTONY AND CLEOPATRA is the analysis, by the popular arts of Antony, but by the cool, keen ruthlessness of Octavius. In this play Shakespeare has not much time for him; but his every line is a power and a portent; the character has taken root, and it is he, because of his unity of purpose and undivided heart, who is to inherit the earth.

The dramatic quality of the play has made it eternally acceptable in the theatre. It shares with the greatest plays that spaciousness of conception which enables any one of twenty interpretations to be applied to it; its political implications can be, and have been, brought into conformity with current issues over the period of more than three hundred years since it was written. Its protagonists remain themselves, but their pulse still beats through the civilized world. We know them in ourselves. They lead Shakespeare to his most universal men and his most ageless dramatization of the spiritual conflict in the soul of man; the heroes will always go down before an Octavius or a Macduff or an Iago, not because of any superior quality in these men, still less through any extrinsic circumstance, but because of the "perilous stuff" within their own hearts.

HAMLET, the first of the four great tragedies, stands apart from the others in conception and treatment, but the essence of Shakespeare's tragic theme has been stated. OTHELLO, KING LEAR, and MACBETH will raise it to a poetic power which is beyond the range of the normal man and give it the dimension of poetic drama on a plane above the level of life. This will set us, in the theatre, a problem different from any which we have before encountered or are to meet again.

In producing any one of the four great tragedies the director and his actors may be forgiven for feeling a trifle overwhelmed. The greatest minds in literary criticism have weightily prestated the case in a continuous march of finely pondered judgments. The greatest actors, designers, directors, and producers have said their theatre say. The majority of any audience to whom the play is presented will have their own ideas about Othello, their particular form of worship for King Lear, and, most decisively, their own especial Hamlet in the mind's eye, with whose beloved lineaments the new Hamlet will tamper at his peril.

Very much that has been written on the four plays will open new angles of vision to the persevering if affrighted director. But he may, after a time, find it hard to preserve his theatre common sense suitably blended with a becoming humility in the presence of so many pundits, and his brain will reel with the effort to assimilate and reconcile their conflicting views. For, on the whole, they tend to make things look much more difficult and alarming than they really are. Perhaps the director will finally be forced to clear himself of all the theories about Hamlet's madness, all the speculations about the double-time scheme of OTHELLO, all the superlatives which have been lavished darkly upon KING LEAR, and simply consider the prosaic business of putting over the texts as we know them.

This can be in no sense a belittling of the greatness of

the material in the plays; for in them the actor will have need of a kind of inspiration. The word genius, so carelessly traded these days over the counters of an artistic ten-cent store, will not be too great in its true essence for the man who can fully measure Shakespeare's Othello or his Hamlet or his Lear. We are growing unaccustomed to the actor whose spiritual caliber enables him to make of himself the medium for a greater power. Perhaps we are afraid of him, or he of himself. We accept instead a set of variations on competence, personality, sweet reason, and sex appeal. We say, half apologetic and a tiny bit relieved, that Duses do not get born any more. Perhaps not. But we no longer demand them; we do not seem to miss them. Shakespeare misses them, for in these tragedies of his there is a greater stature than mere skill will ever reproduce; in them the actor may, as the author did, open the flood-gates to the power and the glory which transcend the appraisal of the logical analyst.

Skill, however, will do much. We cannot know whether Burbage gave wings to the parts he played; but we do know that Shakespeare so fashioned his plays that their melodramatic theatre quality carried them to the tumultuous favor of an Elizabethan audience. It may be well for us to start by getting their theatre structure soundly based and built, to try and recapture their firm, free craftsmanship, their enormous tempo, their passion, their delicate dramatic inflection of stress and relief, and their sweeping impetus of sound.

The director cannot manufacture wings, but he can give the actor space and scope in which to put them on. If the production is planned and patterned to Shakespeare's measurements, it will hold in the theatre under a diversity of different psychological interpretations, for in all of the tragedies there is a universality from which actors and audience may draw just as much or as little as is in themselves. But without theatrical validity a welter of fine mystic or philosophic forethought may totally fail of its effect.

Shakespeare, however startling it may be to remind ourselves of the fact, started with the story. In HAMLET and in LEAR, he had an old play upon which to work, in OTHELLO an Italian romance, in MACBETH the chronicles of his old friend Holinshed, who had seen him through so many medieval battles. The amazing poetic and dramatic genius which enabled him to transform his story material into the essentials of pity and terror is a commonplace of critical praise. But let us remember that he never lost the story.

For about a hundred and fifty years after the first production, nobody saw anything particularly difficult or obscure in the character of Hamlet; they accepted him, dovetailed, as in fact he is, with a thousand invisible links to the dramatic action of the play which bears his name. Gradually, however, critics began a separate analysis of the man himself, growing more obscure and more entangled as he became to them a distinct entity, having a life of his own, related only distantly to the dramatic purpose he serves in the dramatic world which he inhabits. Cut versions, all soliloquies and no plot, added to the murk of conflict. Of recent years, producers have rediscovered HAMLET

in its entirety, and it has been hailed with some surprise
for what it is, an extraordinarily finely jointed piece
of theatre craftsmanship from which no part, other than
a few isolated speeches, can be removed without some
loss. It has been proved, moreover, that Hamlet himself
emerges with infinitely greater clarity among the fuller
contour of his fellows, that audiences will actually feel
the play to move more swiftly in four hours than it
does in two and a half, and that the actor who plays
Hamlet has, by the universal testimony of those who
have played both versions, an easier time in the full one
than he has in the compressed tension caused by cutting.

Surprising things have emerged from these recent
treatments of the play. Rosencrantz and Guildenstern,
long supposed the two prize bores of all Shakespeare's
characters, have acquired identity and purpose; the little
scenes in which they are concerned, between Hamlet's
exit from his Mother's closet and the "How all occasions
do inform against me" soliloquy, have been found to
quicken the play's movement, clarify its plot, and
provide Hamlet with an invaluable ease from strain by
the employment of some beautifully pointed ironic
comedy. Polonius has regained almost his richest comedy
in the brief scene with Reynaldo, and in so doing restores
to the play, still reeling from its ghostly visitation, the
proportion and accent of the humdrum world where
Hamlet's "strangeness" will be so inevitably mis-
interpreted. Claudius, in lines and half speeches usually
dispensed with, in the sequence after the Play, and even
in the scene in which he tempts Laertes to the murder
of Hamlet, takes on a new gloss, a new subtlety of

shading; he becomes a man we understand because the light is turned on every facet of his thinking, and he is not left half effaced in the gloom, with nothing of his features distinguishable except the brand of Cain. Fortinbras rounds out the play, by reference at the beginning and in his own person at the end, with the vivid value of the man who is all Hamlet is not.

When Mr. Evans produced the uncut play in New York in 1938, he had had no intention of playing the entirety version eight times a week; he had felt that most audiences would prefer the more usual brevity of playing time and had planned to give at least half of his performances in a cut version, using, however, a fuller and differently adapted text from the one usually employed. But the demand to see the play that Shakespeare wrote and the response of the public toward it, caused him to drop all cut performances and concentrate exclusively on the full text. The play was the thing. Mr. Shakespeare received universal applause for the scope and sweep of his drama, its impetus, simplicity, and clarity. Mr. Evans's Hamlet was hailed with relief as being bewilderingly unbewildering. Mr. John Anderson wrote in the *Journal American:*

Instead of being a distorted, overly concentrated study of one character, the play becomes a dilated chronicle of melodramatic proportions, fastened securely to its central figure and carried with him in the flooding tide over overwhelming tragedy. The smaller eddies of its plot move inward on a vast centrifugal power until the whole, with all its thrilling momentum, reaches its momentous climax.

Yet Mr. Evans himself, around whose performance

the whole production revolved, would be the last to
claim any part of it as definitive. We aimed at certain
specific values which seemed to us to have become
obscured in the course of time, and these were not
abstract, but concrete. We were fortunate in our in-
terpreters, particularly in Miss Mady Christians, who
made of the Queen a clearly understandable woman
whom everyone in the audience could recognize, caught
by her very weakness in a web of circumstance far
beyond her control. It was our intention to bring the
play close to its hearers, even to lead them by inference
to believe that in this palace of Elsinore people led
everyday lives much like their own, ate and slept and
dressed and listened to music and took an interest in the
theatre and in the skill of riding and horsemanship.
Behind this facade of familiar things moves the spiritual
pulse and emotional conflict of the play.

Within the frame of Shakespeare's dramatic structure,
here as in all his greatest plays, imaginative and psychological values can be related with the greatest possible
freedom. The actor, however, must necessarily choose
one clear line of interpretation and follow it in detailed
application; he may lose, and consciously lose, some
particular high light for the sake of integrity in the
whole. The director too must choose his pattern, and
most carefully in the relation between one character and
another: the interpretation of the actor who plays
Claudius cannot be determined apart from that of the
actress who plays Gertrude. The director, like the actor,
may be forced to some sacrifice of his pet theories in
achieving a homogeneous entity. The whole must be

indivisible; but there will be infinite freedom of choice for both of them in determining what line of interpretation to pursue. Shakespeare, however, constructed his plays with the utmost theatrical skill and care in order that their higher implications might have dramatic cogency. The craft of their structure is mathematical; it is not capable of variation according to taste.

MACBETH, whatever the spiritual or abstract significance with which it has been variously endowed, has always been played for its tremendous dramatic impact. The structural basis of OTHELLO ensures a sweep of movement which, in the theatre, overwhelms all theoretical debate as to the motivation of its principal characters. And it is the lack of this fundamental theatre economy, rather than any insuperable difficulty in the playing of the leading part, that makes KING LEAR, for me, the least actable of the four plays.

Of them all, it is probably the most hypnotic to the reader. In the theatre also there are scenes which stir the heart and trouble the blood, especially the last of them, whose poignant beauty effaces much that has gone before, for it remains vivid and unspoiled in the audience's recollection. There are, moreover, lines and speeches of such magnificance that one's reasoning faculty is stunned by them. If the Lear, and not only the Lear but the Edgar, the Edmund, the Kent, the Gloucester, all three of the women, and indeed practically the whole cast, are superlative actors of superhuman power, they may catch us wholly into a realm of high poetic frenzy, in which we shall gladly abrogate the prerogative of intellectual judgment. Nevertheless, and with infinite respect to the serried ranks of opposed opinion, I cannot believe that KING LEAR ever was or ever will be a good play.

Prof. Bradley, whose lectures on the four tragedies remain among the most profound Shakespearean criticism, has this to say about it:

> When I read KING LEAR two impressions are left on my mind . . . KING LEAR seems to me Shakespeare's greatest achievement, but it seems to me *not* his best play. And I find that I tend to consider it from two rather different points of view. When I regard it strictly as a drama, it appears to me, though in certain parts overwhelming, decidedly inferior as a whole to HAMLET, OTHELLO, and MACBETH. When I am feeling that it is greater than any of these, and the fullest revelation of Shakespeare's power, I find I am not regarding it simply as a drama, but am grouping it in my mind with works like the PROMETHEUS VINCTUS and the DIVINE COMEDY, and even with the greatest symphonies of Beethoven and the statues in the Medici Chapel.

Mr. Granville Barker has devoted one of his most trenchant prefaces to disproving this point, and indeed he does most admirably demonstrate that the stage which Shakespeare used, and of which we can well recapture the essential features, can produce in the theatre a play as fine or finer than the one we have read by the fire, considered in both cases as a play. I think that he assumes, but does not prove, that it was a good play in the first place.

We are forced to clear our minds, to begin with, of the fascination and awe which echo through the writings of poets and critics when they confront KING LEAR and consider just what are the difficulties with which the plain man in the balcony, as well as the plain

actor behind the footlights, are faced. Audiences do
not, as a whole, react on the lines of "I do not understand it, so I suppose it must be great"; their emotions
are seldom engaged without a sympathetic collaboration
of the mind; the greatest actors and the greatest plays
have not seized upon their hearts by baffling them, but
by illuminating them.

Yet KING LEAR seems to me baffling from the very
beginning. There is about the first scene, says Mr.
Barker, "a certain megalithic grandeur, Lear dominat-
ing it, that we associate with Greek Tragedy. Its proba-
bilities are neither here nor there. A dramatist may
postulate any situation he has the means to interpret,
if he will abide by the logic of it after."

If we grant this, we are still faced with a play which
is to describe the tragic progression of retribution and,
if you like, the spiritual rebirth of an old man who has
behaved like an arbitrary, stupid despot, adding to an
admittedly improbable course of action in abdicating his
kingdom, a rejection of the one daughter whose love is
immediately patent to the dullest of us and of the one
subject whose courage and faithfulness are instantly
beyond doubt. That he is megalithic about it does not
make him any the more understandable.

The plain man starts with the inevitable conviction
that Lear will deserve whatever he gets. Nor do I
believe that in the succeeding scene with Goneril he will
appear as anything but a choleric, self-willed old tyrant,
whose presence in the home would be intolerable to the
most dutiful of children. Goneril is apt to emerge with
a very considerable measure of audience sympathy. Lear

drives himself progressively mad. If the audience remain antipathetic, it will be because the gigantic folly of his behavior will have had an immediacy of effect much greater than the imagined terrors of the storm into which his daughters finally thrust him out.

From this point onward, controversy has centered around the question of whether this cataclysmic convulsion of nature can be reproduced in the theatre, or, if it cannot, whether the actor can give us the tempest and turbulence of the convulsion in Lear's soul. Mr. Barker is certainly right in insisting that Shakespeare counted with the actor, and not with competitive technicians. But it is still questionable whether the springs of terror and pity have been adequately unsealed. The greatness of Lear's soul, his alleged genius, have been heavily overlaid.

In the later storm scenes, and still more in the scene with Gloucester, a "deep repentence" and a "compassion for sin" have been remarked in him. To the plain man the change is more likely to seem a gigantic swing of the pendulum of wrath, so that he, the despot who has had no thought for the poor and wretched among his subjects, now rails with equally insensate fury against every representative of riches, authority, or power. We are aghast at the glorious frenzy of his speeches. But do we, yet, pity him? We are overpowered; but do we, truly care? When it comes to his scenes with Cordelia, we shall care; their very quietness, the exquisitely simple writing of them, the touching, homely images, the tender feeling of familiar things, these will at last bring us to capitulation. But we may feel dimly cheated, too.

If the dramatic structure of the play had stood, clean and firm, around this tempestuous center, it would still be actable; Lear himself would be upheld by it. But, in my view, he is not. The subplot of Gloucester and his two sons loads the play with complicating horrors, and, though Shakespeare develops their story with masterly economy, the characters seem at once too fierce and full for the space within which they are confined, and yet too insistent in their interruption of the progress of the main plot. The pattern of Gloucester's folly and its Nemesis, paralleling the story of Lear, may indeed enforce with savage fury the picture of a dark, relentless world, where "machinations, hollowness, treachery and all ruinous disorders follow us disquietly to our graves"; but the compression necessitated by the handling of the two plots adds to the many inconsistencies of the play.

The subplot is especially full of developments inadequately prepared, or arbitrary twists of circumstance, including the major puzzle as to why Edgar does not reveal himself to his blinded father when there is no reason whatever for further concealment, and why he further indulges in a series of differing impersonations which usually defeat the hardiest young actor and bedevil the audience entirely. There surely never was such a young man for burning down the house in order to roast the pig.

With the exception of the chameleon Edgar and of Albany, who is sparely but subtly developed, every one of the dramatis personae steps upon the stage pure white or dead black and continues along a vigorous but all too apparent way, so that we cannot take refuge in the

delayed tension which accompanies the gradual revelation of character, or the unsuspected development of it,
as in HAMLET or MACBETH. Kent, superbly drawn in the
first half of the play, is more or less dropped in the last
third of it. The Fool is dismissed unexplained and apparently unlamented. He has served his purpose in lightening
the gathering strain with a wistful and touching lyric of
fragility; but he has also moved us, and his disappearance is not excused by the simple fact that Shakespeare
has no more need for him.

How are we, in the theatre, to compensate for or to
conceal the fissures and enormous rifts in the structure
of this dinosaur of a play? The practical objections which
I have here outlined may seem picayune to the enthralled
and worshipping reader, but I believe they have almost
always proved fatal to the play in performance, because
Shakespeare has not given us the means to resolve them,
but substituted a cloak of dark magnificence which we
may throw around them, hoping that no one will look
beneath it.

He has done this sort of thing before, of course, in the
lesser plays, sweeping us past an improbable piece of plot
on the impetus of fantasy or of passion. But in LEAR the
magnitude of the attempt will not let us smile indul-
gently and accept a let's-pretend; you cannot smile at
LEAR; either it is sublime or it is ridiculous. Nor is Lear's
Britain a let's-pretend world. Men are savage, lustful,
greedy, evil with a senseless, insatiate appetite; they
set the world spinning toward eternal chaos. But every
one of their actions brings retribution, not exact or just,
but magnified to a vast and horrible doom.

Every character makes some reference to the gods, the heavens, the eternal vengeance, the justicers above, the stars which govern our conditions. But it is the wheel of human action which comes a full and terrible circle. The play has been called one of capricious cruelty; Shakespeare is said to have been thinking himself in terms of Gloucester's famous:

> As flies to wanton boys are we to the gods;
> They kill us for their sport.

But it is as arguable that he is thinking, now as almost always, primarily in terms of humanity, but that here, as very seldom, he is passionately out of love with humanity and supremely doubtful of the civilized veneer with which mankind has succeeded in covering its primeval instincts. The evil in Lear's world is a force liberated by mankind to destroy itself. We may more readily identify Shakespeare with Edmund than with Gloucester, possibly as to his own thought, certainly as to his dramatic credo:

> This is the excellent foppery of the world, that when we are sick in fortune—often the surfeit of our own behaviour—we make guilty of our disasters the sun, the moon and the stars: as if we were villians by necessity, fools by heavenly compulsion, knaves, thieves and trecherers by spherical predominance, drunkards, liars and adulterers by an enforced obedience of planetary influence, and all that we are evil in by a divine thrusting-on: an admirable evasion of whoremaster man, to lay his goatish disposition to the charge of stars! 1, 2, 120

We can never succeed in Shakespeare unless we do so in terms of humanity, and in LEAR we cannot solve the human problem by endeavoring to make a protagonist of the gods. Yet there is in all the tragedies the feeling of a terrible force which the weakness or evil in man sets in motion but whose direction he is powerless to control. We have already seen some incarnation of the supernatural; even in JULIUS CAESAR we have heard of the portents which preceded the death of Caesar, and we have seen his ghost. In HAMLET these prodigies are again referred to by Horatio, whose attitude toward the ghost of King Hamlet most fully sets forth the strong background of superstition and fear which lay behind the enfranchised Renaissance mind. Even Hamlet is not wholly free of it, nor, certainly, Claudius.

Yet one would not think of HAMLET as in any primary sense a conflict between man and the supernatural forces, nor even between man and the larger design of fate. The conflict in this "tragedy of thought," as it has been called, is between man and his own soul; the division is in the very heart of the protagonist.

In the three later "tragedies of passion," the greater force is progressively unleashed, incarnate in human beings who, for the first time since RICHARD III, seem to be indeed the servants of an evil power. In the last of the tragedies, MACBETH, the subtle power of darkness becomes all-pervading; it takes the form of "supernatural soliciting," it employs "instruments of darkness," it drenches the play in blackness and in blood, poisons the air with fear, preys on bloated and diseased imaginings, turns feasting to terror and the innocent sleep to nightmare, and employs a terrible irony of destruction in the accomplishment of its barren ends.

Yet MACBETH contains no villain, no Iago, no Goneril. Evil is alive of itself, a protagonist in its own right.

There is a long theatrical tradition of disaster behind MACBETH, dating back, it seems, to the earliest production of the play. A theatre superstition makes it unlucky even to quote the play inside a theatre, and no actor who believes in this but can quote you a long string of supporting evidence proving the play's fatal influence. Anyone who believes in the darker powers, in whatever form, cannot be wholly incredulous; for no play ever written has more powerfully invoked them.

Yet MACBETH is the best melodrama of them all, and, if you prefer your murders "straight," you can so take them. Its construction is as tight as LEAR's is vast and spreading. Its shortness has led many critics to suppose that the Folio text, which is the only one we have, has been much cut. Yet its design is exact, its pattern as precisely balanced as a Bach fugue, its action taut and muscular, its poetry many times magnificent. As Bradley says of it: "Shakespeare has certainly avoided the over-loading which distresses us in KING LEAR, and has produced a tragedy utterly unlike it, not much less great as a dramatic poem, and as a drama superior."

The producer's problem is therefore a very different one and centers upon three protagonists, the two Macbeths and the power which is behind them. We must at every point be made conscious of the pervasive power of evil suggestion; most clearly we shall feel it through Macbeth himself, so reluctant at first to "yield to that suggestion," yet committed to it more and more deeply, more and more fiercely, as if in action, in blood and more blood, he could kill forever the reproaches his conscience had once heaped upon him. As the quality of his imagination had first shown him the cosmic horror which would follow Duncan's murder in the daring and terrible images of

> . . . pity like a naked new-born babe
> Striding the blast, or heaven's cherubin hors'd
> Upon the sightless couriers of the air,

so this same faculty of perception stretching far behind the concrete aspect of material things is increasingly obsessed by images of blood and death. But now there is no pause between the image and the deed which translates it into action. The tempo increases to the speed of a nightmare; Macbeth cannot stop nor pause in this doomed frenzy of murder lest his imagination should come alive again and significance should flood back over the ashen, relentless path he is traveling. There is no end, any more; there is only the driven, hunted slavery of one who has indeed given "his eternal jewel" to "the common enemy of man."

Through Lady Macbeth we shall be made equally but quite differently aware of the third protagonist. In her very first scene—and it is one of the problems of the part that we neither see nor hear anything of Lady Macbeth before the pressure of climactic circumstance begins to work on her—she reads Macbeth's account of the witches' prophecies, and immediately afterward in comes the news of Duncan's approach.

> The raven himself is hoarse
> That croaks the fatal entrance of Duncan
> Under my battlements.

We can almost hear the soft beat of wings. At once she
begins the terrible invocation:

> . Come you spirits
> That tend on mortal thoughts, unsex me here,
> And fill me from the crown to the toe top-full
> Of direst cruelty . . .
> . . . Come to my woman's breasts,
> And take my milk for gall, you murdering ministers,
> Wherever in your sightless substances
> You wait on nature's mischief. Come, thick night,
> And pall thee in the dunnest smoke of hell,
> That my keen knife see not the wound it makes,
> Nor heaven peep through the blanket of the dark
> To cry "Hold, hold!"   I, 5, 38

And they come, these sightless substances; there
should be no smallest doubt about that. They use her,
possess her, just exactly as she had prayed them to
do; they make of her a creature as relentless as she had
desired, they shroud the stars and charge the blackened
night with terror. And, when the murder is once
accomplished, Lady Macbeth is exhausted, used up,
the vitality and spring of life drained out of her. She
will still summon all the remnant of her power to help
Macbeth when he sees the ghost of Banquo; but he
has gone beyond her, obsessed, blinded, bound to the
treadmill on which she had first set his feet. There is
no contact between them any more, only the feel of the
blood between their hands. The last part of Lady
Macbeth is filled with echoes, ironic echoes, terrible
echoes, inescapable, even through the thick, haunted
nights from which sleep has forever gone.

Toward the end of the play the accelerated pace and

spreading effect of evil is apparent in every scene. All of the minor characters begin to apprehend it: the uneasy guests at the banquet; the mysterious Messenger who comes to warn Lady Macduff but dare not stay to protect her; Ross, describing Scotland as "almost afraid to know itself"; the Doctor and the Gentlewoman, frightened of finding out more than they dare know; the succession of terrified servants who bring to Macbeth the news of Malcolm's approach. Fear is in the ascendant, fear and hate, under whose banners evil has always triumphed. With the victory of Malcolm's army, and Macbeth's death at the hands of the man he had most feared, the spell is broken, suddenly and completely, as the dawn dispels the nightmares of Walpurgis Night.

Every sign and signal of this progression may be carried out in clear theatrical terms, yet it is only in the witches that the evil force is ever actually incarnate, and they present us with the most difficult problem in the play. Shakespeare seems to have taken both the description of their appearance and the abracadabra of their incantations almost verbatim from a contemporary book on witchcraft, and with these generally accepted features his audience was familiar. He was using a symbol of great potency of which there appears to be no equivalent today. Only the most intelligent and enlightened members of his audience would have claimed that they no longer believed in witchcraft, and in doing so they would have rendered themselves suspect. For common belief credited these old hags with undisputed powers. King James himself wrote a treatise against them and encouraged their persecution and savage punishment. It was widely believed that two hundred of them had set out in sieves to try and sink the ship which had brought his Queen from Denmark.

It was not difficult to bring an Elizabethan audience to a state of terrified acceptance before the figures of the Three Weird Sisters. Long after 1606 the average man would still, however hotly he denied it, have felt distinctly uncomfortable had he met three strange old women on a lonely heath. He would have been unable to dismiss a "witch's" curse or blessing freely from his mind. But the most terrifying thing about these old women, especially at their first appearance on the "blasted heath," would have been their apparent harmlessness. Three old women; as simple as that. And suddenly they vanished into air; as incredible as that. What ineluctable force of doom might not lurk behind this phenomenon? A man is paralyzed with fear not so much by some colossal and unheard-of monstrosity as by the more dreadful horror of feeling a familiar thing melt and change beneath his hand.

It is probable that, deep in our hearts, we "moderns" are as vulnerable to superstition as our Elizabethan ancestors, though we deny it more strenuously. But it is almost impossible to find for a modern audience a symbol which will have the effect that Shakespeare's witches had on his. Mr. Orson Welles, in his negro MACBETH, found the perfect equivalent in voodoo; but obviously this is no solution of general application. Gypsies and fortunetellers come somewhere near the mark but not quite up to it. Spiritualist mediums have occasionally been substituted. Other producers have employed mechanical apparitions of grotesque appearance, like the fancier flights of Mr. Disney's imagination.

I do not believe Shakespeare's intention to be truly carried out by such devices, which have, in fact, more often induced laughter than terror in the spectators. We must concentrate on the projection of evil, an incalculable force which expresses itself in all the twisting, echoing pattern of the play. In this design the witches are only a part, and, if the rest of it holds firm, we shall accept them by virtue of what they represent, and not because of any ingenious hocum in their appearance or, for the matter of that, their disappearance.

For even in this, the most supernatural of the four tragedies, Shakespeare does not desert his main principle that drama, be it of thought, of passion, of poetry, or of superhuman forces is expressed in the theatre in terms of human beings and a story. Character under the pressure of circumstance, it has been more grandly termed; the conflict between man and man, man and himself, man and fate. Whatever the improbability of his initial postulate, Shakespeare resolves it with dramatic integrity.

Prof. E. E. Stoll, writing with a vivid sense of theatre, as against literary valuation, disclaims as ''neither here nor there'' the psychological explanations with which analysts have tried to codify and pigeonhole the behavior of Shakespeare's tragic heroes. We shall need, he says, ''that willing suspension of disbelief which constitutes poetic faith." If we do need even this, we shall easily acquire it. For Shakespeare keeps faith with the characters he postulates, and he keeps theatre faith with his audience; in no play does he more clearly demonstrate his mastery than in the most human of the four tragedies, OTHELLO.

There are no ghosts in OTHELLO, no supernatural solicitings, no inexplicable convulsions of nature, no imagery even, as there is so strongly in LEAR, of the primeval characteristics of the animal world to which Lear's world is so nearly akin. There is human passion, of which the germ is in each one of us, raised to its highest pitch, and forged to a white heat of dramatic action.

The postulate which we have in this instance to accept seems to me to be not that of Othello, whom we see transformed before our eyes, but of Iago. Critics have made a great to-do over the nature of Iago, and echoed in many forms Othello's own question:

> Will you, I pray, demand that demi-devil
> Why he hath thus ensnared my soul and body?
>
> v, 2, 308

There is an agreement that the motives which Iago himself successively advances either in soliloquy or to Roderigo, his resentment over the promotion of Cassio, his suspicion of Othello and Emilia, his even more perfunctory suspicion of Emilia and Cassio in no way fully account for his "hatred" of the Moor. He has been described as a man who loves evil for evil's sake and, much more convincingly, as a man with a superiority complex reveling in his own power to destroy someone whom the world has agreed to set above him.

The plain theatre fact, however, is that audiences have never been bothered in the smallest degree by any doubtful "motivation" in Iago. They have accepted him, hook, line, and sinker, and the part has always been effective to the point of stealing the play from Othello himself, probably because it does not make any emotional demands upon the actor which are beyond the normal man's compass.

The universal acceptance of Iago as "honest," another postulate which has been widely questioned, has been often belied in the theatre. Iagos have adopted the sinister mien of a typical Italianate villain to an extent which would cause any sensible housewife to hide the silver spoons the moment he crossed the threshold. There is nothing intrinsically improbable about Iago's apparent honesty, and it is important to the play that it be plausible not only to the other characters but to the audience, if Othello is not to appear unforgivably gullible. Iago is very fully revealed in the text, without the aid of sidelong glances, evil chuckles, and a waxed moustache. The brilliant speed of his small, unscrupulous thinking, the dash of recklessness, the complete worldly armory of his mind, the plentitude of will and the absolute lack of imagination are all full and clear and contrasted unerringly with Othello's utterly alien make-up. A theatrical cast of villainy will ruin both of them.

The very quality of Iago's speech is differentiated from Othello's by every possible means. Except for the soliloquies, it is almost all in prose, light, acute, beautifully phrased, every cynical, easy turn of it unerringly directed. It needs polish, precision, and extreme lucidity in the speaking, little music. Othello, who early says of himself "Rude am I in my speech," is to run an orchestral gamut, always spiced with the flavor of strangeness and enriched with the color of the East and the burnished sun. He is to talk of "antres vast and deserts idle," of sibyls "that had numbered in the world the sun to course two hundred compasses," of Arabian trees and turbaned Turks and Ottomites and anthro-pophagi. But the measured gravity of his first address to the Senate,

> Most potent, grave and reverend signiors,
> My very noble and approved good masters,

will change to a passionate agony of tumbling phrases, to the almost unintelligible ravings of "Lie with her! lie in her!—We say lie on her, when they belie her.—Lie with her! 'Zounds, that's fulsome! Handkerchiefs—confession—handkerchiefs!" And it will change again, under the sway of a great and noble sorrow far transcending the initial passion of jealousy, to the sacrificial majesty of:

> Put out the light, and then put out the light:
> If I quench thee, thou flaming minister,
> I can again thy former light restore,
> Should I repent me: but once put out thine,
> Thou cunning pattern of eternal nature,
> I know not where is that Promethean heat
> That can thy light relume.   v, 2, 7

It is commonly, and as I think erroneously, supposed

that Othello must carry us on a torrent of sound past some intrinsic improbabilities of characterization. Mr. Shaw has said: "The words do not convey ideas—they are streaming ensigns and tossing branches to make the tempest of passion visible . . . Tested by the brain it is ridiculous; tested by the ear it is sublime." It is, of course, the fury of Othello's so-called "jealousy" that strikes Mr. Shaw as ridiculous, which, in Mr. Shaw, can hardly be regarded as surprising.

Many critics have, however, stressed the factual improbability of the situation, the impossible shortness of time, the intervention of fortuitous events, such as the dropping of the handkerchief, which alone makes possible the success of Iago's scheme. And it has been thought that despite the actor's advantage of spoken and magnificent verse, he will be unable to make us believe Othello, but that the audience will simply echo Emilia's "Nay, lay thee down and roar," with as great and callous a contempt.

It is true that many of the cultured gentlemen, reluctantly and faintly disguising from us their familiar features under a layer of becoming coffee-colored grease paint, rather as if they had recently returned from Palm Beach, have seemed to us possessed of far too much intelligence, restraint, and self-control ever to be swept by an uncontrollable passion which is not from the mind at all and only a little from the heart, but principally from the bowels. Mr. Knight says of this emotional situation that "it does not mesh with our minds." It does not, indeed; but then it was never intended to do so.

Othello's emotional functioning is alien to most of us,

though up to a point we may parallel it, upon occasion, in newspaper headlines about some so-called "sex" murderer. But Othello himself is alien; the process of his feeling is as strange to Desdemona as hers to him; the gulf which opens between them once the sympathy of their cooler mental concord is lost, is a gulf between two races, the one old in the soft ways of civilization, the other close to the jungle and the burning desert sands. Iago, even, knowing every twist which can be given to the Moor because of his alien and "inferior" race, does not reckon with the full primitive power of the passion which he unleashes.

For the question of Othello's race is of paramount importance to the play. There has been much controversy as to Shakespeare's intention. It is improbable that he troubled himself greatly with ethnological exactness. The Moor, to an Elizabethan, was a blackamoor, an African, an Ethiopian. Shakespeare's other Moor, Aaron, in TITUS ANDRONICUS, is specifically black; he has thick lips and a fleece of woolly hair. The Prince of Morocco in THE MERCHANT OF VENICE bears "the shadowed livery of the burnished sun," and even Portia recoils from his "complexion" which he himself is at great pains to excuse.

Othello is repeatedly described, both by himself and others, as black; not pale beige, but black; and for a century and a half after the play's first presentation he was so represented on the stage. But after this the close consideration of nice minds began to discern something not quite ladylike about Desdemona's marrying a black man with thick lips. They cannot have been more horrified than Brabantio, her father, who thought that only witchcraft could have caused "nature so preposterously to err," or more convinced of the disastrous outcome of such a match than Iago, who looked upon it as nothing but a "frail vow between an erring Barbarian and a supersubtle Venetian," and declared, with his invincible cynicism, that "when she is sated with his body, she will find the error of her choice: She must have change; she must!"

It is very apparent, and vital to the play, that Othello himself was very conscious of these same considerations and quiveringly aware of what the judgment of the world would be upon his marriage. It is one of the most potent factors in his acceptance of the possibility of Desdemona's infidelity. And she herself loses much in the quality of her steadfastness and courage if it be supposed that she simply married against her father's wishes a man who chanced to be a little darker than his fellows, instead of daring a marriage which would cause universal condemnation among the ladies of polite society. To scamp this consideration in the play is to deprive Othello of his greatest weakness, Desdemona of her highest strength, Iago of his skill and judgment, Emilia of a powerful factor in her behavior both to her master and her mistress, and Venice itself of an arrogance in toleration which was one of the principal hallmarks of its civilization—a civilization which frames, first and last, the soaring emotions of the play.

After these three tragedies, Shakespeare will never again take us into so passion-tossed a world, never set his actors to release themselves so fully from the normal restraints of polite behavior, never pound his audience into submission by the relentless power of words. He will give us a jealous man in Leontes, an ambitious one in Octavius, an embittered outcast in Timon, but it will not be the sacrificial jealousy of Othello, the haunted ambition of Macbeth, or the madness, of Lear. Nothing that happens in the later plays will carry us beyond the sphere where reason is still a comfortable guide. Nor will man ever again cry with such anguish to the stars to shield him from the unbearable responsibility of the world he has fashioned. The theatre will revert to its normal self, its walls solid and comfortably bounding the two hours' traffic of make-believe. There will be plenty of technical problems to be faced. ANTONY AND CLEOPATRA especially will call for a width and range of vision; many of the plays to come will need adroit and lavish handling. But never again will the hearts of players and audience be so swept with the mystery of life and the bitter release of death.

CHAPTER ELEVEN

Plays Unpleasant

UNDER this title I have grouped four plays which the stage has virtually lost, and partly on account of their "unpleasant"-ness. They are ALL'S WELL THAT ENDS WELL, MEASURE FOR MEASURE, TROILUS AND CRESSIDA, and TIMON OF ATHENS. The dates of their composition are in every case uncertain, though we have limiting evidence. It would seem that the first three were written in the period immediately following HAMLET and before OTHELLO and the other tragedies.

TIMON appears to belong some two or three years later, but its spiritual sourness makes one feel it as nearly akin to the other three. The text we have is so garbled and filled out by other hands than Shakespeare's that it is hard to assign it to any definite period of his development. Certainly he left it unfinished; probably his collaborator never fully completed the job; much of the verse is in a rough and chaotic condition, as if it were taken from unfinished notes and first drafts;

240

and there is evidence that it was not originally intended for publication in the complete Folio but was inserted to fill a gap caused by a temporary difficulty in obtaining the rights of TROILUS AND CRESSIDA.

The disintegrating critics have a wide field of conjecture in all these plays, and have done some brilliant bibliographical reconstruction on them. ALL'S WELL bears clear marks of some very early work, and editors conjecture that original material for MEASURE FOR MEASURE and TROILUS was composed some time before either play was finished; all seem to have been cut, revised, and added to at successive times, both by Shakespeare and by collaborating authors.

If the texts are corrupt, the dramatic qualities of the plays are no more satisfactory. I do not think that ALL'S WELL or TIMON will ever return to the theatre, except perhaps as a labor of love for some commemorative festival. ALL'S WELL does acquire in performance a certain warmth; faults in it that are apparent to the analytic student ease themselves past an audience. There is a kind of relativity in the theatre value of a play which works to the advantage of this one.

Helena has strength and beauty in the writing itself, and some most happy lines of verse such as the famous:

> Shall I stay here to do't? no, no, although
> The air of paradise did fan the house,
> And angels offic'd all.   III, 3, 125

and

> But with the word that time will bring on summer,
> When briers shall have leaves as well as thorns,
> And be as sweet as sharp.   IV, 4, 31

She has dignity, and, in a rare moment of softness, a really moving scene of abandoned grief when she reads Bertram's letter to his mother, "Madam, my lord is gone, forever gone." But she is dreadfully strong-minded in her pursuit of the wretched young man, tool of the plot as well as of his own folly, upon whom she has unaccountably set her heart.

Mr. Shaw thinks highly of Helena for being a good doctor and having more brains than most of the heroines. But she is altogether too Shavian, in the manner of Ann in MAN AND SUPERMAN, to warm our hearts. And the stratagem by which she eventually secures her horrible husband must necessarily leave us coldly disbelieving unless we are to be stirred to active dislike of it.

Other characters come out well upon the stage. The Countess of Rossillon is an altogether charming old lady, with the mellow wisdom of age, and the elderly Lord Lafeu, who plays very much better than he reads, partners her with his shrewdness and understanding. He has a trick of very simple speech, which is rare when Shakespeare writes, as he does in this play, without heart. After a scene with the Clown, a rather tedious, acid, pensioner-punster, Lafeu comments "A shrewd knave, and an unhappy." And to the disgraced and discountenanced Parolles, whose pretentious nothingness he had been the first to suspect, he still shows kindness without sentimentality: "Though you are a fool and a knave, you shall eat; go to, follow."

"I praise God for you," replies Parolles. We may deduce the infinite relief behind the words. For Parolles is a weakling in his own braggart kind, a thinly flashy sort of rogue. He too emerges with more substance on the stage than in print. The episode of the drum which his company has lost in battle and which he boasts of being able to recover, to his own ultimate confusion, is vivid and amusing and distracts us from the unbearable Bertram story, but Shakespeare dismisses it perfunctorily, without caring much what happens. The best thing about Parolles is his appearance before the King in the last scene, in which the mixture of fear and bravado, sycophancy and tattered pride offer more to the actor than to the casual reader.

TIMON OF ATHENS seems to me equally unplayable, though for different reasons. Timon himself falls into two halves which Shakespeare has made no attempt to join. Perhaps he intended to, and wrote the two extremes, but never worked on the play to the point where he could achieve the gradations. In the first half everybody flatters Timon and he is witlessly generous to each and every comer. In the second half everybody deserts him, except his steward, and he is as witlessly bitter to and about the whole of mankind. The normal man will be equally mistrustful of him at both times.

Indeed the flood of bitterness in the second half of the play is so relentless that our ears and minds grow dulled to it. The characters vie with one another in cursing mankind and themselves; Apemantus, whose acidity has never changed, does not soften to Timon in misfortune; "a madman first, now a fool," he calls him; and when he is asked what he would do with the world if it lay in his power, replies succinctly "Give it to the beasts, to be rid of the men." The servile little Painter, with his friend the Poet, who have flattered Timon in his heyday, come to him again, hearing he has found gold, and even they have disillusion on their lips: "I will promise him an excellent piece . . . To promise is most courtly and fashionable; performance is a kind of will or testament which argues a great sickness in his judgment that makes it." (Act v, scene 1, line 20) Timon's comprehensive curses blaze through the last two acts like a destructive fire; Shakespeare seems to be unleashing all the tortured hatred of the world; it is magnificent, incomparable rhetoric:

> Rascal thieves,
> Here's gold. Go, suck the subtle blood o' the grape,
> Till the high fever seethe your blood to froth,
> And so 'scape hanging. Trust not the physician,
> His antidotes are poison, and he slays
> Moe than you rob: take wealth and lives together;
> Do villainy, do, since you protest to do't,
> Like workmen. I'll example you with thievery:
> The sun's a thief, and with his great attraction
> Robs the vast sea. The moon's an arrant thief,
> And her pale fire she snatches from the sun.
> The sea's a thief, whose liquid surge resolves
> The moon into salt tears. The earth's a thief,
> That feeds and breeds by a composture stol'n
> From general excrement: each thing's a thief,
> The laws, your curb and whip, in their rough power
> Has uncheck'd theft. Love not yourselves, away,
> Rob one another, there's more gold, cut throats,
> All that you meet are thieves: to Athens go,
> Break open shops, nothing can you steal,
> But thieves do lose it: steal no less for this
> I give you, and gold confound you how soe'er:
> Amen.   IV, 3, 429

Timon is a great operatic part; but the mind of the plain man recoils before the pitiless, raging bitterness of the play. It is surmised that Shakespeare, with all these "plays unpleasant," was going through some experience of extreme personal disillusionment and that with TIMON he reached the breaking point. There can be very little doubt that he was in some way spiritually and intellectually rudderless when he wrote it; and this lack of mental stability deprived him of his sure dramatic sense.

TIMON is bad philosophy and bad theatre, however brilliant the writing. It seems, not surprisingly, that the Globe Company never performed it; and, though the eighteenth century made some halfhearted attempts at adaptations, the first recorded performance of the Folio text did not come till 1851 at Sadlers Wells, London, by Samuel Phelps. It is a pity that we cannot ever hear the great speeches greatly spoken; but we simply cannot take the play, for it never arouses us to participation or to compassion; only very occasionally can we discern a rift in the clouds, as with the fragmentary gleam of:

> Then, Timon, presently prepare thy grave:
> Lie where the light foam of the sea may beat
> Thy grave-stone daily, . . .   IV, 3, 378

and we realize, with a lifting of the heart, that the sea will not always be so savage as it has been, and that Shakespeare will presently wake from this nightmare and find himself once more among his fellows at the Globe.

TROILUS AND CRESSIDA has in it a good deal of the

turbulence of TIMON; it is diffuse, incoherent, difficult
to trim to a recognizable dramatic pattern. A lot of
people are piled into it, and not a single one of them is
wholly likable, with the exception of Troilus himself.
The scurrilous Thersites smears the play with scabrous
jests, though many of them have a good salt sting that
we cannot help appreciating; again, the iteration of
invective is apt to pall. "How now, thou cur of envy,"
say Achilles to Thersites. "Thou crusty batch of nature,
what's the news?" And Thersites replies: "Why, thou
picture of what thou seemest, and idol of idiot worshippers, here's a letter for thee." And later in the same
scene Thersites and Patroclus interchange the following
pleasantries:

PATROCLUS: Why, thou damnable box of envy, thou, what mean'st
thou to curse thus?

THERSITES: Do I curse thee?

PATROCLUS: Why, no, you ruinous butt, you whoreson indistinguishable cur, no.

THERSITES: No? Why art thou then exasperate, thou idle immaterial
skein of sleave silk, thou green sarcenet flap for a sore eye,
thou tassel of a prodigal's purse, thou?   v, i, 24

Shakespeare is not in the romantic vein, certainly.
Achilles is a sulky lout who finally kills Hector by a
cowardly betrayal; Patroclus is a sycophant, Ajax a
boor and a fool, Menelaus a stock cuckold, and Diomed
a "smoothy." Agamemnon comes off rather better.
Ulysses, upon the slightest provocation, will out with
thirty or forty lines of complex trope and metaphor;
for Shakespeare is in his overwriting period, his mind

fecund of pentameters, his heart troubled and unsure. We may have to use a blue pencil with Ulysses, but he has some magnificent things to say. His great speech which begins

> Time hath, my lord, a wallet at his back
> Wherein he puts alms for oblivion,   III, 3, 145

is stuck with platitudinous maxims. "Perseverance, dear my lord, Keeps honour bright." "The welcome ever smiles, The farewell goes out sighing." "The present eye praises the present object" and, startlingly familiar, "One touch of nature makes the whole world kin." This is too much quotability for one speech. We feel that Ulysses has been storing up epigrams for weeks and will not let us off one of them. We appreciate him more when his observation of people is in question, as, of the newly arrived Cressida:

> There's language in her eye, her cheek, her lip,
> Nay, her foot speaks, her wanton spirits look out
> At every joint and motive of her body.
> O, these encounterers, so glib of tongue,
> That give a coasting welcome ere it comes,
> And wide unclasp the tables of their thoughts
> To every ticklish reader! set them down
> For sluttish spoils of opportunity,
> And daughters of the game.   IV, 5, 56

This is recognizable, vivid, the mind engages with it; but it is also a description of "our heroine" and illustrates the problem which confronts us in the play.

We start off, firmly enough, with Troilus in love; he is clearly, maturely drawn, and there is music in him, if, like all the music of the play, it is too elaborately orchestrated. We see Pandarus, lively enough in print but capable of far more likable comedy in the playing, and Cressida, whom we are never led to trust. She is too beautiful, too assured, too "glib of tongue."

Here, with the background of war, are the elements of tragedy. But with the scene of the Greeks in council, Act 1, scene 3, we realize how easy it may be for the lovers and their story to get lost among these "cogging Greeks." For Shakespeare is not in love with war; he is not in love with the men who make wars; he is intent on dissecting, not the bright, flat tapestry heroics of the English chronicle wars, but the battle of power politics, personal jealousies, and faction fights, confusion of issues, confounding of order and sanity, the seamy side of valor.

Having thoroughly discredited the Greeks with one of the least amiable Thersites scenes, he returns to the Trojans in council, discussing a peace proposal. The Trojans are more likable than the Greeks and not quite so long-winded. If any one of them comes near Shakespeare's own thoughts, it must be Hector, who, greatest fighter among them all, uses the most common sense and is the strongest for peace. But Hector-Shakespeare is won over, although his judgment is entirely unconvinced by the arguments in favor of refusing the peace terms. To Troilus and Paris he says that they have argued

> . . . not much
> Unlike young men, whom Aristotle thought
> Unfit to hear moral philosophy.
> The reasons you allege do more conduce

To the hot passion of distempered blood,
Than to make up a free determination
'Twixt right and wrong; for pleasure and revenge
Have ears more deaf than adders to the voice
Of any true decision.   II, 3, 165

But the war must go on, and so must the play, and all the way through it Shakespeare seems to be struggling with an infinite contempt for the whole business of fighting, and the story of Troilus and his false Cressida struggles for breath too, choked with disillusion, occasionally rising to the surface for a long breath of magnificent poetic air. To the facile Cressida, who is fully and unsparingly drawn, he gives one of the most beautiful of his singing speeches:

If I be false, or swerve a hair from truth,
When time is old or hath forgot itself,
When waterdrops have worn the stones of Troy,
And blind oblivion swallow'd cities up,
And mighty states characterless are grated
To dusty nothing, yet let memory,
From false to false among false maids in love,
Upbraid my falsehood!   III, 2, 179

But, if the song is sweet, the irony lies heavily upon it.

Neither the love story nor the war story is ever fully resolved. There is no "pay-off." Cressida is false, Troilus discovers her falsehood; he seeks death in battle but does not find it; finds Diomed, his successful rival, but does not kill him. Hector is slain not in fair fight but in ambush by Achilles and all his gangsters, and Achilles goes off with a couplet of such incredible banality that we cannot help feeling that Shakespeare is nauseated with the whole business. Both sides claim the victory in battle, Thersites threads in and out discrediting everything and everybody, and Pandarus ends the play with some obscure and bawdy rhymed verse; or rather, the play stops because it has already gone on a long time and there doesn't seem to be much left to write about.

All of this leaves us, in the theatre, faced with very great difficulties; the problem of imposing a recognizable form on this shapeless play, of cutting the verbiage away from it, of presenting some sort of conclusion. It might well be worth trying; for there is much fine stuff in the text and much that is possibly closer to our thinking today than it has ever been to any audience before. I feel that we should have to do some very free editing and make a decision, which Shakespeare himself never clearly made, as to whether we are presenting satire, caricature, or a genuine, if caustic, commentary on love and war. The experiment might be worth making. We are up against our usual problem. We have no place to make it.

The last of the four plays, on the other hand, is over-ripe for revival. MEASURE FOR MEASURE is a strong piece of work, less informed with music than the greatest plays, but brimming with life. It is not polite life, nor disciplined life; the comedy characters from the stews of Vienna would not get past the Hays Office; but there is no question as to their reality. Pompey is a fine, fat part, and Elbow, the constable, is in the best Dogberry-and-Verges tradition. Lucio, described in the Folio list of actors as "a fantastic," has a light, showy impudence and a quick tongue.

One of the sourest things in the play is the savagery of the punishment which the Duke imposes on him at the end. They would never have treated him so in Arden or Illyria. But this is not a dream world; it is a hard one, peopled by men and women in the grip of strong, difficult emotions. Spirit and flesh are at war with each other, and their conflict is no more resolved than is the conflict of war in TROILUS AND CRESSIDA. The pattern imposed for its resolution is an arbitrary one. We feel Shakespeare thinking contemptuously that life doesn't solve things so easily, but this is the theatre, and here is your deus ex machina and your last-act curtain, so make the best of it.

There is no doubt that the trick by which one woman substitutes herself for another in a man's bed, always with the noblest intentions, as Helena did in ALL'S WELL and as Mariana does for Isabella in this play, was an accepted artifice with Elizabethan audiences, however difficult we may find it. The impenetrable-disguise business is also put to use, this time by the Duke; and, in reading, we find the Duke's procrastination in revealing himself and meting out the necessary rewards and punishments more than a little irritating. This device, also, is much more acceptable in the theatre; in recent London revivals it has been proved that the Duke, humanized and strengthened by an actor's personality, may be given a variety of thought and feeling which is not immediately apparent from his actual words, and may become much more than "a tall dark dummy," as Mr. Van Doren calls him.

Shakespeare knew, and no doubt counted upon, the

interpretative possibilities of silence. The Duke does quite a lot of listening and quite a lot of learning as he listens; there is, further, much ironic humour implicit in his actual lines. He is dispassionate; he has the power to end all the threatened evils of the play or, rather, to resolve its immediate problems in terms of a pattern roughly just. Over the dark emotions which have caused these problems he has no power. When Shakespeare is writing full tragedy, there will be no Duke to say "Thus far, and no further"; but this play is to be insulated from a consummation of pity and terror, and the Duke will do it for us, interpreting between the audience's normal pulse of thought and the underground currents of emotion which the play so nearly lets loose. He is, supremely, a part for an actor of imagination who has the ability to project unspoken thought.

Angelo is the medium of that ungovernable passion of which Shakespeare wrote in the sonnets with a force that can only come from personal experience:

> The expense of spirit in a waste of shame
> Is lust in action; and till action, lust
> Is perjur'd, murderous, bloody, full of blame,
> Savage, extreme, rude, cruel, not to trust;
> Enjoyed no sooner, but despised straight;
> Past reason hunted, and no sooner had,
> Past reason hated, as the swallowed bait,
> On purpose laid to make the taker mad. Sonnet 152

The degrees of Angelo's yielding to a passion he hates and fears are brilliantly dissected; they carry the first two acts on a flood tide. But in the third act he drops unaccountably from the play and becomes merely the tool of its plot. His last scene is as difficult as ever an actor can have been called upon to play. It is an abandonment to fear and to the most unscrupulous methods of self-defence; it can only be redeemed by the whole-souled truth which the actor can bring, after the ultimate breaking down of all his strategems, to the complete repentance of

> I crave death more willingly than mercy;
> 'Tis my deserving, and I do entreat it.   v, 1, 472

There can be no question of making Angelo "sympathetic"; but we must feel that here is a man who has been "sick unto death" with a fever so terrible that it has left him shriveled to the bone of what he had been, and that clean flesh must grow in the slow process of healing. Shakespeare is not even sure, I think, that this spiritual regeneration can take place; but the artificial devices of the happy-ending plot have at least opened the way for it, and the whole play must be motivated not to the finality of a last-act curtain, but to this speculative conclusion.

For Isabella, swept by the passion of chastity as Angelo by the passion of lust, must also be healed; and the Duke's gentleness to her gives promise that she will be. Diverse judgments have been passed on Isabella, arising, as Dr. Ridley says, "from the diversity of the critics, not from inconsistency in the character." Any attempt to smooth her into a "straight" heroine, any lapse into a smug self-righteousness, will be disastrous. For the balance of the play's second half swings dangerously away from the Isabella-Angelo story toward the comedy of the prison scenes. Lucio, Pompey, and Abhorson threaten to carry it away, with their pungent vitality.

Isabella must play the first half at a pitch of tension which will not cease to tingle in our minds. Angelo has only one soliloquy with which to help her preserve our consciousness of the initial theme, but the Duke, who must never on any account become placid, may also contribute a deepening understanding, which we should share. There should be additional support from Mariana, who, having few lines, must contrive to inform them with the stress of grief and hope, faith and despera-tion; if she does no more than sit, drearily sorry for herself, in her "moated grange," the play will sink down beside her.

MEASURE FOR MEASURE is an adult play. The writing of its emotions is less forthright and more indriven than in almost any other. There are inconsistencies of a minor nature in the text, which skillful staging will easily smooth out. But there is also a feeling of fundamental unease in Shakespeare's mind. At times he seems to be forcing himself to write a comedy. Perhaps the company had begged him for one, thinking back to the prosperous days of AS YOU LIKE IT. But there is no harmony in his soul now, and the comedy he produces is a little acrid and almost too realistic. For this very reason,however, it may be the more easily blended with the turbid emotion of the thematic material. This, again, is a play which has possibly grown more comprehensible as audiences have become

educated to some small appreciation of the importance
and complexity of the subconscious mind.

Like the other "unpleasant" plays, it lacks music.
There are a few notes of harmony; the beautiful song
"Take, O take those lips away"; occasional lines, such
as the Duke's "Look, the unfolding star calls up the
shepherd"; Claudio's famous outburst upon death,
which lifts fear of the unknown into pure poetry, and
catches at our hearts with swift and beautiful imagery.
We cannot, however, take refuge in melody nor be
swept beyond logical analysis, as we are by Othello's
"Wash me in steep-down gulphs of liquid fire." We face
life and people at their least charming and a dramatic
design at its most stubborn. But, in my judgment, the
modern theatre is admirably equipped to grapple with
this play, and it might prove an extremely rewarding
attempt.

CHAPTER TWELVE

"Sad, High, and Working"

I come no more to make you laugh: things now,
That bear a weighty and a serious brow,
Sad, high, and working, full of state and woe:
Such noble scenes as draw the eye to flow
We now present.   HENRY VIII, Prologue

IT seems that in writing the triple magnificence of
OTHELLO, MACBETH, and LEAR Shakespeare had freed
himself from the uncertainties which clog TROILUS
and MEASURE FOR MEASURE. We cannot tell when he
finally cleared his mind of the poison which runs through
TIMON. The suggestion that he wrote it almost simultaneously with LEAR, as if he were peeling emotional
vegetables and throwing all the husks into TIMON and
all the good feeding into Lear, is not wholly convincing.
But at any rate he did at last succeed in purging his mind
and heart, and brought back to his work an even increased
degree of sanity and compassion.

With ANTONY AND CLEOPATRA his intellect is at work

on the problems of high tragedy compressed into the dramatic form which his stage demanded, and he produces what is perhaps his most impressive piece of theatre craftsmanship in the tragic vein. He is free of the over-elaborate and decorated writing of his middle period; his verse is more flexible and more subtly adapted to the rhythms of speech than ever before.

The form remains basic to the end of his life, more involved in CORIOLANUS and A WINTER'S TALE, softened to a gentler modulation in THE TEMPEST. CORIOLANUS follows ANTONY; Plutarch is still in his pocket; it has authority, discipline, little compassion, and no mystery. HENRY VIII brings him back to England. Its characters are nearer home than they have been in the Roman world of CORIOLANUS, which, for the first time, has assumed an almost coldly classical air. The Roman plays steadied his mind; the English one, even though it is written in collaboration with another playwright, warms him again.

The glories and the dramatic problems of ANTONY AND CLEOPATRA, like those of the other great tragedies, defy the easy analysis of a few sentences. The play has been denied a rank with the other four, not because it is inferior, but because it is different in aim and texture, different in the tragic conception, ostensibly less unified. Every critic who has written of it has, himself, been touched to fineness by the majesty of his subject. Strings of superlatives have been heaped together, as if the writer never could express how profoundly the play has moved and awed him.

The unerring power of the text is of such unflagging beauty and of so sure an aim that we may open the play

at any point and fall instantly to quotation, from the
opening lines, as inescapably thematic as the first bars
of the Fifth Symphony:

> Nay, but this dotage of our general's
> O'erflows the measure; those his goodly eyes,
> That o'er the files and musters of the war
> Have glow'd like plated Mars, now bend, now turn
> The office and devotion of their view
> Upon a tawny front. His captain's heart,
> Which in the scuffles of great fights hath burst
> The buckles on his breast, reneges all temper,
> And is become the bellows and the fan
> To cool a gypsy's lust,   I, I, I

to Octavius' epitaph on Cleopatra herself at the play's
end:

> . . . she looks like sleep,
> As she would catch another Antony
> In her strong toil of grace.   V, 2, 345

The aptness and beauty and precision never flag.

Of all the great speeches and famous passages with
which the play is filled, not one may justly be isolated
from its context or from the character who speaks it,
for every line both reveals the speaker and furthers the
play's design. And yet the theatre has signally failed
in productions of it; actors and actresses have been drawn
to the two leading parts like moths towards the candle
flame, and as perilously ventured their reputations.
Fortunately for us this process is likely to continue,
and one day we may see a really great production; but
it will never be one which treats the play as a "vehicle"
for the two actors named on the marquee nor one which

does not appreciate and endeavor to reproduce the original stage design.

A few seasons ago New York suffered, briefly, the production of an extensively adapted text, planned to shape the play to modern needs. The self-styled editors laid violent hands upon this, the most subtle and complex example of Shakespeare's later art. In this play the delicate steel of his dramatic craftsmanship is welded into a machine of tremendous power, each tiny wheel engaging smoothly and beautifully with the main driving shaft. Throw in one monkey wrench, and the machine will run amok and destroy itself. But the editors thought, and the impulse behind their thinking is still widely shared, that the play as it stood was impossible for reproduction on the modern stage. They evidently felt that a process of compression would be beneficial; so they put together lumps of Roman scenes, alternating them with lumps of Egyptian scenes like an endless club sandwich. On the contrary principle they committed several atrocious scene changes in the very middle of a flow of action, even in the midst of Cleopatra's lament over the dead Antony. The result, naturally, was that the actors were blamed for failing in a task which Burbage and Bernhardt together could not have accomplished successfully.

I do not think that the right lessons were learned from this unfortunate episode. It is true that we must have great Antonys and brilliant Cleopatras; it is also true that we must have Shakespeare; and in this play no part will stand unless in its just relation to the whole. If we fear the breadth of its scope and want only the story of how Antony lost all for love of an Egyptian queen, we had better produce Dryden's ALL FOR LOVE, as the eighteenth century producers did, embellishing the easier story with dollops of Shakespeare's verse. For he tells us a different kind of story; he shows us exactly how and why Antony lost the world, what sort of a world it was that he lost, how it was governed and by what caliber of men, and by what process their disciplined strength prevailed over the effete Egyptian civilization, and over the hopelessly unsound resources of Antony, the "lion dying," who had cast himself out from their conventions and abrogated the ability to rule among them.

There is little to take us by surprise in the development of Antony himself. The actor who studies carefully his first two scenes will find the character fully shaped between his hands. Nothing that follows will come upon us unexpectedly, as Cleopatra constantly flashes into new and astonishing self-revelation. The disintegration of Antony is inevitable; it is implicit in the play's very first lines; Enobarbus specifically forecasts it; Antony himself knows in his own heart from the beginning that it is already undermining his greatness. For this reason Antony is a hard part to "act"; the actor must give us, through his own personal quality, a similar abundance of strength from which he can continuously discard as its foundations are sapped by sensuality and passion, and all the old strength of the Roman general softens into confusion and ruin. The actor must never have to "play for" power; he must have it in himself, and let us see the gradual wrecking of it.

Volumes have been written about Cleopatra; she is described in the play, commented upon, discussed, praised, disparaged, loved, hated. No character in any of the plays is more fully analyzed in words or more comprehensively revealed in action. No commentary could amplify that which the text itself provides. There is no mystery here except the high mystery of the attempt to interpret, to convey through the medium of one human being, the "infinite variety" of a being unique in drama as in historical fact. This indeed calls upon the innermost art of acting; and here it must be fortified by the greatest fund of technical and imaginative resource.

But, it cannot be too strongly emphasized, an Antony and a Cleopatra are not enough. "The wide arch of the ranged empire" is the frame within which they move and the action of the play strides the width of it. If ever Shakespeare's imagination wore seven-league boots, it is here.

There is little verbal scene painting, little even to enhance with poetry the wheeling cycles of light and darkness. This is not Romeo's world, star governed, or Titania's, enchanted by the moon. It is a world of men; the discipline and daring of man has discovered it, knows it, moves free and unafraid throughout its vastness. There are no dark corners, no unguessed terrors; light informs the play with reason; there are causes and effects, and they lie in character itself, and character in action.

For this purpose Shakespeare uses a spaceless stage; the thirteen scenes of the third act and the fifteen of the fourth, so marked by the editors, make nonsense of his intention. Heavy scenic settings must drive us away from his extreme flexibility, and we shall lose the careful interlocking of each unit in these scenes, carefully pieced together for the dramatic effect of juxtaposition and contrast. We must recapture this freedom if we are to allow the play unfettered scope. He does not localize, not from carelessness but from extreme deliberation and by right of careful choice. He is arrogant in his demands on actors and audience; from the scene designer he demands nothing.

But we can supply something, and we should; nothing we can achieve with paint and canvas will follow Shakespeare fast enough if we attempt to pin him down to local geography; but we can supply a background to his spirit, a wide sky to his wide empire. We can emphasize, mainly in costume, the differences between Egypt and Rome, for they are important and vital to the play's meaning.

Granville Barker, in what I judge to be the greatest of his prefaces, supplies a detailed analysis of how we may translate this mighty design into the action of the theatre. Any such attempt is outside the scope or purpose of this book. To produce the play and fail is to invite disaster of the first magnitude and to offer oneself up defenceless to endless cheap or caustic witticisms. It is so easy to know what should not have been done and to mock what has been attempted. With this play Shakespeare himself is adamant; he will have no fooling around nor accept anything lesser than himself. If ANTONY AND CLEOPATRA is really unproducible, the theatre must confess itself fallen from its high estate and bankrupt of the ability and devotion to answer greatness with greatness.

In CORIOLANUS, the arch of the Roman world, which we have seen stretched to meet and melt into the infinity of space, becomes a tangible stone structure which we can reproduce as easily as we can photograph Trajan's Column. The passions which move beneath it are as simply analyzed, tabulated, and codified as the episodes of warfare carved on the Trajan monument. We are in no trouble over space and time. They are marked down and divided up. Some simple pillars, some steps, a rostrum or two with a suitable air of immutable Romanness, a set of curtains, a campfire, and we are ready for the actors. They march on; they stride off; they stand and argue; they strike poses and orate; they salute one another, kneel to one another, fight one another; they hardly ever sit down; they never come amongst us nor reach out a hand and take our hearts in it. The theatre will have no trouble in doing justice to this play; we feel unaccountably disappointed in consequence. So, presumably, does Shakespeare; and when he has rung down a grandiloquent last curtain, he throws Plutarch into the River Avon for cold food to the fishes and goes for a long walk through the fields. He will not pass Plutarch's way again. As his hero has said: "There is a world elsewhere."

We wonder what Burbage made of this script. He must have realized that the responsibility lay on him and that it would be no easy task. Whoever was assigned the part of Volumnia had a valiant, heroic, grim time of it.

We guess that "Menenius" chuckled to himself at the first reading and began counting the possible laughs. "Aufidius," not altogether displeased, tentatively tried out his chest notes; the musicians, who hadn't had much fun for a long while, just sighed and went home, all but the trumpeter. The smallest part actors, however, were vastly pleased, for they realized that the burden of the play would lie between themselves and Mr. Burbage, and that whenever the text said "Hoo! Hoo!" for the Citizens, they might look forward to an ad-libbing field day.

Because plays are not usually produced for the benefit of the extras, this one has had a sparse history in the theatre. "Not worth a damn," said Irving, and generations of actor-managers endorsed his view and left the play alone. But to a world deeply engaged in an armed appraisal of totalitarianism and democracy CORIOLANUS may have something to say.

Our rage for "timeliness," however, is not entirely satisfied by this play. It is useless for us to try and make Coriolanus a dictator. He hates and mistrusts the people and the people's tribunes, but he has no wish to rule them. He is content to serve under another general; he runs from public commendation of his own deeds and worth; he is not especially elated over the offer of the consulship; and he cannot bring himself to purchase it by any truckling to the voters or exercise of the demagogic arts. He is a "lonely dragon," glorying in his own power as a fighter and willing, for no reward but the satisfaction of his own pride, to serve it in the most austere tradition of the military caste.

He is not a very satisfactory hero for us. The description

> His nature is too noble for this world
> He would not flatter Neptune for his trident,
> Or Jove for's power to thunder: his heart's in's mouth:
> What his breast forges, that his tongue must vent,
> And, being angry, does forget that ever
> He heard the name of death   III, 1, 254

might fit Hotspur but for that ominous "his nature is too noble for this world." We cannot feel that Shakespeare liked him much, and we are enough of the people to resent him, however illogically. Music is nowhere wrung from him, save, briefly, in the scene where his wife and mother come to plead for Rome; but even the love and yearning of the greeting to his wife is steeled with his obsessing purpose: "O, a kiss, Long as my exile, sweet as my revenge!" Almost the most touching thing about him is the line and the rare stage direction which follow Volumnia's plea: (*After holding her by the hand, silent*) "O, mother, mother! What have you done?"

He fails us as a human being, and he does not provide us with any material for a dictator either. He does, however, voice a potent case against the rule of the many, as against the rule of the few, which is the ground base of the play.

> . . . They choose their magistrate,
> And such a one as he, who puts his "shall,"
> His popular "shall," against a graver bench
> Than ever frowned in Greece. By Jove himself,
> It makes the consuls base; and my soul aches
> To know, when two authorities are up,

Neither supreme, how soon confusion
May enter 'twixt the gap of both, and take
The one by the other.   III, I, 104

And, of "democratic" government:

                         . . . This double worship,
Where one part does disdain with cause, the other
Insult without all reason: where gentry, title, wisdom,
Cannot conclude, but by the yea and no ·
Of general ignorance, it must omit
Real necessities, and give the while
To unstable slightness. Purpose so barr'd, it follows,
Nothing is done to purpose.   III, I, 142

The argument is not for one man, but for an all-powerful
oligarchy, especially in time of war. It is of the highest
interest to us, and the whole of the second and third act
is vibrant with the sway of power between the senators
and the people's tribunes, with Coriolanus' personal
qualities to precipitate the crisis.

The people are nowhere, and by nobody, considered as
an entity worthy of reason or regard. Coriolanus despises
them, Volumnia advises him simply to deceive them
with words that are not from his heart. The demagogic
tribunes, intent on personal power, openly use them
with methods no less blatant. And they themselves
deserve no better treatment; they show, in the scene
where Coriolanus begs their "voices" with a sting of
contempt behind the words, a kind of blunt, bewildered
common sense. But they are, throughout, fickle, stupid,
won and lost by the wrong people for the wrong reasons.
Coriolanus, banished, cries at them:

You common cry of curs, whose breath I hate,
As reek o' the rotten fens . . .
 . . . I banish you,
And here remain with your uncertainty.
Let every feeble rumour shake your hearts:
Your enemies, with nodding of their plumes
Fan you into despair: have the power still
To banish your defenders, till at length
Your ignorance (which finds not till it feels,
Making but reservation of yourselves,
Still your own foes) deliver you as most
Abated captives, to some nation
That won you without blows!   III, 3, 122

Reading such scenes as these, we are not surprised to remember that a few years ago a production of the play at the Comédie Française caused such a storm that rioting broke out and the theatre had to be temporarily closed; time has provided a terrible and ironic coda to that controversy.

There is, then, power and excitement to be derived from this part of the play if we keep the balance accurate and do not try falsely to weight one scale. The handling of the crowd will be even more important than in other crowd scenes. Shakespeare always seems to make his Roman citizens unusually articulate. Here, as in JULIUS CAESAR, many of the citizens have individual lines and individual characteristics. For the rest, the director will have to invent both. A crowd must never be treated in lumps, with lump emotions. Every member of it must feel his own life and be as conscious of himself as the center of surrounding events as is the citizen of today who cheers for Willkie or for Roosevelt with a wholly personal ardor, and for reasons which he at least supposes to be entirely his own. This crowd needs actors; the director conducts the orchestra, but every instrument has its own value, and none of them is easy to play.

The little people in this play are certainly as much alive as its protagonists, with the exception of Menenius, who lives up to his own rich description of himself:

> a humorous patrician, and one that loves a cup of hot wine, with not a drop of allaying Tiber in't . . . hasty and tinder-like upon too trivial motion: one that converses more with the buttock of the night than with the forehead of the morning. What I think, I utter, and spend my malice in breath.

Volumnia, like her son, is noble, but not likable; she is a woman and a mother-in-law in the most blood-curdling tradition, though it must be admitted that the milky Virgilia would irritate a far more tolerant woman than Volumnia. Both of them will take a good deal of humanizing by the actress.

Yet the small-part actors will not infrequently find themselves holding such ripe plums as this, of Aufidius' servant:

> Let me have war, say I, it exceeds peace as far as day does night: it's spritely, walking, audible and full of vent. Peace is very apoplexy, lethargy, mull'd, deaf, sleepy, insensible, a getter of more bastard children than war's a destroyer of men.
>
> IV, 6, 225

On the whole, it seems, we shall have to play this piece for something as near a conflict of what we love to call "ideologies" as Shakespeare ever comes, and focus it around the lofty, unlovable figure of Coriolanus himself.

HENRY VIII occupies a curiously anomalous position
in the canon. It has had a continuous stage history,
as full as that of CORIOLANUS is meager. Its processions,
banquets, halberdiers and citizens and bishops have
provided flourishing, colorful theatre spectacle, with
some rough, lively comedy in between, and plenty of
pathos in the Queen Katherine scenes. Yet the con-
sensus of scholarly opinion, much more unanimous
than usual, admits only four and a half scenes as being
wholly Shakespearen. Whoever wrote the rest of the
play, Fletcher or, less probably, Massinger, was certainly inspired beyond his usual form. For, though the
smoothness of the verse has been criticized as lacking
Shakespeare's muscular flexibility and the conception
of the play condemned as shapeless and over-upholstered,
there is a great deal, even in the non-Shakespearean
portion, that is of sure theatrical effectiveness.

It comes as something of a shock to be reminded that
the last two of Queen Katherine's four great scenes are
Fletcher's, including the famous song "Orpheus with
his lute," and the scene of her death. There may be
nothing in the latter to compare with her outburst
at the Trial:

> . . . I do believe
> (Induc'd by potent circumstances) that
> You are mine enemy, and make my challenge,
> You shall not be my judge: for it is you
> Have blown this coal betwixt my lord and me;
> Which God's dew quench! . . .   II, 4, 75

and the dignified strength of her pleading may have
softened to the humility of her dying, even more than

sickness, sorrow, and a broken life can altogether justify. But the scene with the Cardinals has power and integrity, and her death has, in the theatre, a deeply moving quality, because its oversweetness can be countered and turned to valuable account by the actress who plays it with austerity and truth.

It is equally startling to remember that the most quoted passage in the play, Wolsey's "Farewell, a long farewell to all my greatness," is not supposedly Shakespearean. The part of Wolsey is, however, very equally divided between the two authors, and its design, like its inception, must be Shakespeare's. At all events, it is a fine one, a fine, full chance for an actor, and indestructibly dramatic. Buckingham is almost all Fletcher, Henry himself Shakespearean in the vigorous opening scenes, in the Trial, and in the episode of Wolsey's fall, where Fletcher takes over from the point of Henry's exit.

It seems that Fletcher found the character a hot coal in his hands, for at this juncture Henry fades into a dimmer figure than he has been. Shakespeare picks him up, briefly, and announces to him the birth of the baby Elizabeth, through the mouth of the inimitable "Old Lady," one of the most vigorous little sketches he ever wrote. But from here on the play drags out in a long sequence of conspiracy, most frequently cut upon the stage, and the tableau theatre of the Baptism scene.

It is therefore not surprising that analysis will reveal discrepancies of characterization as well as style and that the construction lacks unity of design. The play must be produced for its pageant values, which are great, and we must contrive such unity of pattern as we can among the principal figures of Wolsey, Buckingham, Henry, and Katherine herself. It seems that the authors knew from the beginning that their play would stand or fall by her, for the Epilogue announces that:

> All the expected good we're like to hear
> For this play at this time, is only in
> The merciful construction of good women;
> For such a one we show'd 'em.

She carried the play then, and has done so since; and, because it presents no such problems in production as many of its worthier fellows, is unlikely to be long absent from the stage.

Shakespeare is generally supposed to have had some share in another collaboration, THE TWO NOBLE KINSMEN, and in yet another play, of which no text survives, entitled CARDENIO; in each case Fletcher was again the collaborator. Many students see more of Shakespeare's hand in THE TWO NOBLE KINSMEN than in HENRY VIII. But the design in this case is evidently Fletcher's, for it follows the exact pattern of his most wearisome romances, and whatever verse Shakespeare wrote for it is wholly inadequate to rescue it from theatrical oblivion. If his name were printed ten times on every title page, its monumental dullness and pomposity would still render it utterly unplayable. Some thirteen years ago, the Old Vic performed a devoted labor of love in presenting it. We may salute the Old Vic and leave well alone.

CHAPTER THIRTEEN

"Music at the Close"

SHAKESPEARE was undoubtedly influenced toward the end of his life by the romantic comedies of Beaumont, Fletcher, and their contemporaries, which were becoming increasingly the fashion. Also, the Burbage syndicate were now working at the indoor theatre at Blackfriars, as well as at the old Globe, and demanded an increase of masques, processions, and other spectacular aids to the drama. In consequence, the stage directions of the last plays are unusually full, and the spectacles unusually elaborate.

Some of them, such as the vision in CYMBELINE, may be regarded as playhouse additions to Shakespeare's text; we should be grateful to get rid of this particular excrescence with such an excuse. The dumb shows in PERICLES are certainly not his, but the whole text of PERICLES is open to grave question. With THE WINTER'S TALE, he had more fully mastered the new form with which he was experimenting, and by the time he wrote THE TEMPEST, probably his last complete play, he had sublimated it to a use exquisitely and unmatchably his own. The four plays are closely knit together as a group, and in them Shakespeare is fancy-free, using the license of the romantic form to give wings to his imagination and to let it roam the "cloud-capp'd towers, the gorgeous palaces" where Fortune is a capricious but kindly deity and man need never resolve unaided the dreadful conflict with his own soul.

It is generally held that the first two acts of PERICLES are by another hand, but in the theatre they do not seem markedly inconsistent with the rest. If Antiochus is a slightly wooden tyrant, Pericles's descriptions of him are pertinent:

> With hostile forces he'll o'erspread the land,
> And with ostent of war will look so huge,
> Amazement shall drive courage from the state,
> Our men be vanquish'd e'er they do resist,
> And subjects punish'd that ne'er thought offence.
>
> I, 2, 24

> To lop that doubt, he'll fill this land with arms,
> And make pretence of wrong that I have done him.
>
> I, 2, 90

The formulas of tyranny have not greatly changed.

Our one glimpse of the "little men," in the Fishermen who rescue Pericles, is lively. But the episode in which Pericles disguises himself as a poor knight and wins the hand of the Princess Thaisa, is pedestrian writing and altogether too naïve for the modern theatre.

With the shipwreck in Act III, matters improve considerably; there is music and true emotion in the scene where Pericles and the old nurse with the honey name, Lychorida, cast the coffined Thaisa into the sea. The opening of the coffin by Cerimon gives us another authentic sequence. He describes himself as "made familiar" with

> . . . the blest infusions
> That dwell in vegetives, in metal, stones;
> And I can speak of the disturbances
> That nature works; and of her cures; which doth give me
> A more content in course of true delight
> Than to be thirsty after tottering honour,
> Or tie my pleasure up in silken bags,
> To please the fool and death.   III, 2, 35

And of course he revives Thaisa.

The story moves on, through Tarsus with its Queen, the "jealous step-mother," Tyre, which stands "in a litigious peace," and Mytilene, where are placed the brothel scenes which Victorian commentators so self-righteously denied to Shakespeare. Thinking back to MEASURE FOR MEASURE, we may be absolved of any serious doubts; they are not pretty, they are extremely outspoken, they sound a harsh discord in the lyric of the play; but it is a Shakespearean dissonance. Marina, decked, like Perdita, with flowers of springtime delicacy, moves through them with a white ardor. When, at last, she and Pericles are reunited, the play is swept up with music, grace, and "all simplicity." The second reunion, between Thaisa and her husband and daughter, is perfunctory by comparison.

The story has meandered a long way; it has been, of

itself, consciously artificial; and, worst theatre fault of all, its diverse episodes, separated widely in space and time, are bridged by no such dramatic scheme as Shakespeare has been at pains to devise for his great plays. They are arbitrarily linked by a narrator, who describes the intervening events in deliberately archaic octosyllabic couplets. If the play is done at all, it must have the quality of an idyll of the golden age and be set luminously and richly. It was a hit, apparently, throughout its early career and retains at least some of the essential elements which made it so. But we should have to cut and tighten, drench the scenes with music, and play it like a decorative tapestry for the eye. It is a play for a relaxed and leisured audience, not too demanding, ready to accept make-believe. Until such time as we evolve a company and an audience who take pleasure in Shakespeare for Shakespeare's sake, we are unlikely to see much of PERICLES.

CYMBELINE is beloved, and rightly so, for Imogen's sake. Imogen is she whom every woman in love would wish to be, free, generous, sane, miraculously happy in the expression of her love. Over and over again she puts feeling into words so just that she seems to express the emotion for all time:

> I did not take my leave of him, but had
> Most pretty things to say: ere I could tell him
> How I would think on him at certain hours,
> Such thoughts and such; . . .
>   . . . or have charg'd him,
> At the sixth hour of morn, at noon, at midnight,
> To encounter me with orisons, for then
> I am in heaven for him;   I, 3, 25

with the ominous letter whose contents, as yet unread, are to lead her toward unsuspected death:

> O, learn'd indeed were that astronomer
> That knows the stars as I his characters;
> He'ld lay the future open. You good gods,
> Let what is here contain'd relish of love,
> Of my lord's health, of his content, yet not
> That we two are asunder; let that grieve him;
> Some griefs are medicinable; that is one of them,
> For it doth physic love; of his content,
> All but in that!   III, 2, 37

and, having read the letter,

> O for a horse with wings! Hear'st thou, Pisanio?
> He is at Milford Haven: read, and tell me
> How far 'tis thither. If one of mean affairs
> May plod it in a week, why may not I
> Glide thither in a day? Then, true Pisanio,—
> Who long'st, like me, to see thy lord; who long'st
> (O, let me bate) but not like me; yet long'st,
> But in a fainter kind: —O, not like me;
> For mine's beyond beyond.   III, 2, 49

Even when she is told of Leonatus' command to have her killed, the music of love is unsilenced:

> . . . Come, fellow, be thou honest,
> Do thy master's bidding. When thou see'st him,
> A little witness my obedience. Look,
> I draw the sword myself, take it, and hit
> The innocent mansion of my love, my heart:
> Fear not, 'tis empty of all things but grief:
> Thy master is not there, who was indeed
> The riches of it.   III, 4, 65

In the disguise of Fidele, Imogen keeps all her own matchless quality, but unfortunately she no longer holds the play, except in the last scene, where she again glorifies it with her integrity and honor; and for the last two acts we are in very serious trouble.

It is difficult to define the reasons for which this play is so extraordinarily unsatisfactory on the stage. The first three acts go with dazzling assurance. It is true that we have to accept a slightly wooden king and a cruel stepmother who reminds us rather too forcibly of SNOW WHITE, though we are mollified by her magnificent speech on the invasion of England, on which subject the ineffable Cloten also has some heart-warming remarks. The rest is brilliant: Iachimo springs alive like coiled steel; in the scenes of his wager with Leonatus, the prose writing is as supple as anything Shakespeare ever wrote, and the character of the two men is unerringly differentiated in it. We are, perhaps, made a little uneasy by the old fairy-tale trick, but we forgive Leonatus for being duped, because Iachimo has engineered his plot with such skill. His speech in Imogen's bedroom while she is asleep is matchless in dramatic poetry. The action moves compactly and surely. If Shakespeare keeps this up, he will give us a masterpiece.

But, in Act III, scene 3, the warning lag begins. It lies, I think, in those two terrible young men, Guiderius and Arviragus. They are, perhaps, part of the romantic convention in which Shakespeare is still not completely at ease. They are the noble savage, but tutored to an unbearable civility by their old guardian, the verbose and pompous Belarius. They go on getting nobler and nobler, and, in case we should miss anything, Belarius stops at regular intervals to tell us just how noble they are. Even their exquisite elegy over the "dead" Fidele leaves us with unforgiving hearts.

To make matters worse, we have lost Iachimo, one speech of whose villainy is worth all their stainless operatic Aryanism, Leonatus is fossilizing slowly but surely, and our old black-and-purple friend, the Queen, is sick unto death in her dressing room. Finally, we are disgusted to discover ourselves launched on an Anglo-Roman war, whose military strategy and fortunes are described in lengthy, complex dumb-show stage directions, with an enormously long narrative speech about the off-stage battle from the unfortunate Leonatus. What a job for a hard-pressed hero! The war business concludes, moreover, in a blaze of appeasement, which inevitably makes us think of the old epitaph,

> Since I was so quickly done for,
> I wonder what I was begun for.

In the last scene, with the utmost dexterity and every resource of the old theatre craftsman Shakespeare rescues himself from the various complications which he has allowed to pile up around the play. We are left enraged that he should have buried our Imogen beneath all this farrago of fairy-tale picture books. Perhaps there is a way to rescue her, mercilessly blue-penciling the whole fourth and fifth act, cutting the episode of Leonatus in prison entirely out, and leaving the audience to make the obvious assumptions about the battle. If we had much less of the noble twins we should like them much more. And we shall have to get an actor who can carry us with him for the shabbily treated Leonatus and another who can make Iachimo's manufactured end join with his admirable beginning.

The mood of the play is evident Renaissance, despite its ostensible setting in ancient Britain; Iachimo is an Italian, not a Roman, and says as much. Togas and woad will be perfectly hopeless for this piece of gilded artifice. "The Family of Darius kneeling to Alexander" will be nearer our mark, if a little over ornate. It is a pretty problem for a producer, but surely there will still be found some knight of the theatre to flaunt Imogen's lovely sleeve upon his billboard.

The stage history of CYMBELINE has, in the past, been fuller than that of THE WINTER'S TALE, and yet the latter play presents fewer difficulties to the producer. Of recent years, both have been neglected, and certainly THE WINTER'S TALE should be seen again. It has no great star part, but three exceptionally fine ones, and half a dozen more which are worth the best talent the theatre can bring to them. It falls, almost exactly, into two halves, the first dominated by Leontes, the second by Perdita; and, in the violence of the contrast, deliberately contrived, lies our difficulty in the theatre, a difficulty further complicated by the fact that the end of Act IV and the first two scenes of Act V move at a snail's pace.

The final reconciliation scene, moreover, depends upon a device much more artificial than anything we have encountered in the play and touches no one of the principal characters to any fresh height of feeling. Its very gentleness and dignity are moving, and their quality, being dependent on visual effect, is much more effective in the theatre than in the study. Visual beauty and the actors' unspoken truth will carry the end of the play, once we have safely negotiated the shallows which precede it.

The first three acts move in a real world, and a harsh one, far distant from the realm of romance, where a happy ending provides every cloud with a discernible silver lining. Sicilia is no Utopia. But in the very first line of verse in the play Polixenes lets slip the fact that there is such a kingdom in his own Bohemia:

> Nine changes of the watery star hath been
> The shepherd's note, since we have left our throne
> Without a burden.   I, 2, I

Presently we are to see the stars and the shepherds; but for three acts they are forgotten in the swirling torrent of Leontes' jealousy, which overwhelms everybody within its reach.

The part is one of the hardest ever written; with almost no preparation, the emotion of it is at flood height. It is an obsession, feeding itself, tortured of itself, relentlessly lashing itself to an insane and superhuman power. We see nothing of what the normal Leontes is like, and almost nothing of the incidents which give rise to this fever in his brain; it is postulated that Hermione and Polixenes are innocent and that Leontes is already nearly helpless in the grip of a passion that no reason can control. Camillo realizes it at once. He thinks for us, in deciding that there is no way of sanity or logic by which this torrent may be dammed.

Polixenes must escape or be destroyed; he escapes, leaving Hermione to her fate with no more than an ineffectual wish that everything may come out all right in the end. Leontes alone can make us appreciate the inevitability of Polixenes' flight, and it will take an actor supremely able to liberate passion. The verse in which the part is written is half the actor's battle; it is tormented, twisted, involved, sometimes deliberately senseless, driven pell-mell from the seething insanity of Leontes' fevered mind. Only an actor who can use the instrument of speech with virtuoso technical command will be able to encompass the reiterated chords of

> . . . Is whispering nothing?
> Is leaning cheek to cheek? is meeting noses?
> Kissing with inside lip? stopping the career
> Of laughter with a sigh (a note infallible
> Of breaking honesty)? horsing foot on foot?
> Skulking in corners? wishing clocks more swift?
> Hours, minutes? noon, midnight? and all eyes
> Blind with the pin and web but theirs; theirs only,
> That would unseen be wicked? Is this nothing?
> Why, then the world, and all that's in't, is nothing,
> The covering sky is nothing, Bohemia nothing,
> My wife is nothing, nor nothing have these nothings,
> If this be nothing. 1, 2, 284

Paulina's outbursts feed Leontes; they have an equal power but a direct and forthright aim. Hermione, in character and speech, holds the play within bounds; her trial scene reminds us a little of Queen Katherine, but with equal dignity it combines a greater beauty of soul, and the verse is level harmony:

> . . . But thus, if powers divine
> Behold our human actions (as they do)
> I doubt not then but innocence shall make

> False accusation blush, and tyranny
> Tremble at patience. You, my lord, best know
> (Who least will seem to do so) my past life
> Hath been as continent, as chaste, as true
> As I am now unhappy; which is more
> Than history can pattern, though devis'd
> And play'd to take spectators . . .
> . . . For life, I prize it
> As I weigh grief, which I would spare: for honour,
> 'Tis a derivative from me to mine,
> And only that I stand for.   III, 2, 28

The part is not a long one, but it is deeply felt and purely written.

Actresses and producers have occasionally agreed to have it doubled with Perdita, a proceeding which seems to me to do great violence to Shakespeare's intention, and to have nothing to recommend it save the possibility that audiences may want to see one woman star through the whole play instead of two in half the play each. The fact that Perdita is "her mother's glass" is the least important thing about her. She brings with her a new world, as far from Leontes' Sicily as May from December. She is sixteen or she is nothing.

With her, the play takes on, quite literally, a new life of shepherds and rustics, and sun and flowers and ribbons and spices and songs; it has dew upon it, and so has Perdita herself. She is the unclouded spirit of youth unstained by sorrow upon which Shakespeare so loved to dwell in his last plays. Florizel too, like Ferdinand, beautifully rounds the picture, gracing her and himself with the exquisite

          . . . What you do
Still betters what is done. When you speak, sweet,
I'ld have you do it ever: when you sing,
I'ld have you buy and sell so; so give alms,
Pray so; and, for the ordering your affairs,
To sing them too: when you do dance, I wish you
A wave of the sea, that you might ever do
Nothing but that.   iv, 4, 135

This is as fresh as it is lovely; this is the daughter
Hermione would have prayed to have; but it is not
Hermione in little. The actress "playing for" youth
cannot, however greatly gifted, achieve the poignant,
transitory loveliness of youth itself.

It is argued that because Perdita at the first meeting
with her father is almost mute, and has only two short
speeches in the scene with her mother, Shakespeare must
have had this doubling in mind. But it is hard to believe
that he would have admitted so clumsy a device; nor do
I think we shall better the disappointing lameness of
these last scenes from Perdita's point of view by sub-
stituting a back-to-the-audience dummy for the actress
who has now reverted to her first role as Hermione. We
shall only add to the handicaps already in the script.

A garland of flowers weaves these last plays together,
linking them with the fragrance of springtime, summer,
and autumn, in the eternal fields where they are set. There
is a curious chime of death behind their sweetness. In
PERICLES, Marina strews Lychorida's grave with flowers:

          . . . the yellows, blues,
The purple violets, and marigolds,
Shall, as a carpet, hang upon thy grave
While summer days do last.   iv, 1, 14

In CYMBELINE, Fidele's grave also is to be decked with a blossoming echo:

> . . . With fairest flowers,
> While summer lasts, and I live here, Fidele,
> I'll sweeten thy sad grave; thou shalt not lack
> The flower that's like thy face, pale primrose, nor
> The azur'd harebell, like thy veins.   IV, 2, 220

And Perdita has flowers of winter, flowers of middle summer; lacking flowers of spring, she brings them beautifully close to our remembrance:

> . . . daffodils
> That come before the swallow dares, and take
> The winds of March with beauty; violets (dim,
> But sweeter than the lids of Juno's eyes,
> Or Cytherea's breath); pale primroses,
> That die unmarried e'er they can behold
> Bright Phoebus in his strength (a malady
> Most incident to maids); bold oxslips, and
> The crown imperial; lilies of all kinds,
> The fleur-de-luce being one! O! these I lack
> To make you garlands of, and my sweet friend,
> To strew him o'er and o'er!
>   What like a corse?
> No, like a bank for love to lie and play on;
> Not like a corse . . .   IV, 4, 118

Shakespeare seems to come back from the fields by the green and quiet Stratford churchyard, where deep bells answer the hour, yet time slips by uncounted as the flowers bloom and die and bloom again with the returning spring.

THE TEMPEST lifts us to another dimension, unique, and last, of Shakespeare's worlds. Ceres' "proud earth," flowers and "turfy mountains," "windring brooks," and "unshrubbed down" is visioned for us, but the play is air and water, always within sound of the sea, always eluding the touch of mortal hands because it belongs to the spirit alone. In LEAR, Shakespeare's overmastering daemon had driven inexorably through the wooden boundaries of his theatre even when they were his daily horizon. In THE TEMPEST we feel that he remembered with an effort that Burbage would want a masque or two and a couple of parts for the comedians; and, having accordingly provided goddesses, nymphs, and reapers, music and dance for the public at Blackfriars, he lifts them on the wings of his genius back to his own region of the soul:

> Our revels now are ended. These our actors,
> (As I foretold you) were all spirits, and
> Are melted into air, into thin air,
> And like the baseless fabric of this vision,
> The cloud-capp'd towers, the gorgeous palaces,
> The solemn temples, the great globe itself,
> Yea, all which it inherit, shall dissolve,
> And like this insubstantial pageant faded,
> Leave not a rack behind: we are such stuff
> As dreams are made on; and our little life
> Is rounded with a sleep.   IV, I, 148

The theatre must handle this fabric with the most delicate hand, and the greatest sensitivity. It is, perhaps, the play above all others where we cannot hope to match the reader's free imagination; yet this very speech was written to be spoken; there is in it as much music as dream. Here, designer, director, and actors must bring much more than theatre competence to the service of the

play, for vision alone will transmit vision. The two
people who will have the hardest task will be the
designer and the actor who plays Ariel. Probably the
setting should be, essentially, as simple and as indicative
as Mr. Jed Harris's OUR TOWN, where the audience was
given a signpost to Grovers' Corners, and left to imagine
its own niche within "the Earth, the Universe, the
Mind of God." The movie of the same play, doing its
representational best, never gave us our spiritual money's
worth as the almost bare stage did. And Shakespeare's
island in "the still-vex'd Bermoothes" wears a different
aspect for each man's differing mind.

We are told little of its physical features, though
Caliban's material mind gives us something, Gonzalo
and his companions a detail or two more. The island is
"of a subtle, tender and delicate temperance"; it is
ringed with sands on which

> . . . the elves with printless foot
> Do chase the ebbing Neptune and do fly him
> When he once comes back.

We cannot reproduce these yellow sands, nor the
cloven pine, nor the spurred cedar. We cannot "'twixt
the green sea and the azur'd vault Set roaring war" at
Prospero's command. It will be hard for our musicians,
even, to give the elusive island echoes, "Sounds and
sweet airs, that give delight and hurt not." Composer,
designer, director, actors, most especially Ariel, must
try to capture a quality once ascribed to David Garrick,
of whose work it was said that "he generally perceives
the finest attitude of things." We must free our audience

to sail their own seas to their own haven, suggesting only the outline it may take.

Writers who have analyzed THE TEMPEST have seen in it a hundred different allegories. They have been touched to beautiful and perceptive flights of the imagination; they have agreed, almost without exception, that there is much more in this play than is yielded from its surface, and symbolic explanations abound. The over-simple pigeonholing of Caliban for the flesh, Prospero for the mind, and Ariel for the spirit has been elaborated in as many different ways as there have been poets and critics to examine it. Mr. Christopher Morley, in preparing a radio version, has suggested a beautiful commentary of politico-social fable. Some allegorical analogy springs to the minds of all who study it; in the theatre we may have to choose one from those already suggested or endeavor to interpret a new one of our own. But we must be as flexible as the play itself, whose wings we dare not attempt to trim to our conception of what a wing should look like and how many feathers it should have.

Mr. Mark Van Doren has put the matter, for me, definitively:

Notwithstanding its visionary grace, its tendency toward lyric abstraction, it keeps that life-like surface and humour with which Shakespeare has always protected his meaning if he had one: that impenetrable shield off which the spears of interpretation invariably glance—or return, bent in the shaft and dulled at the point, to the hand of the thrower. It may well be that Shakespeare in THE TEMPEST is telling us for the last time, about the world. But what he is telling us cannot be simple, or we should agree that it is this or that. Perhaps it is this: that the world is not simple. Or, mysteriously enough, that it is what we all take it to be, just as THE TEMPEST is whatever we would take it to be. Any set of symbols, moved close to this play, lights up as in an electric field. Its meaning, in other words, is precisely as rich as the human mind.

In attempting to preserve the "life-like surface and humour" of the play we must pay due attention to Alonzo, Gonzago, and their companions, who, like the lovers in A MIDSUMMER NIGHT'S DREAM, are often dismissed as bores. Surrounded by Ariel's evanescent grace, Caliban's thick and ominous savagery, and Prospero's probing mind, they may indeed seem ordinary; but this is precisely what they are; just for this reason they, like the lovers in the DREAM, will put all the degrees of strangeness into perspective for us. They must reflect what the ordinary man might feel, shipwrecked on this uncharted island. They perceive, as we might, according to the varying receptivity of their minds, the "quality o' the climate," and feel, as we might, the strange drowsiness in the air. Through them, as clearly as through Ariel the messenger, we too shall sense the awe of powers beyond ourselves, "delaying, not forgetting" in their slow, inexorable wrath. With them we shall make the progress, the pilgrim's progress, through "heart's sorrow" to "a clear life ensuing." They must not be dummies; nor need they be so, for every one is stamped with characteristics of his own, plain enough to the actor with a seeing mind.

The comics, too, must remember the "quality" of the isle. That they are bemused is the essence of their comedy. Stephano and Triculo get drunk with a difference, befuddled with more than wine. The conventional tricks of a "drunk scene" will not do. This wine is headier stuff; it has in it the power to transmute Caliban to an outburst far from comic, the senseless, raging, ungovernable

> 'Ban, 'Ban, Ca-caliban
> Has a new master, get a new man.
> Freedom, hey-day! hey-day, freedom! freedom, hey-day, freedom!
> II, 2, 183

Freedom. Caliban yearns for the freedom to destroy; Ariel sees the freedom of "Merrily, merrily shall I live now, Under the blossom that hangs on the bough"; Ferdinand and Miranda discover a freedom of loving, and Gonzalo a profound one, in finding "all of us ourselves, When no man was his own." Prospero is free of an accomplished task, free to say:

> . . . I'll break my staff,
> Bury it certain fathoms in the earth,
> And deeper than did ever plummet sound,
> I'll drown my book.
> v, 1, 54

This freeing of the spirit we must give to the last, in some sense the loveliest, of the plays. We receive it, as it were, in trust; and, rendering it back to our audience, may well conclude, as Prospero does: "Let your indulgence set me free."

Conclusion

CHAPTER FOURTEEN

Shakespeare Today

I N reviewing thus briefly the potentialities of Shakespeare's plays in our contemporary theatre I have not
attempted to supply a ready-to-wear solution for any
of their problems but simply to point out certain aspects
of those problems. In doing so, I am acutely aware of the
danger of generalizations. Every producer, designer,
director, every company of actors will bring qualities of
mind and spirit to bear on the texts which will illuminate them from a different angle. Every play, self-evi-
dently, requires a particularized treatment. Each separate
text presents its own specific difficulties; settings and
costumes must be considered in relation to the mood and
emotional pattern of each. The musical accompaniment,
whether it be indicated or required by the script itself, or
added to it as a supplementary factor, must equally be
devised to enhance and vivify the essential spirit of each
play. So the actors' personal gifts or shortcomings must
be welded together into an interpretative whole, not

violating the author's intention, but translating it anew into the living language which is shared by actors and audience alike. No part of the theatre is machine-made, and no part may be governed by mathematical formulas. Human fallibility being what it is, none of us may be assured of encompassing our vision; all we can do is to try to bring this vision into focus with Shakespeare himself and pursue it with such integrity as we may.

If a modern producer were dealing with an author with thirty-seven plays to his credit, most of them successes and a dozen or so smash hits, he would at least listen with respect to what that author had to say and take some trouble to appreciate the workings of his mind. Shakespeare is still one of Broadway's most successful playwrights. His pay checks, if he still received them, would top the lists of Dramatists' Guild members; although the Hollywood market offers him little, the amateur rights are worth a fortune. He is worth consulting, worth understanding, as a man, as a man of the theatre, and this will take something a little wider in scope than a cursory perusal of the text, even of the New Cambridge edition.

There is a German play in which Goethe, reincarnating himself as a college student about to take an examination on Goethe, fails hopelessly to answer the questions put to him. Either he does not remember at all incidents which the examiners seem to consider of supreme importance, or his replies run directly counter to the textbooks of accepted criticism. It is probable that we should be appalled by Shakespeare's inability to satisfy some of our burning inquiries and that he

would be at a loss to understand why we should get
so exercised over seeming trifles.

But it is unlikely that we should ever find him without
an explanation of the purpose of his stagecraft, or a
reason for his dramatic intention. I think we are justified
in assuming that he would readily suggest modifications
to suit our revivals; he would probably understand our
audiences as well as or better than we do. We are perhaps
too ready to accept current shibboleths as to what an
audience will or will not like, what it will pay to see,
and what it will stay away from in overwhelming
numbers. He probably would find no difficulty in adapt-
ing the practice of his theatre to the usage of ours, and,
if he found it unnecessary to make all the changes we at
first demanded, we might well discover in the end that
he was right. However, because we cannot claim his aid,
we must do our best to think with his mind and bring
his standards into harmony with our own.

The principles on which a director must base his
approach to a Shakespearean play are, after all, no
different from those which govern his approach to any
other play. His method will vary, because the technique
of directing is itself subject to every degree of personal
idiosyncrasy. I believe that he should determine first
the mood of the play, its material and spiritual atmosphere, its structural pattern, the wholeness of its effect.
What kind of a world is this of Arden or Elsinore, Illyria
or Verona? What forces are at work in it? What values or
what standards hold good within its confines? Shakespeare will have employed certain dramatic devices
whose origin and purpose we must learn to recognize

through a knowledge of the material, human or in-
animate, which he employed. But what was the intention behind these theatre devices? Knowing his method,
we may guess at his mind; perceiving the familiar, we
may divine the transcendental. With the former, we
must sometimes take liberties of adaptation, the latter
we may not violate, except at our own peril.

The bridge over which we shall travel to Shakespeare's country, like the bridge we ourselves shall build
from stage to auditorium is built of human beings. Who
are these people? From King Lear to the Third Citizen,
we must know them. They have a certain background,
sometimes of historical fact, sometimes of tale or
legend; they have an Elizabethan background in
Shakespeare's Elizabethan mind. These we shall want
to understand, for they will bring light into shadowed
places. But, above all, what qualities in their minds
and hearts do we share? What is their kinship with us,
What is it in their blood which we also feel to be in our
own?

The tangible things by which they are surrounded, the
hats and cloaks they wear, the weapons they use, their
food and drink, may belong almost exclusively to
Shakespeare's England. Even the conventions of love
and honor, hate and merriment, may differ from our
own. But we can still lay our hands upon the pulse of
each one of them; Shylock's speech may still stand for
the universality of man, annihilating the gap of time as
easily as the division of race. We too have "organs,
dimensions, senses; affections, passions." We are "subject to the same diseases, healed by the same means,

warmed and cooled by the same winter and summer . . .
If you prick us do we not bleed? if you tickle us do we
not laugh? if you poison us do we not die? and if you
wrong us, shall we not revenge?" It is always a sense of
closeness at which we should aim, rather than an
emphasis of separation.

We shall not need to dress Hotspur in the uniform
of the R.A.F. in order to invest him with life; we underrate both our author and our audience in supposing that
they can only be dragged into accord by distorting
Coriolanus to the image of General Franco, slyly
insinuating that there have been abdications of the
English throne more recent than that of Richard II, or
claiming with gleeful shouts that Enobarbus is an
anticipatory Rudolph Hess. The truth of the plays is a
timeless truth, and similarity of external circumstances
no more than a fortuitous, though sometimes poignant,
reminder that the returning paths of history have been
trodden by many feet.

In these days those who love the theatre and are
jealous for its power and prerogative are rightly eager
that it should prove itself as a contemporary force. But
Shakespeare is not an escapist; he aims straight for the
heart. There is singularly little hatred in the plays, and
infinite understanding. It would be a barren world which
ever felt that it had gone beyond his wisdom and
compassion.

It will also be a sterile theatre which cannot extract
from his plays the very best entertainment value. The
quality of it will depend on the spell we are able to
weave through the eyes and ears of our audiences. It is

part of the theatre's legitimate business to draw the eye with pictorial beauty. Shakespeare's men knew it. Although they had no resources in scenery and lighting, they made up the decorative deficiency by lavish expenditure on costume.

We are well equipped to satisfy our audience's eyes; but we must do it by going a little deeper than "something pretty to look at." The interpretative vision must govern our sets and costumes. The actors too must interpret to the eye. A man may carry away a picture in his mind even when the words have faded. It may be the impression of a background, a flight of steps, a shaft of light, a crimson curtain; it may be a group, a massing of people, in action or repose; or it may be a gesture, an attitude, a "piece of business" silently executed. We must see to it that all these things have significance; there is drama in the pictorial composition on which a curtain rises, and equally in the line and tension of an actor's body as he listens, as he waits, as he stands in thought, or as he unleashes action.

It is instructive to find that all through theatre history the writers whose comments are preserved for us have been vividly impressed by what their eyes remembered. Kean, as Richard, stooped and "drew in the dust with the point of his sword"; Sothern, as Romeo, reeled across the stage with his "O! I am fortune's fool!"; Charles Laughton as Angelo, in the present writer's recollection, stood crouching over Isabella, his arms outstretched like an evil black bird of prey. These things sound trivial in print, because the emotion with which they were informed defies recapture. But they can illuminate the very essence of a character or of a play.

On the other hand, this does not mean that we need, or should, seek first for that elusive "something different." Many of the keenest young minds in the theatre are inclined to assume that external eccentricity denotes fundamental vitality and to mistake novelty for growth. Once in several generations will arise a genius like Meierhold, whose creative imagination expresses itself instinctively and spontaneously in unusual and particular external forms. Imitations of such a model are likely to become precious, pretentious, and altogether sterile. The work of a man like Stanislavsky, however, has a lasting influence and an enduring value, not because of its emphasis on "realism" (that frayed and battered word), or through any pictorial or theatrical formula, but because of the fierceness and intensity of his drive for truth in the dramatic interpretation of human beings.

With Shakespeare, or any great classic playwright, the importance of the settings by which he is surrounded assumes, in some sense, a different proportion. The function of design, as of direction, is not the same as it might be with a contemporary play, in a new contemporary idiom. The vigor and liveness of the theatre at any given period is not, in its presentation of Shakespeare, to be gauged by the extent to which its productions are "radical" or "original." It is to be measured against interpretative truth and the actors' ability to project their author's vision. It is probable that, if you could put Edwin Booth onto a bare Elizabethan stage, John

Barrymore among some eighteenth-century perspective "wings," Richard Burbage into a production of the Belasco school, or Edwin Forrest upon some architectural formation evolved by Norman Bel Geddes, in each case the actor would stare for a few moments and presently get back into the skin of Hamlet. The lines that have echoed through three hundred years would begin to exercise their old power. Dramatic truth has many faces, many voices; it is more important than any of its backgrounds.

Shakespeare, above all dramatists who have written in English, has given us the magic means to enchant our audience's ears, whether with a grace and delicacy which is Mozart in speech, or with the sweeping orchestration of sound which lifts LEAR and OTHELLO to a dimension beyond the mind. But the actor must not forget that no impression of lasting truth will be achieved by "sound and fury signifying nothing." There must be thought and feeling imprinted upon the music of the human voice.

We need actors with minds and lungs and vocal chords trained to this use of speech, who will not use it as a foreign language, a barrier between themselves and their normal mode of expression, but will welcome it as a rich inheritance which they know how to spend richly. It is possible that we also need audiences trained so to listen, though it is my belief that all we need, if the actors are good enough, is that they should be "still and willing."

Shakespeare does not demand audiences of students, though we have frequently found schools and colleges to be our most "understanding auditory." He did not write for the intelligentsia; he provided entertainment for an assorted crowd of noisy, eager, demanding citizens. When the Old Vic, in the slums of London's "South suburbs at the Elephant," first launched the Shakespearean phase of its development from the rowdy music hall it had been, it had a company of unknown actors and an audience which paid sixpence to come in. There were no stuffed shirts, no sophisticated high-hat opening nighters, no critics, even, except such as had a morbid passion for slumming. It is now occasion-ally admitted, in a rather fearful whisper, that some of the Old Vic productions have not been up to the very highest standard; it should, in fact, be clearly stated that many of them have been terrible. Yet no pro-duction, even of so difficult a play as CYMBELINE, can be considered to have failed when a member of the gallery is so moved that he calls frantically to Imogen during her scene with Iachimo: "Don't you trust 'im, Mrs. Casson! 'e's up to no good!"

"The best in this kind are but shadows, and the worst are no worse if imagination amend them," says Theseus of the amateur players. "It must be your imagination then, and not theirs," replies Hippolyta, sourly giving utterance to a profound truth. We need the imaginative cooperation of audiences. We have not recently asked them for it. The commercial theatre has narrowed itself to the belief that they will pay to see only Miss So-and-so *as* Juliet or Mr. Such-and-such *in* Othello; we have not expected them to appreciate simply a company of fine actors, and Mr. Shakespeare. We have limited our audiences for the great plays and lost them for the lesser ones through this excessive caution. Yet Shakespeare has given us every means for providing entertainment, and he has never lacked a generous response from the public.

In the old days repertory companies playing only Shakespeare abounded in the United States and in England. They were not very good, in many regrettable cases. They were actor-managed, and they paid little attention to what we now recognize as standards of textual accuracy or fidelity to the author's intention. They went at the plays simply and wholeheartedly and met with a similar response. We like to flatter ourselves that we have bettered their production methods; but we have lost their audiences, the very ones with whom Shakespeare himself would probably have felt most at home. In America the Shakespearean repertory company no longer exists, and in England wartime conditions alone have driven it from the entrenchments of Stratford-on-Avon or its South London shrine to village halls and small-town meetinghouses over the length and breadth of Great Britain.

With the passing of such companies as these, the greater part of the Shakespearean canon has become lost to the commercial theatre. Only such playhouses as the Pasadena Theatre can perform the less popular plays. The highly trained professional theatre can neither afford to risk on the uncertain money-makers the enormous investment which modern conditions dictate nor bring even the great plays to the audiences which should see them at prices which those audiences can afford to pay. In this respect Shakespeare is not the only sufferer; he is strangled by the same forces which are gradually squeezing all initiative and enterprise from the American stage. Indeed, he has the edge on his competitors in the sense that, being unimpeachably "classic," producers have a reasonable assurance that if the play is adversely criticized, it will at least be treated more in sorrow than in anger. It will not be received by the critical fraternity as if it were a personal affront to be expiated only by the author's blood. It will not therefore die the morning after its birth, "with twenty trenched gashes in its head," inflicted by the merciless ax of print.

On the other hand, potential backers will view Shakespeare even more warily than is their custom. There are no royalties to be paid, but there are also no picture rights to be envisaged. This will be no one-set show with six characters which cannot land anybody deeply in the red. Shakespeare will need settings, at fixed rates to the designer for each unit set, and additional rates for every variation of such a set, if it be no more than the addition of a column or a piece of tapestry. This scenery will have to be handled by a fixed, and large, number of stagehands, to be determined at their, not the producer's, discretion. Not all of these men will be skilled, and they will be replaceable in rotation by "relief" men who have never set eyes on the scenery until the moment they are required to move it.

To swell this alarming budget, Shakespeare will need musicians, and on the road union requirements will force the producer to pay not only his own costly orchestra but, in some cities, an equal and, in some, a double set of local men. Shakespeare will need a large cast, of whom the least apprentice spear carrier, who has either to speak or to understudy the line "No, indeed, my lord," must be paid a salary higher than the normal earnings of a trained and experienced young doctor with years of intensive study to his credit. Finally, he will probably be dependent for his drawing power on the services of one or more stars who must be lured from their Hollywood lairs at a price which may totally imperil the economics of the whole enterprise.

We may surmise that Shakespeare, could he revisit our theatre, would be a little stunned by all this. He had the imagination of a poet; he was used to inventing non-existent kingdoms and creatures of magic power. Neither the existence of the North American continent nor its mechanical wonders would necessarily leave him very greatly at a loss. He could conceive the miracle of expansion. The black magic of spiritual contraction might be harder for him to understand. He was used to a theatre where everybody did everything, from sheer love of the job. We wonder what he would make of: "I'm sorry, Mr. Shakespeare, but you may not help us to move that throne-chair; you are not a member of the I.A.T.S.E."; or "We should very much like to have you repeat your performance as the Ghost in HAMLET. You will understand that you must join Equity. We will deduct the necessary $100 from your royalties, and 5 per cent of your weekly salary. You will, of course, be an alien member." "We regret that we cannot venture upon a production of your play, KING JOHN. It would involve us in the outlay of a sum of money considerably greater than the probable sum total of your life's earnings." "We understand the eagerness of your young friends from the East Side to witness your work. But you will appreciate that we could not conceivably admit anyone to our theatre for a dime, as you somewhat idyllically suggest."

Shakespeare, like all classical dramatists and many modern ones as well, cannot reasonably hope to survive a system in which costs of production drive costs of admission to a point where his rightful audience is debarred from the theatre. If we wish to preserve for him the service of all that is most skilled in our theatre, or to continue to use his plays in our current repertoire, we shall be forced to make a choice; it is a choice which the American theatre as a whole will have to make in any case, in order to take the place to which it is entitled as the finest in the world.

If the organizations which represent its component parts continue their one-eyed battle to take as much as possible for themselves, and to give as little, then the theatre as a whole must accept the limitation of activity which is increasingly and inevitably clamped down upon it. Otherwise its constituent members must necessarily cooperate in a concerted attempt to lessen costs of production, to widen the geographical field of production throughout the forty-eight states, to appeal to vastly increased audiences, and to offer them dramatic wares which will justify the theatre's claim to existence. Hollywood is in a far better position to beglamor a synthetic commercial product and open the way to an audience for it by the Panzer divisions of publicity.

Hollywood cannot preserve Shakespeare or Ibsen or Chekhov or Sheridan or Sophocles; and unless the theatre becomes conscious of its responsibilities they will become dead dramatists indeed.

Eva Le Gallienne's great experiment with the Civic Repertory Theatre, saluting Shakespeare with productions of TWELFTH NIGHT and a memorable ROMEO AND JULIET, was the last occasion upon which the professional theatre has attempted to keep pace with its responsibilities in the matter of playing, at moderate prices, a repertoire of classic plays. Possibly, too, it was the last time that a professional company has been enabled to feel the electricity, the sting, and the zest, which hard work and continuous high challenge alone bring to an actor.

Even though "the Civic" never envisaged itself as a profit-making business, it failed, finally, to pay its way. Nobody has tried since; and theatre costs and conditions in the intervening years have imposed steadily increasing penalties upon initiative and enterprise. People sigh for "an Old Vic in America." There could be no such thing at present; the economic conditions necessary for its operation, the freedom and receptivity in collaboration, do not exist.

Many members of the audience who would, however, welcome the resurrection of the classic dramatists envisage some sort of national theatre in which their works would hold an honored place. It is, of course, shameful that the English-speaking nations, alone in the world, do not seem to consider the theatre as an art worthy of national, or even civic, endowment. But the fact remains that at the present time the hope for any such subsidy would be a piece of wishful thinking.

I am not even certain that Shakespeare, for one, would recognize himself as an institution. He wrote of the people and for the people; his preservation must be by the people. His plays should not be performed as a cultural duty, but because they are worth doing and worth seeing and will provide any audience with its money's worth, provided the price of admission does not soar to nonsensical heights. Any national theatre in America must be a people's theatre; and it must be a multiple institution, not isolated in one particular building but represented by different companies in different regions of the country. In a healthy, sanely organized theatre such as this Shakespeare would again be enabled to meet his public.

As a small initial contribution toward the task of restoring to the American people a knowledge of the living Shakespeare, it seems to me possible that a repertory company could be organized, not in competition with the commercial theatre, but geared to play mainly in school and college auditoriums, from which its basic scope might well widen to include a more general public. This it would necessarily have to do, in the end, if its potential value was to be realized. Productions so presented would be compelled to use the utmost economy of physical means, and this might easily result in a method of staging not far removed from Shakespeare's own.

The playing of Shakespeare is as fine a training as any young actor can wish for and remains an inexhaustible delight to the most experienced. There would, in my view, be no fear of failing to recruit a fine personnel for such a company. It would, and should, maintain the high standards of production which modern audiences expect and to which they are entitled. The numberless classrooms, our audiences of the future, to whom the study of the inevitable Bard is a weariness of the spirit, might discover a surprising liveliness about him. They might even enjoy themselves.

For there is a reward in playing Shakespeare and in seeing his plays well done. There is food alike for the poet, the philosopher, the business man, and the truck driver. Each will take from the plays what his mind and heart will carry, just as everyone concerned in their production will bring to them all he has and find it fully absorbed. Shakespeare's stamp and seal of honor has been set on every actor who has achieved a lasting reputation of greatness. In America today the finest traditions of civilized mankind have taken refuge; we face the high responsibility of handing on to succeeding generations a way of thought, an interpretation of free living. Shakespeare is part of the stuff from which our civilization has been forged. It is for the theatre to claim its rightful share in his immortality.

Index

educational